Social Enterprise

Social Enterprise

Empowering Mission-Driven Entrepreneurs

Marc J. Lane

AMERICAN BAR ASSOCIATION
Defending Liberty
Pursuing Justice

Cover design by ABA Publishing

15 14   5 4

Library of Congress Cataloging-in-Publication Data

Lane, Marc J.
    Social enterprise / by Marc J. Lane. — 1st ed.
    p. cm.
    Includes bibliographical references and index.
    1. Social entrepreneurship. 2. Industrial management. I. American Bar Association. II. Title.
    ISBN: 978-1-60442-739

HD60.L326 2011
658.4'08—dc22   2011006900

Dedication

For Allison, Amanda, and Jennifer, with love—and for the principles that guide their lives.

Acknowledgments

I gratefully acknowledge the hard work and extraordinary contributions of my colleagues at The Law Offices of Marc J. Lane, P.C.—Timothy P. Fitzgerald, Joshua S. Kreitzer, Lisa Sklenicka, and Cory White—without whose thorough research and careful scholarship this work would be a far less useful resource for those who will rely on it.

I am also very appreciative of the time and care taken by my friend and colleague Tom Triplett, who painstakingly reviewed my manuscript.

Of course, any errors or omissions are mine, and mine alone.

Contents

Preface: A Word to My Colleagues xv

𝖾𝖆 Chapter One

Empowering the Social Sector 1

What Is a Social Enterprise? 3

    Competing Definitions 4

    Defining through Organizational Structure 6

    The "Social Good" Trap 6

    Our Definition for the Purposes of This Book 7

The Origins of Social Enterprise 7

    The Nonprofit, Tax-Exempt Sector 7

    The For-Profit Sector 8

Recent Trends in Social Enterprise: New Legal Forms and

   Concerns 9

    New Legal Structures for Social Enterprises 11

    The Emergence of Venture Philanthropy and New

      Funding Sources 13

Overview of the Book 15

    Chapter 2: Vetting the Social Enterprise Business

      Model 15

    Chapter 3: Zeroing In on the Right Business Form . . . 15

    Chapter 4: Governing the Nonprofit Social Enterprise . . 15

    Chapter 5: Governing the For-Profit Social Enterprise . . 16

    Chapter 6: Multi-Organizational Structures 16

    Chapter 7: Funding 16

    Chapter 8: Securing Certification 17

    Chapter 9: To What End?: Measuring the Impact of

      the Social Enterprise 17

ટ Chapter Two
Vetting the Social Enterprise's Business Model **19**
Finding the Right Cause and Determining the Desired
  Social Impact 21
    Assessing the Opportunities and Risks Involved 21
    Forecasting the Potential Social Impact 23
Selecting the Business Form: 24
Available Funding and Allocation of Resources 24
    Entity Choice and Available Income Streams 24
    Entity Choice and Resource Conservation 26
    Saving Resources through the Use of Volunteers 27
Sustainable Demand for Mission-Driven Products 29

ટ Chapter Three
Zeroing In on the Right Business Form **31**
Hybrid Organizations 31
    L³Cs (Low-Profit Limited Liability Companies) 32
    Benefit Corporations 43
    Flexible Purpose Corporations 49
    Michigan Public and Triple Benefit Corporations 52
    Minnesota Community Enhancement Corporations ... 52
Cooperatives (Co-ops) 53
    Producer Cooperatives 55
    Consumer Cooperatives 57
    Multistakeholder Cooperatives 57
    Cooperatives—Formation Issues 58
    Cooperatives—Federal Taxation Aspects 59
    Cooperatives—Governance 60

ટ Chapter Four
Governing the Nonprofit, Tax-Exempt Social Enterprise **65**
Advantages to Tax-Exempt Status 65
Nonprofit, Tax-Exempt Corporations 66
    Ownership and Management 67
    Tax-Exempt Status 67
    Fiduciary Duties Owed in Nonprofit, Tax-Exempt
      Corporation Settings 67
Sample Conflict of Interest Policy 79
Unincorporated Nonprofit Associations 83
    Background 84

Model Acts 84
Tax-Exempt Status 86
Duties of Members and Managers 87
Distributions and the Threat of Private Inurement for Tax-Exempt Social Enterprises 88
Private Inurement 88
Private Inurement—Multi-Organizational Structures . . 89
Commercial Reasonableness 90
Compensation Considerations 90
Excess Benefit Transactions 92
Exempt Organization Checklist 95
Political and Legislative Activities 95
Political Activities 95
Lobbying Activities 98
Volunteer Labor—Unrelated Business Income Exception 101
State Laws Dealing with Charitable Organizations 101
Illinois' Approach 102
Maryland's Approach 106
New York's Approach 107
The Unified Registration Statement (URS) 109
State-Specific Registration Requirements 109

Chapter Five
Governing the For-Profit Social Enterprise 117
The Business Corporation 119
Ownership and Management 120
Tax Status 120
Fiduciary Duties Owed in Traditional For-Profit Corporate Settings 120
The Benefit Corporation 127
Ownership and Management 128
Tax Status 128
Fiduciary Duties Owed in Benefit Corporate Settings 128
The Limited Liability Company 129
Ownership and Management 130
Tax Status 130
Fiduciary Duties Owed by Managers and Members . . . 131

"L³C": The Low-Profit Limited Liability Company 134
    Ownership and Management 135
    Tax Status 135
    Fiduciary Duties of Loyalty and Care Owed in
        the L³C Setting 135
Constituency Statutes 137
Compensation and Benefits in the For-Profit Social Enterprise 141
    Business Judgment Protection 141
    Federal Law and Executive Compensation 143

≈ Chapter Six
Multi-Organizational Structures **145**
Unrelated Business Taxable Income (UBTI) Considerations . . 146
Corporation or Flow-Through Entity? 147
    Corporate Considerations 148
    Flow-Through Considerations 152
Sharing Personnel 155
    Employee Benefit Plan Considerations 160
Sharing of Office Space/Furniture/Equipment 160

≈ Chapter Seven
Capitalizing the Social Enterprise **163**
Access to Capital 163
    Grants and Contributions 164
Attracting Private Foundation Investments 166
    Program-Related Investments 166
    Mission-Related Investments 171
    Socially Responsible Investments 173
    Cause-Related Marketing 173
    Sponsorships 175
    Endorsements 177
    Fiscal Sponsorship 178
Governmental Assistance 180
    Community Development Financing Fund 180
    United Farm Credit System 181
    Economic Development Companies 182
    Community Advantage 183
    Startup America 184
    Catalog of Federal Domestic Assistance 184

Issuance of Securities 185
   Federal Securities Law Compliance 185
   State Securities Law Compliance and Preemption by Federal
      Securities Laws 187
Funding Networks: Social Enterprises Helping Each Other ... 188
   Venture Philanthropy 188
Pay-for-Success/Social Impact Bonds 193
Additional Funding Sources 197

ᏮᏮ Chapter Eight
Securing Certification 203
Social Enterprise Accreditation 203
Fair Trade Movement Certifications 206
"Green" Companies 208
Certified Economic Development Companies 212
   Certification Requirements under the Small Business
      Investment Act 212
   Certification Requirements under SBA Rules and
      Guidelines 213
B Corporation Certification 217
   B Lab Certification Process 218

ᏮᏮ Chapter Nine
To What End? Measuring the Impact of the Social Enterprise .. 223
Revisiting the Social Impact Theory: Knowing Where You
   Are Going 224
   Performance Measurement 225
Creating a Universal Method of Measuring Social Impact and
   Ultimate Value 227
   The Iris Model 227
   Center for What Works Model 233
The Gates Foundation and Actionable Measurement 237
   Supply and Demand Model: Looking to Value without
      Direct Reference to Social Impact 239
The Importance of Measuring Social Impact 241

Bibliography **243**
    Primary Sources 243
        Table of Cases 243
        Administrative and Legislative Materials 245
    Secondary Sources 246
    Social Enterprises and Related Organizations 249

Glossary **255**

Index **263**

About the Author **283**

A Word to My Colleagues

Charles Hamilton Houston, Howard University Law School's legendary dean and a champion of civil rights, famously observed, "A lawyer is either a social engineer or a parasite on society." Restating Dean Houston's provocative message in a less incendiary but equally instructive way, we're all in the empowerment business.

Our responsibility to empower others—and to lead by example—may be greater today than it ever has been in the past because, now more than ever, the social sector desperately needs our help.

The deepest recession in modern times has left one in seven working-age Americans in poverty. Yet the nation's charities have cut their services to the disadvantaged. Their operating costs have skyrocketed; grants and subsidies, more competitive than ever, have been cut back; and charitable giving is down—by 3.6 percent in 2009, the steepest decline in current dollar terms since Giving USA first published its annual report in 1956. Worse still, federal and state governments, faced with staggering budget deficits, have had no choice but to pull back on their support of the social sector.

Nonprofits have prudently implemented austerity measures, inevitably leaving their beneficiaries without the basic services they require. But nonprofits have also been innovative. And, more and more, they've become entrepreneurial, on their own and in collaboration with other nonprofits and even for-profit businesses.

They see earned revenue strategies, ideally those directly tied to their mission, as a reasonable contributor to sustainability. Some, discounting the reliability of government subsidy and philanthropy, pursue self-sufficiency—reliance on earned revenue alone.

The results have been extraordinary. Nonprofits have launched customer-focused substance abuse recovery centers, literacy initiatives, supportive housing developments, adult day-care facilities, hospices, and supplemental educational services. They have also created employee-focused social enterprises that offer disadvantaged and disabled people job training, mentoring, and a path to permanent employment.

Increasingly, for-profit social-purpose businesses are also addressing social needs. They see merit in defining success in terms of both financial and social returns. And new business models and even entity forms are emerging to encourage the social entrepreneur to drive positive social change.

Many social enterprises, both for-profit and nonprofit, have already tapped into market efficiencies and achieved scale. They are affecting the lives of thousands of people. But so much more can and will be done.

If Dean Houston were still walking Howard's halls, he would inspire each of us to be an agent of change. Please join me in sharing the social enterprise's potential with those you counsel—nonprofits, entrepreneurs, socially conscious individuals, foundations, and institutional investors. By empowering them, you will empower those you may never meet, but whose lives you'll change forever.

Marc J. Lane
March 2011

CHAPTER ONE

Empowering the Social Sector

SOCIAL ENTERPRISES ARE everywhere around us. More and more mission-driven organizations, both nonprofits and for-profits, are applying market-based strategies to achieve a social purpose.

When Bangladeshi economist Muhammed Yunus and his Grameen Bank were jointly awarded a Nobel Peace Prize in 2006 "for their efforts to create economic and social development from below," the world's attention was irresistibly drawn to the twin phenomena of microcredit and microfinance. In the United States, social enterprises that are successfully addressing critical social and environmental problems are hidden in plain sight, including these notable examples:

- The Women's Bean Project (www.womensbeanproject.com), employing chronically unemployed women in the manufacture of gourmet foods.
- Juma Ventures (www.jumaventures.org), operating businesses specifically to offer job opportunities to economically disadvantaged teens.
- Better World Books (www.betterworldbooks.com), collecting and selling books online to fund literacy initiatives around the world.
- Benetech (www.benetech.org), allowing people with print disabilities to legally download over 40,000 books and periodicals to be read as Braille, large print, or synthetic speech.

- Open Books (www.open-books.org), combining book donations, a retail bookstore, e-commerce, and volunteers to help support its literacy program for students of all ages.
- Harborquest, Inc. (www.harborquest.com), and its subsidiary, Civic Staffing L^{3}C, helping low-income, inner-city workers earn a living while serving businesses that need reliable, lower-skilled workers.
- A Safe Haven (www.asafehaven.com), providing and coordinating supportive recovery home housing, job training, and job placement services for people in recovery from alcoholism and drug addiction.
- Wisconsin Women's Business Initiative Corporation (www.wwbic.com), offering small-business loans and also managing a catering business and bakery.
- Materials Matter (www.materialsmatter.org), diverting construction waste and materials from landfills and then selling the products at discounts to nonprofits working in housing and community development.

The social enterprise field has taken off, and new business forms and models have been developed in the contemporaneous pursuit of profits and positive social change. Entrepreneurial practices have evolved in the social sector, and socially conscious entrepreneurs have designed new entity forms, including the low-profit limited liability company (L^{3}C) and the "benefit" corporation. Moreover, new business structures have emerged that link for-profit ventures with tax-exempt charities or foundations to achieve the socially impactful goals they share. Not surprisingly, the lawyer's role in counseling social entrepreneurs, organizing their ventures, and structuring their transactions has become more challenging. Issues surrounding entity design, governance, funding, taxation, and statutory and regulatory compliance are more nuanced, yet more important than ever. [1]

Yet the social enterprise is misunderstood, and even controversial. So the place to start is to define our terms.

---

1. *See generally* MARC J. LANE, ADVISING ENTREPRENEURS: DYNAMIC STRATEGIES FOR FINANCIAL GROWTH (John Wiley & Sons, Inc., 2001).

What Is a Social Enterprise?

Just as the sculptor reveals his work by chiseling that which it is not, the social enterprise, commentators will generally agree, can best be understood by distinguishing it from other, sometimes complementary strategies.

- Social enterprise is not corporate social responsibility (CSR). While CSR is a form of self-regulation that businesses can embrace to monitor and control their activities' impact on the environment and stakeholders, social enterprises have social impact built into their DNA. But for their intent to achieve positive social impact, specifically and directly, they would not exist.

- Neither does social enterprise include socially responsible investing (SRI) or its institutional variant, mission-related investing (MRI). Although foundations and socially conscious investors may favor business practices that promote environmental stewardship, consumer protection, human rights, or diversity, social enterprises aren't merely concerned about the environment and social justice; they do something about it.

- What's more, socially responsible investing seeks to maximize both financial return and social good. But social entrepreneurs may reject the notion that profit and social impact are equally important. They acknowledge that without profitability a venture cannot be sustained, but they place social mission above money.

- Still, social enterprises are not exclusively the business arms of nonprofits. Although nonprofits continue to dominate the social enterprise community, for-profit social purpose businesses are conspicuously staking out their claims.

- Not every business that a nonprofit adds to its portfolio is a social enterprise. Even if a business activity helps support the nonprofit's operations, it won't qualify as a social enterprise unless its overarching purpose is itself meant to drive positive social change.

Yet academics and institutions have not coalesced around a single definition.

Competing Definitions

Defining Through Mission Motive

In Professor Yunus's view, a "social business," the model he promotes, should be dedicated entirely to achieving a social goal. He would allow investors to recover their investment but never to receive a dividend. A prime example of the social business is the Grameen Bank, whose borrowers are its shareholders.[2]

More typically, a social enterprise can be viewed as one not motivated by profit, in that any profit motive takes a back seat to a mission centered on curing an acute social malady. The specific nature of the social mission is not as important in this definition as the fact that it remain front and center, and that profit motives are secondary.

Take an enterprise whose social mission is to help the organic farmer. Whether the enterprise accomplishes its mission directly (by giving planting supplies to the organic farmers) or indirectly (by funding charities that give planting supplies to organic farmers) would not affect its status as a social enterprise. What is important to understand is that a business need not lack a profit motive to be considered a social enterprise. Indeed, financial viability—and sustainability—require financial performance.

Defining through Mission Execution and Earned Income

Social Enterprise Alliance (SEA) (www.se-alliance.org), the only membership organization in North America to bring together nonprofits that use business models to pursue their missions and for-profits whose primary purposes are social, sees a social enterprise as "an organization or venture that achieves its primary social or environmental mission using business methods." SEA's definition of social enterprise turns on two things: 1) how the social mission is executed, and 2) how the venture's revenue is generated.

(a) Execution of the Mission

According to SEA, a social enterprise *directly* addresses social needs by pro-

---

2. *See generally* MUHAMMAD YUNUS, BUILDING SOCIAL BUSINESS: THE NEW KIND OF CAPITALISM THAT SERVES HUMANITY'S MOST PRESSING NEEDS (Public Affairs, 2010).

viding products or services to disadvantaged people.[3] The mission must be centered on helping people who are mentally, physically, economically, or educationally disadvantaged.[4] For the purposes of this definition, the term "disadvantaged" includes, but is not limited to, individuals who are developmentally disabled, mentally ill, former convicts, undereducated, substance abusers, recovering substance abusers, gang members, living below the poverty line, on welfare, elderly and in need of hospice care, and anyone else who may stand outside the socioeconomic mainstream.[5] The social enterprise accomplishes that mission by providing products or services that address a social need directly to individuals as customers; providing job and career training services directly to individuals as employees; or by combining both approaches.[6] This forecloses the possibility of simply giving money, or facilitating the giving of money, to accomplish the social mission.

(b) Earned Revenue Strategies

SEA has also defined social enterprise by reference to a venture's "earned revenue" strategy. Earned revenue strategies are programs taken on by enterprises with social purposes, such as nonprofit tax-exempt corporations, that produce revenue from the sale of goods or services.[7] It is "earned" revenue because it comes from the business operations of the enterprise rather than through donations or contributions.[8] For a particular organization to be considered a social enterprise, this needs to be a primary method of raising money. The key term here is "enterprise." In order to be truly entrepreneurial, a venture must be self-sustaining and able to generate streams of revenue on its own—that is, it must be a business.[9]

---

3. Social Enterprise Alliance (SEA), *Social Enterprise: A Powerful Engine for Economic and Social Development* (last visited Oct. 4, 2010), at 1, *available at* http://www.sageglobal.org/files/pdf/social-enterprise-white-paper.pdf.

4. *Id.* at 2.

5. *Id.* at 3.

6. *Id.* at 2–3.

7. Jerr Boschee, *Eight Basic Principles for Nonprofit Entrepreneurs*, NONPROFIT WORLD, July/Aug. 2001, at 15, *available at* http://www.socialent.org/pdfs/8BasicPrinciples.pdf.

8. *Id.*

9. *Id.*

SEA's definition of social enterprise is demanding: the social enterprise must help a certain segment of society and must do so in a particular way. To SEA, all other attempts at doing social good in a businesslike way, such as running a business with a social mission that indirectly addresses a problem, is considered "social entrepreneurship" rather than social enterprise.[10] SEA's more exacting definition allows social entrepreneurs[11] to better identify their businesses as social enterprises and more easily associate them with the legal and financial concerns discussed at length in the coming chapters.[12]

Defining through Organizational Structure

Another method of defining social enterprise hinges not on how the organization is run, but on how it is organized as a legal entity. This "organizational" method looks at what type of entity the social entrepreneur chooses to form. Entity choice, discussed at length in Chapter 3, has important governance and tax consequences that will affect the ability of the social enterprise to complete its mission. Entities range from the traditional for-profit corporation on one end of the spectrum to the nonprofit, tax-exempt corporation on the other. An entity may choose to forgo a profit motive based on its entity choice, which would indicate that the entity is a social enterprise.

The "Social Good" Trap

Most commentators agree that a social enterprise isn't merely a venture that purports to pursue or promote a "social good." Were that the case, every business corporation and every charity could fairly be characterized as a social enterprise. After all, businesses employ people, fulfill the needs and wants of their customers, and pay taxes. Similarly, charities perform altruistic and humanitarian services that would otherwise be performed by government or not at all.

---

10. SEA, *Social Enterprise: A Powerful Engine for Economic and Social Development* 2 (2010), *available at* http://www.sageglobal.org/files/pdf/social-enterprise-white-paper.pdf.

11. *See generally* MARC J. LANE, ADVISING ENTREPRENEURS: DYNAMIC STRATEGIES FOR FINANCIAL GROWTH (John Wiley & Sons, Inc., 2001).

12. Social Enterprise Alliance, *Social Enterprise: A Powerful Engine for Economic and Social Development* (2010), *available at* http://www.sageglobal.org/files/pdf/social-enterprise-white-paper.pdf.

Instead, the social enterprise involves a disciplined community of people who are thinking about social impact every day and, in that quest, are going about the serious business of applying strategic planning and management tools to social causes.

Our Definition for the Purposes of This Book

Without regard to the way in which a social enterprise is defined, the reader should find one common thread that runs through all the definitions presented—a significant commitment to better the lives of others. This, at the bare minimum, is needed to classify an organization as a social enterprise. Accordingly, for the purposes of this book, "social enterprise" will refer to any business model that, to a significant degree, has a mission-driven motive. This mission-driven motive may be exclusive of a profit motive or blended with one. The mission-driven motive may be primary and the profit motive may be secondary, or vice versa.

This definition includes all legal entity types available in any and all United States jurisdictions. It does not depend on the tax status of the entity, nor does it depend on how the entity chooses to pursue its mission-driven motives. Accordingly, the practitioner should consider the advice provided in this book as applicable to various types of legal entities and various types of organizational models.

The Origins of Social Enterprise

The concept of voluntarily helping those who need help is embedded in the American character. Philanthropic organizations had been operating in the United States even before independence was declared. Social enterprise is not only about doing good, but about doing good through the application of sound business principles. Thus, the origins of social enterprise can properly be traced back to the arrival of organizational and legal structures that promoted social welfare, either to the exclusion of a profit motive or concurrently with a profit motive.

The Nonprofit, Tax-Exempt Sector

The nonprofit, tax-exempt organization is a creature of statute, both federal and state. The Internal Revenue Service (IRS) has afforded these entities tax exemption when they comply with the requirements imposed by section 501 of the Internal Revenue Code (IRC). The nonprofit section 501(c)(3) organization, usually organized as a corporation, must have the sole purpose of engaging in a charitable, educational, or other benevolent purpose defined in the statute.[13] While the nonprofit, tax-exempt organization often conducts businesslike activities and seeks profits from those activities, those activities must at all times be substantially related to the tax-exempt purposes of the organization, and at no time can the production of profits be more than an insubstantial purpose.[14] Nonprofit, tax-exempt entities, since the early days of their existence, have depended on government and public philanthropic support, but over the past 30 years they have relied more heavily on revenue generated from business ("earned" revenue) that is substantially related to their social purposes.[15] SEA has identified several probable reasons that nonprofits are increasingly pursuing earned revenue:[16]

- Nonprofit operating costs have been steadily escalating over time.
- Philanthropic and governmental support has waned.
- The growth of the nonprofit sector has increased competition for increasingly scarce available charitable funds.
- The demand for nonprofit services has expanded.

Although the legal and organizational principles underlying the social enterprise rightfully have their genesis in the nonprofit, tax-exempt organization, for-profit enterprises soon began developing mission-driven objectives of their own, often in concert with their profit-seeking motives.

The For-Profit Sector

Social mission and profit-making motives can, and increasingly do, coexist. The case of William C. Norris is instructive. Mr. Norris was the founder of Control Data Corporation, a major computer manufacturer from the 1950s

---

13. I.R.C. § 501(c)(3).

14. *Id.*

15. *See* Social Enterprise Alliance, *Social Enterprise: A Powerful Engine for Economic and Social Development* (2010), *available at* http://www.sageglobal.org/files/pdf/social-enterprise-white-paper.pdf.

16. *See id.* at 7.

to the 1980s. In 1967, he opened production plants in several impoverished cities and rural areas to create jobs for depressed segments of the population.[17] Mr. Norris saw pursuing socially beneficial purposes as a path to achieving greater profitability. Since then, more and more for-profit businesses have embraced socially responsible corporate practices. To name just one example among thousands, Valspar, the paint company, recently donated 1 million gallons of paint to Habitat for Humanity to help keep housing prices affordable.[18] Companies ranging from Nike to Johnson & Johnson have adopted socially responsible policies to ensure the safe and humane production of their products.

Still, it is important to understand that corporations and other profit-driven enterprises are generally obliged to maximize the profits of their owners.[19] The duties of managers are informed by this singular objective. As such, pursuing a social purpose at the expense of profits may lead to legal liability, as further discussed in Chapter 5.[20] For that reason and others, new entity types, notably the benefit corporation and the L³C, have been created to afford legal protection to managers who make decisions based on socially conscious and mission-driven motives.[21]

Recent Trends in Social Enterprise: New Legal Forms and Concerns

As the appeal of social enterprise grows, new and innovative organizational structures are emerging that not only blend mission with profit motives but also aim at confronting the governance, tax, and funding challenges the social enterprise continues to face. While most social enterprises still exist as nonprofit, tax-exempt organizations, new hybrid entities allow fiduciaries to manage them with an eye toward both social concerns and profit motives. These new business entities present complex and interesting legal

---

17. *See id.*

18. Press Release, Valspar Corp., Valspar Celebrates Donation of 1 Million Gallons of Paint to Habitat for Humanity International (Sept. 15, 2010), *available at* http://www.csrwire.com/press_releases/30575-Valspar-Celebrates-Donation-of-1-Million-Gallons-of-Paint-to-Habitat-for-Humanity-International.

19. *See infra* Chapter 5.

20. *Id.*

21. *Id.*

questions that every attorney who is seeking to design a social enterprise must consider.

Hybrid structuring models are also becoming more common, often where a tax-exempt, nonprofit organization will have an interlocking relationship, such as a parent-subsidiary relationship, with a for-profit organization. This method of structuring the social enterprise presents advantages in funding and access to capital but, without careful planning, may also put the parent organization's tax-exempt status at risk.[22]

There has been enhanced interest in venture philanthropy—a charity's or a social enterprise's collection of funds from private investors and donors, followed by the distribution of those funds to other social enterprises that meet certain investment and donative criteria. This process resembles venture capital investing, which has a results-oriented approach demanding measurable results. As is true of venture capital investing, venture philanthropy requires social enterprises to deliver measurable results—but results that are significantly defined not by profits, but rather through social impact. An entire field of social impact valuation—with its own performance metrics—has developed in response to this need.

Microfinance agencies are starting to become more prominent as a method of funding and creating sustainable businesses. Microfinance is generally defined as providing financial services to impoverished populations and communities. The key component of microfinance is microcredit, or lending small amounts of money to underserved individuals, thereby enabling them to create their own self-sustaining business. These loans, although small (usually less than $100), have payback rates upward of 95 percent.

The business world is also beginning to see the emergence of local and national securities exchanges that list and trade the securities of social enterprises. Importantly, these exchanges must comply with applicable federal and state securities law as well as the rules and regulations of a self-regulatory organization known as the Financial Industry Regulatory Authority (FINRA).

---

22. *See infra* Chapter 3.

New Legal Structures for Social Enterprises

Although the nonprofit, tax-exempt organization remains the most popular entity form for social enterprises, those enterprises looking to pursue profit-driven operations may prefer to organize in another form for both funding and governance reasons.[23] It may be difficult for managers of for-profit entities to pursue social purposes without incurring liability for failing to meet their profit-maximization duties, which, in turn, inform their core duties of loyalty and care.[24] That explains why hybrid entities have been developed and are authorized in several jurisdictions that permit fiduciaries to manage businesses with both profits and mission in mind.

Two of the new hybrid structures to consider when planning the social enterprise are:

- The L³C—the low-profit limited liability company—is a variant of the LLC organized significantly for charitable or educational purposes. The managers (or members) may still manage the enterprise with a secondary profit motive. Eight states and two Native American nations have enacted L³C statutes.
- The benefit corporation, sanctioned in Vermont and Maryland, requires its directors and officers to take "public benefits" into account when running the business. ("Public benefits" produce material and positive impacts on society and the environment, as measured by a third-party standard.) The corporation may be run with a profit motive, and that motive need not be secondary to any social motive.[25] Similar bills passed the New York Senate in 2010[26] and both houses of the New Jersey legislature in 2011,[27] and have been introduced in other states as well.[28]

---

23. See infra Chapter 4.

24. See infra Chapter 5.

25. See generally MD. CODE ANN. CORPS. & ASS'NS § 5-6C-01(c); 11A VT. STAT. ANN. § 21.03(a)(4).

26. S. 7855B (N.Y. 2010).

27. S. 2170 (N.J. 2010).

28. See B Lab, Benefit Corporation Legislation (last visited Jan. 21, 20110, available at http://www.bcorporation.net/publicpolicy, for updates on the current status of such bills. See also S.B. 11-005 (Colo. 2011).

Other legislation has been introduced in California and Michigan, and is under consideration in Minnesota, which would afford social entrepreneurs still more options:

- Like the benefit corporation, the flexible purpose corporation that has been proposed in California would require its directors to pursue social interests (which could include the concerns of employees and other non-shareholder stakeholders) in running the corporation. Profit motives would not need to be secondary to any social purpose of the corporation.

- A bill authorizing the public benefit corporation and the triple benefit corporation was introduced in Michigan's legislature in September 2010 but was not enacted.[29] Such corporations would significantly further charitable or educational purposes with the production of income as a secondary purpose (similar to an L³C). Among other proposed statutory requirements, the corporation would need to balance the interests of both people and the planet while pursing a profit. As this book goes to press, the bill has not been introduced into the legislature's 2011 session.

- The Minnesota Community Enhancement Corporation Act would authorize the boards of a new breed of corporations to balance the economic returns paid to shareholders with the interests of other stakeholders and society at large.

B Corp. Certification

As part of the movement of blending social and profit motives into sustainable business forms, B Lab (www.bcorporation.net), a nonprofit in its own right, has created a "B (Beneficial) Corp. certification" for for-profit enterprises that are run for social purposes. B Lab's certification process requires that the enterprise be specifically organized, through inclusion of applicable language in its governance documents, for the promotion of a social purpose.[30] There are two things that every attorney must be aware of when looking into B Corp. certification. First, any for-profit entity—not just corporations—is eligible. Second, certification holds no legal weight. All the

---

29. H.B. 6454 (Mich. 2010).
30. *See infra* Chapter 8.

duties applicable to the for-profit's management in a particular jurisdiction will continue to apply, even with B Corp. certification.[31] Details on the requirements for B Corp. certification can be found in Chapter 8.

Constituency Statutes and Their New Uses

Constituency statutes from various jurisdictions, originally enacted in reaction to Delaware's ruling in *Revlon v. MacAndrews & Forbes Holdings Inc.*,[32] were intended to allow managers to take nonshareholder stakeholder concerns into consideration during certain sale-of-control transactions, such as a merger or asset sale.[33] Certain jurisdictions have interpreted these statutes to allow management (including managers of an LLC and directors and officers of a corporation) to take nonshareholder stakeholder concerns into consideration in making day-to-day business decisions.[34] Accordingly, these statutes may allow for-profit entities to be run for socially beneficial purposes, depending on how the state's statute is interpreted. Fiduciaries of traditional for-profit entities that choose to seek B Corp. certification will rely on these statutes when managing their businesses for social purposes. These issues are tackled in Chapters 5 and 8.

The Emergence of Venture Philanthropy and New Funding Sources

Venture philanthropy invites charities and social enterprises to collaborate to create funding networks. Venture philanthropy organizations can themselves be classified as social enterprises for the purposes of this book. These organizations manage funds which are then distributed to other social enterprises based on both social and financial returns. Many venture philanthropic organizations, such as the Acumen Fund (www.acumenfund.org)[35] and REDF (www.redf.org),[36] receive grants, contributions, and investments into their funds, the assets from which are invested in, or donated to, targeted social enterprises. The creation and management of these funds raise tax, securities, and governance issues, which are addressed in Chapter 7. The managers of these venture philanthropic funds are also attempting to

---

31. *Id.*
32. Revlon v. MacAndrews & Forbes Holdings Inc., 506 A.2d 173 (Del. 1986).
33. *See infra* Chapter 5.
34. *Id.*
35. *See* http://www.acumenfund.org/.
36. *See* http://www.redf.org/.

make investment and donation decisions based on the measurable impact of the target social enterprise.[37]

The Calvert Foundation (www.calvertfoundation.org) is one example of a social enterprise that engages in philanthropic investing.[38] This social enterprise is an IRC section 501(c)(3) tax-exempt organization that maintains a fund, including both investments and contributions from donors, which makes loans to qualified organizations engaged in community development and socially beneficial activities. The Calvert Foundation, like many philanthropic funding enterprises, is interested in the measurable social impact of the enterprises it funds.

Measuring Impact

Measuring the impact of a social enterprise can be very difficult. Several novel concepts for measuring social impact have been created by the Young Foundation,[39] the Acumen Fund, B Lab,[40] and other participants in social-purpose investing.[41] The various theoretical models created by the Young Foundation (www.youngfoundation.org) and the Impact Reporting and Investment Standards (IRIS at http://iris.thegiin.org), created by the Acumen Fund and its partners, look to concepts that move past traditional measures of profitability. These new methods (and others) of measuring impact are detailed in Chapter 9.

Social Investing Securities Exchanges

Financial intermediates have begun setting up securities marketplaces in the United States and abroad, listing the securities of socially conscious companies. The listing standards for these markets generally require, as one of their core requirements, a commitment to a socially driven purpose. Companies such as Mission Markets, Inc. (www.missionmarkets.com) have set up and maintain these marketplaces, which, in the United States, must comply with applicable SEC and FINRA regulations.[42]

---

37. *See infra* Chapter 9.
38. *See* http://www.calvertfoundation.org/invest/community-investing.
39. *See* http://www.youngfoundation.org/.
40. *See* http://www.bcorporation.net/.
41. *See infra* Chapter 9.
42. *Id.*

These new trends in funding have been bolstered by a precipitous dropoff in philanthropic contributions and grant making. And new funding sources, much like traditional investors, are demanding that social enterprises develop and implement sustainable business models.

Overview of the Book

The following will provide a brief chapter-by-chapter overview of the balance of this book. In general, the book is divided into three themes: 1) creating and developing a business model for the social enterprise with due attention paid to the relevant legal issues, 2) organizing and running the social enterprise, and 3) measuring the social enterprise's impact.

Chapter 2: Vetting the Social Enterprise Business Model

This chapter addressed the questions that must be asked during the initial stages of organizational planning. It tracks the steps necessary to identify a viable and impactful social opportunity. After these initial stages of idea formation, questions of entity choice, funding, and sustainability are considered.

Chapter 3: Zeroing In on the Right Business Form

This chapter evaluates the entity choices available to the social entrepreneur, including the emerging hybrid entities that blend mission and profit motives, such as the L³C and the benefit corporation.

Chapter 4: Governing the Nonprofit Social Enterprise

Most nonprofit social enterprises will seek tax exemption from federal and state income taxes. This chapter will contrast the advantages and disadvantages of maintaining tax exemption, followed by a discussion of the governance principles that are specific to the nonprofit, tax-exempt corporation. The duties of care, loyalty, and obedience are described in detail. Also discussed are legal requirements applicable to unincorporated nonprofit associations as well as a treatment of the tax rules and regulations concerning the compensation of managers, directors, and officers of nonprofits. Next, there is a comprehensive review of the duties and requirements under the representative charitable solicitation laws of Illinois, Maryland, and New

York. Finally, this chapter identifies the statutes governing the charitable solicitation requirements within each state.

Chapter 5: Governing the For-Profit Social Enterprise

This chapter examines the organizational and governance principles unique to for-profit social enterprises. From traditional profit-driven entities, such as corporations and LLCs, to hybrid forms, such as the L³C and the benefit corporation, the fiduciary duties of for-profit entities are spelled out. Hybrid entities, mixing for-profit and mission-driven motives, will have a different set of concerns from primarily profit-driven entities. This chapter explains those differences. Finally, an expanded discussion focuses on the usage of constituency statutes in organizing a for-profit social enterprise.

Chapter 6: Multi-Organizational Structures

Social enterprises may consist of one entity or of various entities working together. The interconnected entities may consist of a combination of for-profit and tax-exempt entities. This is known as "hybrid structuring." Hybrid structuring is a new spin on an old approach to corporate structuring that can give social enterprises access to revenue streams not otherwise available to them.

Special issues arise when for-profits and tax-exempt entities are structurally linked. The majority of these issues deal with the ability of the tax-exempt entity to maintain its tax-exempt status while having an ownership interest in a for-profit entity that carries on business activities that may be unrelated to the tax-exempt purposes of the tax-exempt entity. This chapter looks at structuring models that combine pass-through, disregarded entities with tax-exempt entities as well as models that combine corporate, dual-taxed entities with tax-exempt entities.

Chapter 7: Funding

How and where to secure initial capitalization—and continuing access to capital as the enterprise grows—are primary drivers when planning any venture. Social enterprises share these universal concerns with the rest of the business community.

But the social enterprise's funding opportunities are unique in their sourcing, and often in the motives of their funders. Traditional commercial investors have profit-driven motives and will be likely to invest only in a social enterprise that can generate market-rate financial returns. Philanthropic donors are concerned exclusively with the social good achieved by the social enterprise, and will not be motivated by financial returns. But other sources of funding have mixed motives, both social and financial. Reconciling funders' disparate objectives often falls to the attorney who shapes the venture and manages the stakeholders' expectations.

This chapter looks at philanthropic, commercial, and government funding opportunities, examining what is needed to secure each type of funding.

Chapter 8: Securing Certification

A social enterprise may find it advantageous to get its products or the organization itself certified as a promoter of social good. Certification of products and services as complying with fair trade or other socially conscious standards can help investors and contributors identify the social enterprises most deserving of their funding. Certification can also help consumers of the enterprise's products and services determine which enterprise to patronize. Some types of certification are necessary for certain social enterprises to move ahead with their business plan and structure.

Chapter 8 looks at various forms of certification, including Social Enterprise Alliance's certification of "Accredited Social Enterprises," "green" branding initiatives, Fair Trade certification, B Corporation certification, and certification mandated by the U.S. Small Business Association for economic development companies.

Chapter 9: To What End?: Measuring the Impact of the Social Enterprise

Measuring the social enterprise's impact is important. More and more donors, investors, governmental agencies, policy makers, and other decision makers are demanding evidence of the social enterprise's social impact. Yet traditional benchmarks are of little utility. This chapter looks at the analytical methods of measuring the social enterprise's impact.

*   *   *   *

The social enterprise field is gaining traction. Pursing double and triple bottom lines poses unprecedented challenges for social enterprises and their lawyers. From new hybrid organizational models to new and emerging funding sources, the realm of social enterprise is teeming with both complexity and opportunity.

The formation and operation of a successful social enterprise require a comprehensive analysis of a host of business and tax issues, and advisors to social enterprises will need to counsel clients about all of them to ensure success. However, the first step in this process requires the vetting of the social enterprise's business model to assess whether an opportunity actually exists in the marketplace.

Vetting the Social Enterprise's Business Model

ENGAGING IN A SOCIALLY beneficial enterprise is generally a choice made with the intent to make a difference. While social entrepreneurs have the desire to see their enterprises address social problems, their attorneys can help them determine whether their enterprises can become functioning and viable organizations.

The business plan and its implementation must be taken one step at a time. Each entrepreneur and his or her counsel must answer three basic questions:

1) What type of business is to be launched (which includes the issue of entity choice), and what it will accomplish?
2) How will the funding and resources necessary to run the business successfully be obtained?
3) How will the business's resources be utilized and conserved?

The social entrepreneur's attorney has an important role in addressing each of these questions.

The first concern of the social entrepreneur should be to determine the viability of the social opportunity that he or she wants to pursue. The feasibility of the proposed social enterprise needs to be tested against real-world judgments:

- Will the venture have a meaningful social impact (and, if the venture is to be launched by a nonprofit organization, will that impact help drive the nonprofit's mission)?
- Is the social entrepreneur (or the nonprofit) competent and committed to achieving the venture's promise?
- Does the social entrepreneur have the skills and experience to produce and deliver the product or services?
- Is the target market clearly defined and likely to view the venture's product or service as superior to the available alternative at the price to be charged?
- Are adequate start-up costs on hand or reasonably available?
- Has the social entrepreneur defined "success" realistically?
- Are the financial forecasts based on reasonable assumptions and reasonably achievable?

Assuming the embryonic business idea appears viable, business planning should begin in earnest. An effective business plan will articulate the enterprise's mission; define its strategy; establish performance targets; identify resources; project revenues and costs over time; and serve as actionable, durable yet flexible implementation guidelines. The product of exhaustive market research and collaboration among the venture's key stakeholders, the business plan will systematically address every relevant financial, operational, marketing, production, and human resource issue.

Once the opportunity for a social enterprise has been carefully planned, its legal form must be determined. The social entrepreneur should understand all of the available options. From the traditional business corporation to the IRC § 501(c)(3) nonprofit, tax-exempt organization and everything in between, the legal options available are varied. And each option comes with its own governance, tax, funding, and resource allocation concerns, all of which must be deliberated. As the social entrepreneur will quickly learn, each decision will likely affect the others.

This chapter will introduce the major legal considerations in developing the social enterprise's business plan. The more technical aspects of funding, governance, and business structure will be explored in greater depth in later chapters.

Finding the Right Cause and Determining the Desired Social Impact

Whether or not a social enterprise is worth pursuing ultimately turns on two factors:

1) Confirmation that the opportunity is based on a tangible and workable social idea that responds to actual social needs.
2) Confirmation that the opportunity is reasonably likely to positively impact a social problem sufficiently to justify the requisite investment in time, money, and energy.

A social venture will be worth pursuing if the likely impact of the enterprise outweighs the cost of the necessary resources needed to launch and run the enterprise and reasonably ensure its survival.

Assessing the Opportunities and Risks Involved

Many promising social ideas are born of the entrepreneur's personal experiences. For instance, Geoff Cramer, the co-founder and principal of Futures for Kids (www.f4k.org), was a high school wrestling coach who discovered that many of his student-athletes did not understand or know about the full spectrum of post–high school opportunities that were available to them.[1] Cramer provided his students with the resources and guidance to improve their chances for success in the real world.

Curtis Sliwa was already running Guardian Angels (www. guardianangels.org), a nonprofit organization that promoted safe streets for children and families, when he founded CyberAngels (www. cyberangels.org), a nonprofit organization that works with local law enforcement to curb predatory Internet practices. Sliwa used the knowledge he gained from his work with Guardian Angels, and identified and responded to a new need—Internet safety. Taking personal experiences and marrying them with social needs is often how workable social ideas are created.

A social need can be defined in many ways, but Ayse Guclu, Gregory Dees, and Beth Battle Anderson of the Fuqua School of Business have defined "social need" as the gap between the current existing reality and

---

1. *See Futures for Kids*, Center for the Advancement of Social Entrepreneurship, at 1 (2002), *available at* http://www.caseatduke.org/documents/f4kfinal.pdf.

optimal socially desirable conditions.[2] Because social needs are based on a particular social outlook, those needs in turn are based on social values that inform that outlook.[3] Thus, where one group of individuals may place a high value on parental involvement in the educational process, another may believe that greater value should be placed on a teacher's ability to independently guide the student. There is more than one way to approach each problem, and the social entrepreneur must have an open mind and be imaginative.

The key to creating a workable social idea is to identify values that a significant number of people agree on, thus ensuring that the social enterprise will respond to a sustainable social need. In today's climate, many state and local governments are experiencing budgetary shortfalls. In times like these, common sense tells us that most people would think that government should scale back certain initiatives in an effort to save resources. Scaling back would save valuable resources, thus putting government in a better position to balance the budget. What if, instead of scaling back during difficult economic times, government and businesses actually took proactive steps to implement additional initiatives that would save money and promote positive social values? That could create a workable social idea that a significant number of people could agree on.

An outstanding example of accomplishing multiple objectives through a single social enterprise is illustrated by BigBelly Solar (www.bigbellysolar.com), based in Needham, Massachusetts. BigBelly Solar has developed an innovative way to collect, compact, and haul away garbage through the use of solar-powered trash compactors. Innovative technology provides on-demand information as to when trash bins are full, thereby reducing unnecessary pickups, resulting in less use of fossil fuels, carbon dioxide, and other greenhouse gases. As a result, the company increases cost-efficiency of waste-collection services while developing more environmentally sustainable practices.[4] This innovative idea has enabled this social enterprise to save governments and businesses money while promoting sustainable environmental practices.

---

2. AYSE GUCLU ET AL., THE PROCESS OF SOCIAL ENTREPRENEURSHIP: CREATING OPPORTUNITIES WORTHY OF SERIOUS PURSUIT 3 (Center for the Advancement of Social Entrepreneurship 2002), *available at* http://www.caseatduke.org/documents/seprocess.pdf.

3. *Id.* at 3.

4. *See* http://bigbellysolar.com/about/.

BigBelly Solar is just one example of an innovative social enterprise. Thousands more are already in existence, and an untold number of worthwhile social ventures are waiting to launch. Determining the opportunities and risks involved takes time and dedication, but what can be accomplished is virtually without limit.

Forecasting the Potential Social Impact

The first step in ensuring positive impact is to develop what some have called a "social impact theory" (impact theory).[5] The impact theory is a tool by which the social entrepreneur can predict whether or not his or her workable idea will have the impact necessary to become a viable social opportunity. Accordingly, the impact theory is the engine that drives the process by which any workable social idea evolves into a fully functioning social enterprise.

An impact theory requires a clear definition of the enterprise's desired outcomes. More precisely, it posits how enterprise inputs will produce a sequence of desired outcomes, both long-term and short-term. This framework provides a defined set of desired outcomes against which the social enterprise's inputs can be tested. Moving from the idea stage, this will give the social enterprise a purpose that can be tested for the potential impact it will have on society. Once the desired outcome is identified, the next step is to gauge the potential impact of a proposed social enterprise on society through an analysis of the available inputs. Testing for social impact involves comparing the desired outcomes to relevant and real inputs taken from the field in which the social enterprise will operate. If the desired outcomes cannot be tested against the current social reality, they should tested by using new research and analysis.[6]

So, if the social entrepreneur is starting an enterprise that will provide clothing to a city's homeless population during the winter months, an impact theory should be developed that contemplates the planned size of the enterprise and then, based on the breadth of the expected operations, the percentage of the city's homeless population that will be reached and serviced within a given time. The social entrepreneur should then take this desired outcome and consider the following inputs:

---

5. AYSE GUCLU ET AL., *supra* note 2, at 7, *available at* http://www.caseatduke.org/documents/seprocess.pdf.

6. *Id.* at 7.

1) the outlets available for acquiring the clothing;
2) the number of homeless people in the city;
3) the cost associated with acquiring the clothing and other resources required to run the enterprise;
4) the legal requirements the enterprise must meet; and
5) any factors that could hinder the operation of the enterprise.

The desired outcomes would be tested against these inputs.

Whenever possible, the impact theory should be tested before the enterprise is organized. Still, the impact theory may need to be reevaluated and reshaped if desired outcomes are not achieved. In adjusting the impact theory, the social entrepreneur may also realize that what once appeared to be a workable idea simply did not have the necessary social impact to justify pursuing or continuing the enterprise.

Selecting the Business Form: Available Funding and Allocation of Resources

Once the proposed venture's impact theory has been successfully tested, the social entrepreneur and his or her legal counsel need to select the optimal business form for the venture from among a wide range of entity choices. The social enterprise's organizational and business form will be the product of planning relating to funding, governance, taxes, and other relevant concerns.

Entity Choice and Available Income Streams

Traditional Profit-Driven Entities

Every business initially needs to be funded and then have access to continuing sources of capital. The best way to gain and retain capital may be through a traditional for-profit business—a traditional business corporation or limited liability company. Running a for-profit business with one ultimate bottom line, generating profits, will be very attractive to investors looking to contribute both debt and equity. For-profit businesses, many of which are organized to operate for any legal purpose, have definite, well-established legal rules concerning formation and governance. This opens up the possibility of securities offerings and other capitalization options, both initially and after the business has begun operation.

Mission-Driven Entities

A for-profit enterprise's duty to drive shareholder value may be inconsistent with the mission-driven motives of the social enterprise. Where profit is subordinated to mission, keeping investors happy can understandably be tricky.

(a) Tax-Exempt Entities

Organizing as a tax-exempt entity, typically as a nonprofit corporation, will necessarily limit third-party investment, both because most nonprofit corporations cannot issue shares and are thus ineligible for entity investments, and because they must be organized and operated exclusively for charitable purposes. However, tax-exempt entities, unlike traditional for-profit entities, will avoid income tax on income generated from any trade or business that is significantly related to the tax-exempt purpose of the entity.[7] Moreover, tax-exempt entities may find fertile funding opportunities from philanthropic donors who are willing to contribute to meaningful social enterprises.[8] (Most jurisdictions have stringent requirements for the solicitation of charitable contributions. Charitable enterprises must register with the state and provide continuing financial reports on the use of funds solicited and raised.[9]) Government grants and aid may also be available for these types of entities.[10]

In addition, the products or services offered by social enterprises that sport a tax-exempt purpose may be particularly appealing to consumers and a growing segment of investors who are not in it only for the money.[11] (It is also possible to organize as a nonprofit entity within a particular jurisdiction but not apply for tax exemption. However, doing so is usually an ineffective strategy for the social enterprise, as it creates funding issues

---

7. *See generally* I.R.C. §§ 511–512.
8. *See infra* Chapter 6.
9. *See infra* Chapter 3.
10. *See infra* Chapter 6.
11. See materials concerning the slow money investing movement at http://www.slowmoney.org/.

without the benefit of tax exemption.) Nonprofit, tax-exempt entities may also be able to tap into funding provided by venture philanthropic organizations.[12]

(b) Hybrid Entities and Hybrid Structuring

A social enterprise may also choose to organize as a hybrid entity that would allow for the pursuit of both mission-driven and profit-driven motives. There are two statutorily allowed hybrid entities, the "benefit corporation" and the "low-profit limited liability company" (L³C).[13] Each is only available in relatively few states.[14] Both entity forms require mission-driven motives and, in the case of the L³C, motive must be a "significant" purpose of the enterprise.[15] Although mission-driven motives are present and must be memorialized in the organizational documents of the hybrid entity, it will be a for-profit entity under both federal and state laws.[16]

Because of their permitted profit motives, these types of entities may be more attractive to traditional investors than nonprofit, tax-exempt entities. Because of their mission motives, they may also find support from philanthropic donors. However, they may not draw as many investors as traditional profit-driven entities, or as many philanthropic donors as nonprofit entities. The tax, legal, and governance issues around these entities are also in flux, which can make actions and outcomes hard to predict.[17]

Increasingly, nonprofits are collaborating with for-profits, running for-profit subsidiaries, and entering into joint profit-making ventures with for-profit businesses.

Entity Choice and Resource Conservation

Resource conservation and management is critical to the success of the social enterprise. For the social enterprise, organizing as a tax-exempt entity will ensure that any money gained from operations that substantially relates to the tax-exempt purpose will be safe from taxation on the federal

---

12. *See infra* Chapter 6.
13. *See infra* Chapter 4.
14. *Id.*
15. *Id.*
16. *Id.*
17. *Id.*

level.[18] All states also offer tax exemption if certain requirements are met, most of which mirror the federal requirements for tax exemption.

Organizing the venture as a for-profit hybrid entity, such as an L³C or a benefit corporation, may allow greater access to capital but will subject the social enterprise to taxation. The social entrepreneur must be guided to find the right balance between using what limited capital is available to accomplish the social mission and conserving capital to ensure that the mission can continue. While funding is critical, other resources, such as labor and good will, must also be considered when establishing the social enterprise.

Saving Resources through the Use of Volunteers

Staffing a social enterprise with the right personnel to accomplish the mission is another key contributor to success. Generally speaking, a person who works for a business can be classified as an employee, independent contractor, volunteer, partner, officer, or director. No matter how large or small the enterprise is, the persons who work there must be classified into one of these categories, and that classification will affect compensation, payroll administration, and qualification for insurance and other benefits.

Using volunteers in a social enterprise setting is an exciting way to accomplish tasks within the organization while saving significant financial resources. These resources can be diverted and utilized in other, more strategic ways, allowing the social enterprise to advance its overall mission.

The most recent information provided by the U.S. Bureau of Labor Statistics indicates the trend toward volunteerism has been increasing in recent years. In fact, for the year ended September 2009, roughly 27 percent of the United States population (63.4 million people) volunteered through or for an organization at least once between September 2008 and September 2009.[19] Social enterprises that are able to tap into this resource may find that people are eager to work toward the advancement of a cause that is dear to them, despite the fact that they are not remunerated for their time.

There are many online organizations aimed at promoting the utilization of volunteers and making it easier for people and causes to connect. A

---

18. Rev. Rul. 81-178, 1981-2 C.B. 135.

19. *See* Economic News Release, U.S. Bureau of Labor Statistics, Volunteering in the United States, 2009 (Jan. 26, 2010), *available at* http://data.bls.gov/cgi-bin/print.pl/news.release/volun.nr0.htm.

few interesting organizations working to connect people and businesses through volunteerism include Volunteer Match (www.volunteermatch.org), UN Volunteers (www.unv.org), Idealist.org (www.idealist.org), and Foundation Center (www.foundationcenter.org). There are, of course, numerous other opportunities available, and the trend suggests this will only continue.

The utilization of volunteers may or may not enable social enterprises to avoid compliance with the Fair Labor Standards Act (FLSA), which sets forth, among other employee rights, minimum wage requirements. Compliance with the FLSA will vary, depending on whether the social enterprise is organized as a for-profit or nonprofit venture. Under the FLSA, for-profit sector employers are prohibited from accepting volunteer services. Therefore, for-profit social enterprises attempting to use volunteers will be required to comply with the minimum wage requirements imposed by the FLSA.

The FLSA is intended to cover only employees; as a result, depending upon whether a nonprofit's workers are classified as employees or volunteers, compliance with the FLSA may be required. Ascertaining whether a worker is a volunteer or employee is not always easy to do, as the FLSA defines "employ" very broadly—"to suffer or permit to work."[20] However, the Supreme Court has made clear that the FLSA was not intended "to stamp all persons as employees who, without any express or implied compensation agreement, might work for their own advantage on the premises of another."[21]

The Department of Labor follows the Supreme Court's guidance in the case of individuals serving as unpaid volunteers and has stated that individuals who volunteer or donate their services, usually on a part-time basis, for public service, religious, or humanitarian objectives, not as employees and without contemplation of pay, are not considered employees of the religious, charitable, or nonprofit organizations that receive their services.[22] As a result, if such workers are not considered employees, but rather volunteers, compliance with the FLSA is not required.

---

20. 29 U.S.C. § 203(g).

21. Walling v. Portland Terminal Co., 330 U.S. 148 (1947).

22. United States Department of Labor, *Fair Standards Act Advisor: Volunteers, available at* http://www.dol.gov/elaws/esa/flsa/scope/er16.asp.

Sustainable Demand for Mission-Driven Products

Despite the state of the economy, consumer demand for mission-driven products and services is growing. The next generation of purchasers, through social-purpose branding, will be more educated and better informed about their purchasing decisions. Qualifying businesses of every variety are likely to benefit from branding and positioning as a social enterprise.

For example, the astronomical growth and positive publicity of TOMS Shoes (TOMS at www.toms.com) illustrates purchasers' commitment to support mission-driven organizations. Founded in 2006 by Blake Mycoskie, TOMS Shoes shows how taking compassionate actions today can create a better tomorrow. Its mission is simple: for every pair of shoes purchased from TOMS Shoes, TOMS will provide a pair of shoes to a child in need.

Utilizing the national media, social networking sites, and college campus clubs, TOMS has worked hard in getting its message out. During its first year, TOMS sold 10,000 pairs of shoes and provided 10,000 pairs of shoes to children in desperate need. In September 2010, TOMS announced that it had given its one millionth pair of new shoes to children in need.[23]

Aside from its own online store, TOMS shoes are sold in high-end retailers around the world, thus proving that consumers are willing to support mission-driven organizations.

The attorney's role in helping to shape the venture—to balance mission and profit, to help achieve the social impact it seeks, and to connect funders and investors with the social enterprise—is extraordinarily challenging, but extraordinarily worthwhile.

*   *   *   *

Once it has been determined that a viable social enterprise is possible, its advisors should then focus on the proper legal vehicle from which the enterprise should operate. A wide range of options is available, and guidance in selecting the proper form is provided in the following chapter.

---

23. *And Now: TOMS Reaches an Incredible Milestone,* Toms.com (Sept. 16, 2010), *available at* http://www.toms.com/blog/node/988.

CHAPTER THREE

Zeroing In on the Right Business Form

SELECTING THE OPTIMAL legal form for a social venture can be among the most difficult and important early decisions faced by an aspiring social entrepreneur. Although social enterprises are often operated as traditional corporations, limited liability companies, or nonprofit corporations, certain business forms are uniquely suited to the social enterprise.

Hybrid Organizations

Recently, several entity types have emerged that blend for-profit and mission-driven motives. Such hybrid organizations are not run *exclusively* for charitable, educational, or benevolent purposes. As a result, the Internal Revenue Code (IRC) does not provide these organizations with tax-exempt status. For tax purposes, hybrids are for-profit entities.

Recent trends indicate that investment in hybrid ventures that clearly focus on and promote social purposes may be gaining significant momentum. For example, the world's largest private foundation, the Bill and Melinda Gates Foundation (www.gatesfoundation.org), announced at the end of 2009 that it would begin extensive use of program-related investments (PRIs) as a way to leverage the foundation's resources and encourage broader financial support for its mission.[1] (See Chapter 7 for a comprehensive discussion of

---

1. David T. Leibell, *Gates Embraces Philanthro-capitalism*, TRUSTSAND ESTATES.COM (Dec. 30, 2009), *available at* http://trustsandestates.com/wealth_watch/gates-foundation-venture-philanthropy1230/.

program-related investments.) The Gates Foundation has stated that PRIs are the right instruments to use in situations in which the foundation's program strategies are best served by partnering with revenue-generating enterprises, such as non-government organizations, financial institutions, or companies.[2] Because organizations formed as L³Cs and benefit corporations encourage program-related investment, the potential for expansion of their usage may increase. With the Gates Foundation's pledge to invest roughly $400 million in PRIs, it is likely that other foundations and private investors will follow suit in coming years and invest in hybrid organizations.

There are two types of hybrid entities that are currently available and becoming increasingly popular: the low-profit limited liability company, or L³C, and the benefit corporation. Organizing as a for-profit entity, whether as an L³C or benefit corporation, will allow the social entrepreneur greater access to capital, but will, at the same time, subject the social enterprise to federal and state income taxation. These hybrid entities are discussed in detail in the following section.

L³Cs (Low-Profit Limited Liability Companies)
• **Tax Considerations**—Income and expenses will generally flow through to members. Tax-exempt members must consider the impact of unrelated business income.
• **Governance & Management**—May be (i) member-managed either by the members collectively or through a management committee selected by the members, or (ii) manager-managed by an outside third-party manager. The rights, duties, and responsibilities will be defined in the operating agreement and/or the articles of organization.
• **Capital Sources**—Equity or debt investment permitted by both tax-exempt and for-profit sources. Designed to be a recipient of program-related investments made by private foundations.

2. BILL AND MELINDA GATES FOUNDATION, PROGRAM-RELATED INVESTMENTS: LEVERAGING OUR RESOURCES TO CATALYZE BROADER SUPPORT FOR OUR MISSION, *available at* http://www.gatesfoundation.org/about/Pages/program-related-investments-faq.aspx.

> - **Distributions/Liquidation**—Distributions to members in accordance with provisions contained in the operating agreement. Liquidation proceeds flow to members after satisfaction of outstanding liabilities owed to creditors.

The "L³C" is a legal form intended to bridge the gap between for-profit and nonprofit functions. The L³C combines the financial advantages and governance flexibility of the traditional limited liability company with the social advantages of a nonprofit entity. The primary focus of the L³C is not on earning revenue or capital appreciation, but on achieving socially beneficial goals and objectives, with profit as a secondary goal. The L³C thus occupies the space that exists between the for-profit and charitable sectors.

L³C Example—The Paradigm Project

An important example of the L³C in action is The Paradigm Project (www.theparadigmproject.org), an L³C formed to create sustainable economic, social, and environmental value within the developing-world communities through the use of a member-driven collaborative network of leading businesses, charitable organizations, and others. With a diverse membership base of both for-profits and nonprofits, The Paradigm Project combines donor funds, grants, and low-interest loans with traditional investment tools to create unique public/private partnerships for funding projects.

Many of the projects are aimed at eliminating poverty in the developing world—proof that L³Cs can be used to solve social problems around the globe. A current project assists families in rural Kenya and Haiti. Because meals have historically been cooked over an open fire in these countries, women and children have had to walk great distances to obtain firewood, subjecting them not only to backbreaking labor but also putting them in a position where they could be attacked or harmed while venturing into dangerous woodlands.

In addition to the physical toll inflicted obtaining firewood, danger also lurks during the preparation of the meal. In fact, because meals are typically cooked indoors where there is no proper ventilation, respiratory diseases are commonplace. It is estimated that every day more than 2,500 women around the world die from respiratory causes related to indoor smoke.

In order to solve this problem, The Paradigm Project plans to distribute over a million or more efficient stoves over the next 10 years to rural villages so that families will no longer have to obtain firewood and cook in unsafe conditions. This is a classic example of a relatively simple fix to a large problem.

While this is just one example of the work that The Paradigm Project performs, it shows how positive change can be effected throughout the global community by L³Cs. Drawing funding from both for-profit and nonprofit sources has enabled The Paradigm Project to begin to solve a global problem.

The Clinton Global Initiative (www.clintonglobalinitiative.org) recently singled out The Paradigm Project as representing "an exemplary approach to addressing challenges in environment and energy."[3] This is a significant advancement toward further utilization of the L³C as The Clinton Global Initiative, part of the Clinton Foundation, facilitates the collaboration of heads of state, management of multinational companies, philanthropists, foundations, and many other non-governmental organizations to develop solutions to the world's most pressing social problems.

The use of L³Cs to drive positive social change is gaining momentum. As this book goes to press, L³Cs have been authorized in eight states and two Native American nations. Bills to authorize such entities have been introduced in at least 11 other states.[4] Once an L³C has been formed in any of these jurisdictions, it may operate in all 50 states and beyond.

---

3. Press Release, The Paradigm Project Featured at Clinton Global Initiative (Sept. 20, 2010), *available* at http://www.reuters.com/article/idUS83330+20-Sep-2010+PRN20100920.

4. Americans for Community Development, *Legislative Watch* (last visited Jan. 23, 2011), *available at* htt://www.americansforcommunitydevelopment.org/legislativewatch.php.

The first state to adopt L³C legislation was Vermont, where the law introducing L³Cs was passed and took effect in April 2008. Subsequently, seven more states have enacted L³C legislation, namely Michigan (enacted and effective January 2009), Wyoming (enacted February 2009, effective July 2009), Utah (enacted and effected March 2009), Illinois (enacted August 2009, effective January 2010), Maine (April 2010, effective July 2011), Louisiana (enacted June 2010, effective August 2010), North Carolina (enacted and effective August 2010), as well as the Crow Indian Nation of Montana (enacted and effective January 2009) and the Oglala Sioux Tribe of South Dakota (enacted and effective July 2009).

North Dakota and Oregon have enacted laws authorizing further study of L³Cs. In addition, other states, including Arkansas, Louisiana, Missouri, Montana, North Carolina, Tennessee, and Washington, are reportedly looking into the possibility of authorizing the organization of L³Cs.

The governing statutes of those states that have already authorized L³Cs are very similar in all respects. In general, in order to qualify as an L³C, the entity's articles of organization and operating agreement must contain the requirements listed below. These requirements have been designed to enable investments in L³Cs to qualify as program-related investments (discussed below):

- **Charitable or Educational Purposes.** L³Cs must operate with the primary (but not sole) motive to significantly further the accomplishment of one or more charitable or educational purposes within the meaning of IRC § 170(c)(2)(b), and the L³C would not have been formed but for its relationship to the accomplishment of such purpose(s).
- **No Significant Purpose for Production of Income.** No significant purpose of the L³C shall be the production of income or the appreciation of property, but the fact that the L³C may produce income or that property appreciates does not conclusively mean that a significant purpose of the L³C is to produce income or appreciate.
- **No Purpose to Accomplish Political or Legislative Purposes.** An L³C must not be organized to accomplish any political or legislative purposes, attempt to influence legislation, or intervene in any political campaigns on behalf of any particular candidate for public office.

Investment Strategies and Program-Related Investments

The foregoing requirements deliberately mirror the program-related investment (PRI) provisions contained in the Internal Revenue Code (IRC), which allow for private foundations to make investments in for-profit business ventures to support the foundation's charitable or educational purposes. Because of the primarily socially beneficial nature of L³Cs, an investment in an L³C may more easily qualify as a PRI for the private foundation investor than might otherwise have been the case.[5] The structure of the L³C facilitates investments in these socially beneficial, for-profit ventures while attempting to simplify compliance with the IRS's stringent and outdated rules pertaining to PRIs. A detailed discussion of PRIs, including the statutory requirements of making a PRI, the characteristics of a PRI, advantages and drawbacks to making a PRI, and the recent trends in that area, are discussed in greater detail in Chapter 7.

As a hybrid business form that encompasses aspects of both for-profit and nonprofit organizations, L³Cs are able to leverage private foundations' PRIs and access market-driven capital for ventures with modest financial prospects but also the possibility of major social impact. This affords the L³C the potential to solve major social problems through creative financing by both tax-exempt and for-profit investors.

L³Cs are intended to make investment in socially beneficial businesses more attractive to for-profit investors by strategically allocating risk among the private foundation and for-profit investors. This may be accomplished through a multilayered investment strategy that uses PRIs to fund the L³C's initial capital needs.

This strategy is best illustrated through a simplified example. When an L³C is organized, a private foundation can invest in the business by making a PRI. Because the private foundation is most concerned that its investment further its charitable mission, the financial returns provided to the private foundation can be structured at less than market rate. Utilizing a private foundation for the initial capital investment in the L³C lowers the risk to subsequent for-profit investors who invest in the L³C. Thus, the L³C provides an attractive investment opportunity with limited risk, while

---

5. Robert A. Wexler, *Effective Social Enterprise — A Menu of Legal Structures*, 63 EXEMPT ORG. TAX REV. 565 (2009), *available at* http://www.se-alliance.org/resources_wexler09.pdf.

at the same time providing competitive market-rate returns for second- (and later) tier, for-profit investors. This flexibility accommodates the interests of both tax-exempt and for-profit investors.

The IRS has not opined that an investment in an L³C will automatically qualify as a PRI. However, the IRS has issued private letter rulings permitting PRIs that were structured as LLC equity investments, and the L³C is merely a specialized LLC. In a 2006 private letter ruling, a tax-exempt private foundation invested in a private for-profit pharmaceutical company formed to discover and invent solutions to solve global health problems. The IRS ruled that such an investment constituted a qualifying distribution under IRC § 4942(g).[6] In another 2006 letter ruling, a private foundation's capital contributions to an LLC organized to invest in businesses in low-income communities qualified as a PRI under IRC § 4944(c).[7] In these examples, private foundations made direct investments into an LLC with for-profit co-investors, and such investments were held to constitute qualifying distributions under IRC § 4942.

Although the investments described in these examples were made in entities formed as LLCs (and not L³Cs), it can be inferred that if such an investment were instead made in an L³C, the IRS would reach the same conclusion. In fact, in a letter written to the IRS Commissioner—where additional PRI examples were provided to the IRS for consideration—the chair of the American Bar Association Section of Taxation stated that if an investment in an LLC would qualify as a PRI, then *a fortiori*, an investment in an L³C should also qualify.[8] This belief appears to be generally accepted.

Groups within the social enterprise movement have been working to introduce a bill in Congress that would expedite the process for obtaining a private letter ruling. (As of this writing, no such bill had been introduced.) In specific, a "Philanthropic Facilitation Act" has been drafted and could serve as a template for future legislation. The act would improve the ability of private foundations to use the PRI exception more efficiently,

---

6. Priv. Ltr. Rul. 200603031 (Jan. 20, 2006).

7. Priv. Ltr. Rul. 200610020 (Mar. 10, 2006).

8. Letter from Stuart M. Lewis to Hon. Douglas Shulman, Commissioner, Internal Revenue Service (Mar. 3, 2010), *available at* http://www.abanet.org/tax/pubpolicy/2010/Comments_Concerning_Proposed_Additional_Examples_on_Program_Related_Investments.pdf.

thereby opening up additional capital for investment in economically distressed industries.[9]

The following specific amendments to the Internal Revenue Code would be included within the act:

- Amending Code Section 4944(c) to create a rebuttable presumption that an investment in an entity qualified under state law or under the law of a federally recognized tribe as an L^3C qualifies as a PRI.[10]

- Amending Code Section 4944(c) to clarify that PRIs are considered qualifying distributions under Code Section 4942 and are not considered business holdings under Code Section 4943.[11]

- Amending Code Section 4944(c) to offer a voluntary procedure to entries seeking to qualify as recipients of PRIs under which such entities could receive a determination from the IRS that investments in them will qualify as PRIs for private foundations with a common purpose. If such investments are deemed to qualify, all private foundations would be able to rely on such a determination unless and until the Secretary of the Treasury publishes a revocation of the determination. The fee charged for such a determination would be the average fee charged for an organization seeking recognition of tax-exempt status under Code Section 501 (c)(3).[12]

- Amending Code Section 7428(a) to allow entities seeking to quality as recipients of PRIs to appeal an adverse determination by the IRS to the U.S. Tax Court, the U.S. Claims Court, or the U.S. District Court for the District of Columbia, as can be done by organizations seeking to appeal denials of tax-exempt status under Section 501(c)(3).[13]

- Adding a new section to the Code to require each for-profit entity receiving PRIs to file and make public an information return disclosing its gross income, its expenses, its disbursements for the ex-

---

9. Philanthropic Facilitation Act of 2010: Final Draft, at 1, *available at* http://www.americansforcommunitydevelopment.org/downloads/Philanthropic FacilitationAct2010.pdf.

10. *Id.* at 8.

11. *Id.*

12. *Id.*

13. *Id.* at 9.

empt purposes of the organizations that have made PRIs in the entity, a narrative statement of the results achieved from the use of such investment funds, for charitable purposes, its assets, liabilities and net worth, the names and addresses of all private foundations holding PRIs in the entity during the year, a statement of the portion of the entity's liabilities and net worth attributable to the PRIs, and a statement of all distributions paid to the entities holding PRIs during the year.[14]

In addition to the above, the act would also direct the Department of the Treasury to amend its regulations by providing that the dissemination of news furthers educational and literary purposes and clarify that the activities of a news organization in disseminating news do not constitute lobbying (so as to facilitate the operation of newspapers and other news organizations as L³Cs).[15] The Treasury Department would also be instructed to provide examples of investments in L³Cs that would qualify, and those that would not qualify, as PRIs, and to provide a procedure for private foundations to divest investments in PRIs that cease to qualify as such without incurring excise tax.[16]

Because the IRS has not stated that an investment by a private foundation in an L³C will qualify as a PRI, private foundations that wish to make PRIs in L³Cs may obtain private letter rulings from the IRS stating that investments in such for-profit ventures will qualify as PRIs. This would be the safest approach and would provide the private foundation with the most comfort. Because of the costs involved in both money and time, obtaining such a ruling is not practical in most cases. For that reason, foundations commonly rely on opinions of counsel in lieu of private letter rulings.

Tax Considerations

The L³C is not a tax-exempt entity, but rather a for-profit organization that will ordinarily be treated and taxed as a partnership, requiring the filing of IRS Form 1065 for income tax purposes, unless the L³C elects to be taxed as a corporation by filing IRS Form 8832. This means that, absent a special election to be treated as a corporation for tax purposes, an L³C will be taxed

---

14. *Id.* at 8-9
15. *Id.* at 9-10.
16. *Id.* at 10.

as a "flow-through" entity for federal and state income tax purposes, just as any LLC would normally be taxed. The equity holders or members of the L³C are then taxed on their allocable shares of its income.

Tax-exempt organizations that invest in "disregarded" entities such as an L³C must keep in mind that the flow-through nature of its income may cause a tax-exempt investor's income from the venture to be characterized as unrelated business income (i.e., income from an activity engaged in by a tax-exempt organization that is not substantially related to its tax-exempt purpose). That said, because L³Cs are formed with the primary motive of accomplishing a charitable or educational purpose within the meaning of IRC § 170(c)(2)(B), it is likely—and recommended—that the L³C's purposes be substantially related to the purposes of the tax-exempt investor, thus allowing the tax-exempt investor to escape unrelated business income tax.

Despite the fact that L³Cs are formed to advance charitable and educational purposes, they are not formed as charitable entities under the IRC. Because the L³C is not a tax-exempt entity, it is not eligible to receive tax-deductible charitable contributions under IRC § 170.

Governance and Management

L³Cs provide significant flexibility with respect to both membership and management characteristics. There are no limitations on who may become a member in an L³C, except to the extent that the members decide to restrict ownership through provisions in the operating agreement.

The L³C may be member-managed or manager-managed, with fiduciary obligations being owed by those who take on a management role. If member-managed, the L³C will resemble a partnership, in that all members will have the right to manage the organization and will take on fiduciary duties in doing so. If manager-managed, the L³C will resemble a corporation, and there will be a split between ownership, represented by the members, and management, represented by managers. In this latter instance, only the managers will bear fiduciary responsibilities.

Because L³C provisions have generally been added as "friendly" amendments to states' preexisting LLC statutes, the fiduciary obligations of the managers and members of an L³C will be controlled by the LLC statute of the state of organization. The fiduciary duties of L³C managers may be defined almost entirely through the operating agreement, meaning profit maximization need not be the primary motive of the enterprise, allowing the enterprise to be run effectively for charitable, educational, religious, or other IRC § 170(c)(2)(B) purposes.[17] This flexibility in assigning fiduciary obligations allows those obligations to be tailored to the specific purpose(s) of the enterprise and, in effect, may make the L³C an optimal hybrid business model for running a social enterprise. The core duties of care and loyalty owed by L³C managers can ultimately be colored by an enterprise's socially beneficial purposes.

Controversy Surrounding the L³C

As the L³C continues to gain traction, it's important to note that the form has not been without controversy. Its critics have raised a number of serious concerns about the L³C's utility and efficacy, including those that follow.

- L³C laws are unnecessary at best and a gimmick at worst. One can easily organize a traditional LLC and limit its Articles of Organization's purpose clause to mirror the PRI requirements established by the Tax Reform Act of 1969.
- Unless and until Congress or the IRS sanctions the use of the L³C as a favored recipient of PRIs, the form will mislead foundations and other investors who will unjustifiably believe that L³Cs will always qualify for program-related investments.[18]
- To the extent that private foundations forgo market-rate returns and thus subsidize returns to private-sector investors, the L³C will be unable to demonstrate that the production of income is not a significant purpose of the venture.
- L³C managers may be put in an untenable position as they seek to account to the venture's various stakeholders.
- L³Cs may encourage the diversion of charitable assets away from the non-profit sector. NASCO, the National Association of State Charitable Officials (www.nasco.net), has raised this possibility and

---

17. *See* 805 ILL. COMP. STAT. 180/15-5(a).

18. J. William Callison & Allan W. Vestal, *The L3C Illusion: Why Low-Profit Limited Liability Companies Will Not Stimulate Socially Optimal Private Foundation Investment in Entrepreneurial Ventures*, 35 Vt. L. Rev. 273, 291 (2010).

has also argued for supervision by state charity officials of L³Cs and other for-profit recipients of charitable dollars, as some states already require.

As the L³C evolves, it will be tested against legal and market challenges, as it should be. For now, an objective defense of the form would include these early observations.

- Those who question the utility of the form when an LLC can do the same job overlook the reality that the L³C's Articles, which track federal PRI standards, may simplify foundation investors' due diligence, thus facilitating their investment.
- Their argument also disregards the form's branding appeal when the venture reaches out to consumers, investors, and other counterparties.
- And it ignores the L³C's unique capacity to sensitize foundations to the genuine opportunity to invest rather than only to grant, thereby capturing the financial—and social—multiplier effect of an investment made for social purposes that may be recovered, with its proceeds redeployed over and over again.
- The advent of the L³C demands that all those who may find merit in the form be educated about the nature and scope of the opportunities it offers.
- Unlike the traditional LLC, the very form signals to all its stakeholders that their discrete objectives and fiduciary obligations must be harmonized, thus inviting a candid harmonization of goals at the outset.
- Whether or not a proposed investee is an L³C, a foundation should only make a PRI after performing careful due diligence which takes into account the foundation's mission, the terms of the investment, its risk, its structure, and how it fits into the foundation's investment portfolio.

Already, L³Cs are earning broad acceptance:

(1) for social ventures seeking to secure PRI support from foundations that forgo market-rate returns and thus subsidize private-sector investors who can thereby earn market-rate returns;

(2) as single-purpose, wholly owned subsidiaries of tax-exempt organizations;

(3) for ventures that seek to draw consumer and funder attention to their status as social enterprises; and

(4) for coalitions of nonprofits that join forces to tackle a social problem through the application of business principles.

Benefit Corporations
• **Tax Considerations**—Net income is taxed at corporate rates. Double taxation of net income must be considered, as net income is first taxed at the corporate level and subsequently at shareholder-level distribution of dividends.
• **Governance and Management**—Board of Directors elected by the shareholders. Officers appointed by the Board of Directors. Both the Board of Directors and officers are permitted to consider multiple factors—stockholders; employees, workforce, subsidiaries, and suppliers; consumers; community and societal considerations; and local and global environment—when making corporate decisions.
• **Capital Sources**—Shareholder equity (stock purchases). Debt issuance. May be recipient of program-related investments by private foundations.
• **Distributions/Liquidation**—Dividend distributions to stockholders. Liquidation proceeds flow to stockholders after satisfaction of outstanding liabilities owed to creditors.

Another new legal form is the "benefit corporation." Two states authorized this form in the spring of 2010,[19] with Maryland enacting a benefit corporation law on April 13, 2010,[20] followed by Vermont on May 19.[21]

---

19. John Tozzi, *Maryland Passes 'Benefit Corp.' Law for Social Entrepreneurs*, BUSINESSWEEK.COM (Apr. 13, 2010), *available at* http://www.businessweek.com/smallbiz/running_small_business/archives/2010/04/benefit_corp_bi.html.

20. *See* B Lab, *Benefit Corporation Legislation* (last visited Jan. 21, 2011), *available at* http://www.bcorporation.net/publicpolicy, for updates on the current status of such bills. *See also* S.B. 11-005 (Colo. 2011).

21. S. 2170 (N.J. 2010).

Several other states are considering such legislation,[22] including New Jersey, where both houses of the legislature unanimously approved a bill authorizing benefit corporations in January 2011.[23] The bill was awaiting the governor's signature as this book went to press.

Under both the Maryland and Vermont laws, a benefit corporation is a corporation that will have the purpose of creating a "general public benefit," in addition to any other purpose for which it may be established.[24] Such a corporation may also specify in its charter or articles of incorporation that its purpose includes the creation of one or more "specific public benefits."[25]

Both states define a "general public benefit" as "a material, positive impact on society and the environment, as measured by a third-party standard" through activities that promote a combination of specific public benefits.[26]

Both states, in turn, define "specific public benefit" as including the following: promoting economic opportunity for individuals or communities beyond the creation of jobs in the normal course of business;[27] preserving the environment;[28] improving human health;[29] promoting the arts, sciences, or advancement of knowledge;[30] increasing the flow of capital to

---

22. Act of April 13, 2010, ch. 98 (codified at MD. CODE ANN. CORPS. & ASS'NS §§ 5-6C-01 to 5-6C-08). The Maryland law took effect October 1, 2010.

23. Vermont Benefit Corporation Act, No. 113 (May 19, 2010) (codified at 11A VT. STAT. ANN. §§ 21.01 to 21.14). The Vermont law takes effect July 1, 2011.

24. MD. CODE ANN. CORPS. & ASS'NS § 5-6C-06(a); 11A VT. STAT. ANN. § 21.08(a).

25. MD. CODE ANN. CORPS. & ASS'NS § 5-6C-06(b); 11A VT. STAT. ANN. § 21.08(b).

26. MD. CODE ANN. CORPS. & ASS'NS § 5-6C-01(c); 11A VT. STAT. ANN. § 21.03(a)(4). The Maryland law uses the phrase "a combination of specific public benefits," while Vermont refers to "some combination of specific public benefits."

27. MD. CODE ANN. CORPS. & ASS'NS § 5-6C-01(d)(2); 11A VT. STAT. ANN. § 21.03(a)(6)(B).

28. MD. CODE ANN. CORPS. & ASS'NS § 5-6C-01(d)(3); 11A VT. STAT. ANN. § 21.03(a)(6)(C). The Vermont law refers to "preserving or improving the environment," whereas the Maryland law refers only to "preserving the environment."

29. MD. CODE ANN. CORPS. & ASS'NS § 5-6C-01(d)(4); 11A VT. STAT. ANN. § 21.03(a)(6)(D).

30. MD. CODE ANN. CORPS. & ASS'NS § 5-6C-01(d)(5); 11A VT. STAT. ANN. § 21.03(a)(6)(E).

entities with a public benefit purpose;[31] or accomplishing any other particular or identifiable benefit for society or the environment.[32] In addition, while Maryland lists as a specific public benefit "providing individuals or communities with beneficial products or services,"[33] Vermont lists in its similar provision "providing *low income or underserved* individuals or communities with beneficial products or services."[34]

The requirement for a "third-party standard" in both states refers to a standard[35] for defining, reporting, and assessing corporate social and environmental performance.[36] Such a standard must be developed by a person or entity independent of the benefit corporation.[37] Furthermore, it must be "transparent" in the sense that the following information about the standard must be publicly available: (1) the factors considered when measuring the performance of a business; (2) the relative weightings of those factors; and (3) the identity of the persons who developed and control changes to the standard and the process by which those changes are made.[38]

In both Maryland and Vermont, the standards of conduct applicable to directors of benefit corporations require that such directors, in determining what they reasonably believe to be in the best interests of the corporation, consider the effects of any action or inaction on (1) the corporation's stockholders; (2) the corporation's employees, workforce, subsidiaries, and suppliers; (3) the interests of consumers as beneficiaries of the corporation's general or specific public benefit purposes; (4) community and societal considerations, including those of any community where the corporation,

---

31. MD. CODE ANN. CORPS. & ASS'NS § 5-6C-01(d)(6); 11A VT. STAT. ANN. § 21.03(a)(6)(F).

32. MD. CODE ANN. CORPS. & ASS'NS § 5-6C-01(d)(7); 11A VT. STAT. ANN. § 21.03(a)(6)(G). The Maryland law uses the word "particular" while the Vermont law uses "identifiable."

33. MD. CODE ANN. CORPS. & ASS'NS § 5-6C-01(d)(1).

34. 11A VT. STAT. ANN. § 21.03(a)(6)(A) (emphasis added).

35. In Vermont, the standard must be a "recognized" standard. 11A VT. STAT. ANN. § 21.03(a)(8).

36. MD. CODE ANN. CORPS. & ASS'NS § 5-6C-01(e); 11A VT. STAT. ANN. § 21.03(a)(8). In Maryland, the standard must be for defining, reporting, and assessing "best practices" in corporate social and environmental performance.

37. MD. CODE ANN. CORPS. & ASS'NS § 5-6C-01(e)(1); 11A VT. STAT. ANN. § 21.03(a)(8)(A).

38. MD. CODE ANN. CORPS. & ASS'NS § 5-6C-01(e)(2); 11A VT. STAT. ANN. § 21.03(a)(8)(B).

its subsidiaries, or its suppliers have offices or facilities; and (5) the local and global environment.[39] In addition, Vermont requires directors of a benefit corporation to consider the corporation's long-term and short-term interests, including the possibility that those interests may be best served by the corporation's continued independence.[40] Both states also allow the directors of a benefit corporation to consider any other pertinent factors or the interest of any group that they deem appropriate.[41]

Vermont, but not Maryland, requires at least one member of a benefit corporation's board of directors to be designated as a "benefit director." The benefit director must be independent of the corporation and is responsible for preparing the corporation's "annual benefit report" (see below).[42] Vermont also allows (but does not require) a benefit corporation to have an officer designated as the "benefit officer" who shall have the authority and perform the duties in the corporation's management related to creating public benefit.[43] The same person may serve as both benefit director and benefit officer.[44]

One particularly distinctive aspect of benefit corporation laws is that they require (in both Maryland and Vermont) a benefit corporation to provide each stockholder with an "annual benefit report."[45] Such a report must also be posted on the corporation's public website (or, if the corporation does not have a public website, provided free of charge to anyone upon request).[46]

The annual benefit report must include the following information for Maryland benefit corporations: (1) the ways in which the corporation pursued a general public benefit during the year and the extent to which the general public benefit was created; (2) the ways in which the corporation pursued any specific public benefit mentioned as a purpose in the

---

39. MD. CODE ANN. CORPS. & ASS'NS § 5-6C-07(a)(1); 11A VT. STAT. ANN. § 21.09(a)(1).

40. 11A VT. STAT. ANN. § 21.09(a)(1)(F).

41. MD. CODE ANN. CORPS. & ASS'NS § 5-6C-07(a)(2); 11A VT. STAT. ANN. § 21.09(a)(2).

42. 11A VT. STAT. ANN. § 21.10.

43. 11A VT. STAT. ANN. § 21.12.

44. 11A VT. STAT. ANN. § 21.10(b).

45. MD. CODE ANN. CORPS. & ASS'NS § 5-6C-08; 11A VT. STAT. ANN. § 21.14.

46. MD. CODE ANN. CORPS. & ASS'NS § 5-6C-08(c); 11A VT. STAT. ANN. § 21.14(d).

corporation's charter and the extent to which that specific public benefit was created; (3) any circumstances that have hindered the corporation's creation of the public benefit; and (4) an assessment of the corporation's societal and environmental performance prepared in accordance with a third-party standard, applied consistently with the prior year's benefit report or explaining the reasons for any inconsistent application.[47]

For Vermont benefit corporations, the annual benefit report must include (1) a statement of the corporation's specific goals or outcomes for creating general public benefit and any specific public benefit for the year; (2) a description of the corporation's actions taken to attain those goals or outcomes and the extent to which the goals or outcomes were attained; (3) a description of any circumstances that hindered the attainment of the goals or outcomes and the creation of general or specific public benefits; (4) specific actions the corporation can take to improve its social and environmental performance and attain the goals or outcomes identified; (5) an assessment of the corporation's societal and environmental performance prepared in accordance with a third-party standard, applied consistently with the prior year's benefit report or explaining the reasons for any inconsistent application; (6) a statement of specific goals and outcomes identified by the corporation and approved by the shareholders for creating general and/or specific public benefit for the following year; (7) the name and address of the benefit director(s) and the benefit officer, if any; (8) the compensation paid to each director for their service as directors; (9) the name of all beneficial or record owners of at least 5 percent of the corporation's shares; and (10) a benefit director's statement.[48] The benefit director's statement shall consist of a written opinion as to whether the corporation acted in accordance with its general public benefit purpose and any specific public benefit purpose in all material respects during the year, and whether the directors and officers acted in accordance with the applicable standards of conduct.[49] If the benefit director believes that the corporation failed to act in accordance with those purposes, or if the directors and officers failed to act in accordance with those standards of conduct, the benefit director's statement shall include a description of those failures.[50]

---

47. MD. CODE ANN. CORPS. & ASS'NS § 5-6C-08(a).
48. 11A VT. STAT. ANN. § 21.14(a).
49. 11A VT. STAT. ANN. § 21.10(c)(3).
50. 11A VT. STAT. ANN. § 21.10(c)(4).

Among those who have acclaimed the creation of the benefit corporation as a new legal form are Ben Cohen and Jerry Greenfield, founders of the Vermont-based ice cream company Ben & Jerry's Homemade, Inc. (www.benandjerrys.com), which was sold to Unilever in 2000.[51] Under traditional corporate law, had Cohen and Greenfield rejected Unilever's offer at the time, they could have been sued by shareholders. However, if the ice cream company had been a Vermont benefit corporation, the directors would have been required to take into account, in deciding whether the corporation should be sold, the corporation's long-term and short-term interests, including the possibility that those interests might have been best served by the corporation's continued independence. They would also have been required to take into account the effects on the company's employees and the community where the company's facilities were located. Cohen has commented, "The more defenses that you have and the more legal roadblocks to having the company taken over by an entity that doesn't share that social mission, the better it is for keeping the interests of the community at heart."[52] (However, commentators have suggested that the risk of a successful shareholder lawsuit against the directors of Ben & Jerry's was slim given its capital structure, with 47 percent of the stock being owned at the time by Cohen, Greenfield, and another director, and the existence of the corporation's anti-takeover defenses.[53])

Still, the benefit corporation is a fragile new entity, yet to be tested in the courts. Although its directors are intended to have "immunity from liability" in the "reasonable performance of [their] duties," litigants may disagree about what is "reasonable," and directors could be attacked by shareholders for not doing enough to benefit the public, ironically expanding rather than limiting the directors' fiduciary obligations. That said, the benefit corporation is clearly a step in the right direction, adding a significant design choice to the attorney's inventory.

---

51. Dave Gram, *States Move to Let Firms Pursue Social Mission*, SEATTLE TIMES, Apr. 11, 2010, *available at* http://seattletimes.nwsource.com/html/localnews/2011582541_apusbenefitcorporations1stldwritethru.html.

52. Antony Page & Robert A. Katz, *Freezing Out Ben & Jerry: Corporate Law and the Sale of a Social Enterprise Icon*, 35 VT. L. REV. 211, 233–34, 237–38 (2010).

53. *Id.*

Flexible Purpose Corporations

A flexible purpose corporation is a new type of entity that has been proposed in legislation in California, but as this book goes to publication, has not yet been enacted into law.[54] A bill to authorize flexible purpose corporations was introduced into the California Senate on February 19, 2010, but a committee hearing was postponed on April 5, 2010, and no further action was taken on the legislation.[55] In 2011, a similar bill was reintroduced in the state senate on February 8.[56]

The bill was originally drafted by a group known as the California Working Group for New Corporate Forms (the Working Group).[57] The Working Group is a group of corporate lawyers from private law firms, nonprofit law firms, and academia.[58] The group began to seek alternatives to traditional corporations and LLCs in 2008, after Governor Arnold Schwarzenegger vetoed California Assembly Bill 2944.[59] A.B. 2944 would have allowed the directors of all California corporations, in considering the best interests of the corporation and its shareholders, to take into account both the long-term and short-term interests of the corporation and its shareholders, as well as the effects of the corporation's actions on its prospects for potential growth, development, productivity, and profitability; the economy of the state and the nation; the corporation's employees, suppliers, customers, and creditors; community and societal corporations; and the environment.[60]

After the veto of A.B. 2944, the Working Group came up with the plan of creating a different type of corporate form. The bill pertaining to flexible purpose corporations would require that any corporation wishing to elect such a classification would have to include in the corporation's articles of incorporation a statement that the corporation is organized as a flexible purpose corporation and include the words "flexible purpose corporation" or an

---

54. S.B. 201 (Cal. 2011).
55. S.B. 1463 (Cal. 2010).
56. S.B. 201 (Cal. 2011).
57. W. DERRICK BRITT ET AL., FREQUENTLY ASKED QUESTIONS: PROPOSED AMENDMENTS TO THE CALIFORNIA CORPORATIONS CODE FOR A NEW CORPORATE FORM: THE FLEXIBLE PURPOSE CORPORATION 1 (Jan. 5, 2010).
58. *Id.* at 1.
59. *Id.* at 2 (Jan. 5, 2010).
60. A.B. 2944 (Cal. 2008).

abbreviation thereof in the corporate name.[61] The corporation would also have to include a statement that the corporation's purpose is to engage in a lawful activity or profession "for the benefit of the long-term and the short-term interests of the flexible purpose corporation and its shareholders."[62] Also required to be included would be a statement that the corporation's purposes included engaging in one or more of the following purposes: (a) "[o]ne or more charitable or public purpose activities that a nonprofit public benefit corporation is authorized to carry out"; (b) "[t]he purpose of promoting positive short-term or long-term effects of, or minimizing adverse short-term or long-term effects of, the flexible purpose corporation's activities upon" the corporation's employees, suppliers, customers, and creditors; the community and society; and/or the environment.[63]

A flexible purpose corporation would also be required to provide an annual report to its shareholders containing a management discussion and analysis (MD&A) relating to the corporation's stated purposes as set forth in its articles of incorporation, known as the "special purpose MD&A."[64] The special purpose MD&A would include an identification and discussion of short-term and long-term objectives of the corporation relating to its special purpose or purposes, and an identification and explanation of any changes made in those special purpose objectives during the fiscal year.[65] The corporation would identify the material actions it had taken during the fiscal year to achieve its special purpose objectives, the impact of those actions, the relationships between the actions and the reported outcomes, and the extent to which those actions achieved the corporation's special purpose objectives during the year.[66] The corporation would further identify the material actions it intended to take in the short term and long term with regard to achieving those objectives and the intended impact therefrom.[67]

Moreover, the special purpose MD&A would include a "description of the process for selecting, and an identification and description of, the financial, operating, and other measures used by the flexible purpose corporation during the fiscal year for evaluating its performance in achieving its

61. S.B. 201, sec. 11, § 2602(a), (b)(3) (Cal. 2011).
62. S.B. 201, sec. 11, § 2602(b)(1) (Cal. 2011).
63. S.B. 201, sec. 11, § 2602(b)(2) (Cal. 2011).
64. S.B. 201, sec. 11, § 3500(b) (Cal. 2011).
65. S.B. 201, sec. 11, § 3500(b)(1) (Cal. 2011).
66. S.B. 201, sec. 11, § 3500(b)(2) (Cal. 2011).
67. S.B. 201, sec. 11, § 3500(b)(3) (Cal. 2011).

special purpose objectives, including an explanation of why the flexible purpose corporation selected those measures and identification and discussion of the nature and rationale for any material changes in those measures made during the fiscal year."[68] The corporation would also be required to identify and discuss any material operating and capital expenditures made during the fiscal year in furtherance of achieving its special purpose objectives, and estimate the additional material expenditures that would be required over the ensuing three years in doing so.[69]

The special purpose MD&A would have to be sent to shareholders at least 15 days before the stockholders' annual meeting.[70] It would also have to be made available to the public on the corporation's website or by similar electronic means.[71]

On the other hand, flexible purpose corporations with fewer than 100 stockholders of record would be exempt from preparing a special purpose MD&A if the corporation held waivers of compliance from holders of at least two-thirds of the corporation's shares.[72]

Should the flexible purpose corporation be enacted into law in California, it would be possible for corporations to elect such a form and thus give directors and management protection to act according to a social or environmental mission that may be as important as, or more important than, profits.[73]

As of this writing, it is unclear whether the flexible purpose corporation will ever be established in California. Perhaps the state may choose to adopt a benefit corporation law, similar to those enacted in Maryland and Vermont in 2010 and discussed elsewhere in this chapter, that would accomplish many of the same goals as the flexible purpose corporation legislation is expected to provide. However, the flexible purpose corporation bill is intended, as its name implies, to give corporations greater flexibility by not defining specifically what a corporation must do to qualify as "ben-

---

68. S.B. 201, sec. 11, § 3500(b)(4) (Cal. 2011).
69. S.B. 201, sec. 11, § 3500(b)(5) (Cal. 2011).
70. S.B. 201, sec. 11, § 3500(c) (Cal. 2011).
71. S.B. 201, sec. 11, § 3500(b) (Cal. 2011).
72. S.B. 201, sec. 11, § 3502(h) (Cal. 2011).
73. Joel Makower, *California's Bold Move to Legitimize Sustainable Business,* GreenBiz.com (Feb. 14, 2011), *available at* http://www.greenbiz.com/blog/2011/02/14/california%E2%80%99s-move-legalize-sustainable-business.

eficial."[74] Hence, the flexible benefit corporation form would more likely be adopted by larger and publicly traded corporations, compared to benefit corporations, which tend to be smaller and privately held.[75]

Michigan Public and Triple Benefit Corporations

A bill was introduced in 2010 in the state of Michigan that would have amended its Business Corporation Act to allow for the creation of "Public Benefit Corporations" and "Triple Benefit Corporations."[76] The proposed legislation generally mirrored the requirements for forming an L³C and required that such corporations balance the interests of both people and the planet while pursuing profit.[77] In doing so, such corporations would be required to serve the interests of all stakeholders equally, including shareholders, employees, contractors, creditors, customers, suppliers, society at large, and the physical world in which they operate.[78] The bill was referred to committee and made no further progress before the legislative session expired. As this book goes to press, it has not yet been introduced again in the 2011 session.

Minnesota Community Enhancement Corporations

Minnesota State Senator John Marty has proposed legislation that would require a director of a community enhancement corporation to "seek the best interests of the corporation: (1) in good faith; (2) in a manner the director reasonably believes to be in the best interests of the corporation; and (3) with the care an ordinarily prudent person in a like position would exercise under similar circumstances." "The best interests of the corporation means those goals and objectives which are reasonably thought to provide for long-term community and enhancement or to advance one or more interests of stakeholders." Stakeholders include shareholders, employees, customers, "communities of interest," and creditors. Senator Marty's bill has not yet been considered by the Minnesota legislature.[79]

---

74. *Id.*
75. *Id.*
76. H.B. 6454 (Mich. 2010).
77. *Id.*
78. *Id.*
79. Draft copies of *Minnesota Community Enhancement Corporation Act*, MINN. STATS. Ch. 304 A.

Cooperatives (Co-ops)

As an alternative to utilizing a hybrid entity form, social enterprises may seek to form a cooperative to accomplish a social mission. Conceptually, cooperatives could be viewed as businesses owned and controlled by groups of individuals or businesses united to promote their common economic and social needs. If a social enterprise seeks to grapple with and respond to social needs, cooperatives can easily be said to qualify. They provide an outlet for producers of goods and services, often farmers, to better their livelihood through cooperation. The purpose of the cooperative is to provide benefits to its constituents through programs that allow producers to receive marketing services at low prices, receive supplies below cost, and better control the price that they eventually charge to the end consumer of the products or services.

The Rochdale Society of Equitable Pioneers, founded in Rochdale, England, in 1844, established the model for the modern cooperative movement. Its members, 28 weavers and other artisans, each contributed one pound sterling to capitalize a store that would sell goods that they themselves could not afford to purchase. At first they stocked butter, sugar, flour, oatmeal, and a few candles, but within three months their Toad Lane shop also offered tea and tobacco, and quickly gained a reputation for high-quality, unadulterated goods. Others took notice of the society's success and, by the mid-1850s, 1,000 cooperatives had been launched in England, signaling the start of a worldwide movement.[80]

The Society's Rochford Principles, a set of ideals for the operation of cooperatives that guide cooperatives around the world to this day, were adopted by the International Co-operative Alliance (ICA), "an independent, non-governmental organization which unites, represents and serves cooperatives worldwide," in 1937, and have since been updated to form a part of ICA's "Statement of the Co-operative Identity."[81]

---

80. John K. Walton, *Co-operative Movement*, THE OXFORD COMPANION TO BRITISH HISTORY (Oxford Univ. Press 1997).

81. *Available at* www.ica.coop/coop/principles.html.

International Co-operative Alliance's Statement on the Co-operative Identity

Definition

A co-operative is an autonomous association of persons united voluntarily to meet their common economic, social, and cultural needs and aspirations through a jointly owned and democratically controlled enterprise.

Values

Co-operatives are based on the values of self-help, self-responsibility, democracy, equality, equity and solidarity. In the tradition of their founders, co-operative members believe in the ethical values of honesty, openness, social responsibility and caring for others.

Principles

The co-operative principles are guidelines by which co-operatives put their values into practice.

1st Principle: Voluntary and Open Membership

Co-operatives are voluntary organizations, open to all persons able to use their services and willing to accept the responsibilities of membership, without gender, social, racial, political or religious discrimination.

2nd Principle: Democratic Member Control

Co-operatives are democratic organizations controlled by their members, who actively participate in setting their policies and making decisions. Men and women serving as elected representatives are accountable to the membership. In primary co-operatives members have equal voting rights (one member, one vote) and co-operatives at other levels are also organised in a democratic manner.

3rd Principle: Member Economic Participation

Members contribute equitable to, and democratically control, the capital of their co-operative. At least part of that capital is usually the common property of the co-operative. Members usually receive limited compensation, if any, on capital subscribed as a condition of membership. Members allocate surpluses for any or all of the following purposes: developing their co-operative, possibly by setting up reserves, part of which at least would be indivisible;

benefiting members in proportion to their transactions with the co-operative; and supporting other activities approved by the membership.

4th Principle: Authority and Independence

Co-operatives are autonomous, self-help organizations controlled by their members. If they enter into agreements with other organisations, including governments, or raise capital from external sources, they do so on terms that ensure democratic control by their members and maintain their co-operative autonomy.

5th Principle: Education, Training and Information

Co-operatives provide education and training for their members, elected representatives, managers, and employees so they can contribute effectively to the development of their co-operatives. They inform the general public—particularly young people and opinion leaders—about the nature and benefits of co-operation.

6th Principle: Cooperation among Co-operatives

Co-operatives serve their members most effectively and strengthen the co-operative movement by working together through local, national, regional and international structures.

7th Principle: Concern for Community

Co-operatives work for the sustainable development of their communities through policies approved by their members.

Producer Cooperatives

One common purpose of cooperatives is to allow workers and producers of goods, such as farmers, to exert more control over the prices at which their goods are sold,[82] leading to a better value proposition for consumers.[83] This method of price control has been made possible largely through exceptions found in the federal antitrust laws, such as the Clayton Act.[84] If the social entrepreneur is seeking to provide aid to farmers or other producers of

---

82. Suzanne K. Golden, Comment, *Board of Directors' Fiduciary Duties: Are They Compromised in Agricultural Cooperatives?*, 10 SAN JOAQUIN AGRIC. L. REV. 201, 203 (2000).

83. *Id.* at 203.

84. *See* 15 U.S.C. § 17.

goods, a cooperative endeavor is a near-perfect tool to ensure fair labor and business practices.

Although consumer cooperatives are formed for the benefit of the member-consumers, most American cooperatives are "producer side" cooperatives, the majority of those being agricultural cooperatives. In fact, one of the largest and most famous cooperatives in the United States is a producer cooperative: Land O'Lakes, Inc. (www.landolakes.com). Land O' Lakes was organized as a cooperative enterprise in 1921 and serves dairy farmers, who make up the cooperative's membership.[85] The cooperative provides customer-members with supply services, supplying feed specifically tailored to dairy production.[86] As one of the largest dairy cooperatives in the world, it also supplies marketing services to its many members. From the board down to the CEO and other officers, Land O' Lakes' managerial structure is uniquely corporate, yet the essential elements of a cooperative remain: (1) providing benefits to members as its purpose; (2) having a one-member/one-vote dynamic, regardless of equity interest; and (3) having earnings allocated to membership based not on equity holdings but on business done by the member with the cooperative.[87]

Another instructive example of a producer cooperative that has found its own market niche is Big Tree Organic Farms (www.bigtreeorganic. com), a marketing cooperative of almond growers.[88] This co-op was formed in 1998 to promote almonds grown organically in California's San Joaquin Valley.[89] Big Tree has 20 farmer-members with a combined total of 700 acres; although the farms range from 11 to 150 acres, each farmer has one vote.[90] In addition to providing a single brand name for the farms to market their almonds, the co-op handles almond processing itself and provides training sessions and workshops to help its members and attract new ones.[91] Big Tree processed approximately 1.5 million pounds of al-

---

85. *See* http://www.landolakesinc.com/.

86. *See id.*

87. *See* http://www.landolakesinc.com/company/corporateresponsibility/default.aspx.

88. Big Tree Organic Farms, *available at* http://www.bigtreeorganic.com/BigTreeOrganicFarms/Homepage.html.

89. Equal Exchange, *Big Tree Organic Farms* (Oct./Nov. 2008), *available at* http://www.equalexchange.coop/big-tree-organic-farms-1.

90. *Id.*

91. *Id.*

monds in 2008 and has grown to be the second-largest organic handler of almonds in the state.[92]

Consumer Cooperatives

Consumer cooperatives, which are less prevalent than producer cooperatives, are organized to provide the end users of certain products and services with greater information before purchasing products and services. Generally speaking, consumer cooperatives operate on principles similar to producer-side cooperatives—that is, to provide services to members, to have the members democratically control the cooperative, and to have any distributions made based on business done with the cooperative.[93]

Although this type of cooperative is beginning to catch on in the United States, the majority of these cooperatives exist abroad. One of the largest consumer cooperatives in the world is the Co-operative Group (www.co-operative.coop), organized and operating in the United Kingdom.[94] The group has more than 4 million members and serves as an umbrella organization for smaller cooperatives that purchase membership interests in the larger group.[95] The cooperative serves consumer-members in various areas of consumer spending, such as purchasing cars, food, health-care products, and insurance.[96]

Multistakeholder Cooperatives

Multistakeholder cooperatives serve various membership groups, or stakeholders. For instance, in producer cooperatives, there may be various types of producers that a single cooperative serves.[97] These cooperatives are organized and governed by the same principles discussed throughout this section but may serve a variety of small producers who produce different goods

---

92. *Id.*

93. John Winward, *The Organized Consumer and Consumer Information Cooperatives, in* THE AUTHORITY OF THE CONSUMER 76–77 (Russell Keat et al. eds., 1994).

94. *See* http://www.co-operative.coop/.

95. *See id.*

96. *See id.*

97. Elisabeth Mattsson, *Social Economy and New Cooperatives Create Jobs,* COPAC OPEN FORUM, *available at* http://www.copacgva.org/about/2000/cecop-text.pdf.

or services, such as local community-based micro enterprises.[98] Such cooperatives may focus on serving all the business in a particular community.

Cooperatives—Formation Issues

In jurisdictions such as Illinois and Wisconsin, cooperatives are organized under laws that specifically deal with cooperatives. In such instances, there may or may not be any distinction based on the seeking of profits. For instance, in Illinois, cooperatives are organized under the Illinois Cooperative Act.[99] Under this act, a cooperative is organized by incorporating as a corporation that specifically serves its shareholders by providing certain goods and services to those shareholders.[100] There are strict constraints placed on the ownership of shares and the numbers of shares issued, ensuring that no one shareholder has effective control of the cooperatives.[101]

In Wisconsin, one of the states that pioneered cooperative legislation, a cooperative is organized specifically through the filing of articles of incorporation and bylaws.[102] Under Wisconsin law, a cooperative must be designated specifically as such and distinguished from any other type of entity.[103] In Wisconsin, the essential feature of a cooperative is the distributions made to its patrons.[104]

In addition to the traditional cooperative law, in 2006 Wisconsin passed a second statute dealing with cooperatives, the Wisconsin Cooperative Association Act, which works in conjunction with the earlier statute and provides an alternative act under which to organize.[105] The main differences in the 2006 act center on limiting the purposes of the co-op and having certain restrictions placed on membership.[106] The 2006 act still requires a filing with the secretary of state of Wisconsin.

---

98. *Id.*
99. 805 ILL. COMP. STAT. 310.
100. 805 ILL. COMP. STAT. 310/1.
101. 805 ILL. COMP. STAT. 310/2.
102. WIS. STAT. § 185.01.
103. WIS. STAT. § 185.01.
104. WIS. STAT. § 185.02.
105. Dorsey & Whitney, *Wisconsin Adopts Second Cooperative Statute: The Wisconsin Cooperative Statute Act* (Mar. 2007), *available at* http://www.dorsey.com/agribusiness_news_mar_2007/.
106. WIS. STAT. § 193.01.

Regardless of how and where it is organized, a co-op is defined by its membership, the services provided to and by that membership, and the types of distributions made to that membership.

Cooperatives—Federal Taxation Aspects

Cooperatives have a special designation within the Internal Revenue Code. The term "cooperative association" includes any corporation operating on a cooperative basis and allocating amounts to patrons on the basis of the business done with or for such patrons.[107] Stated differently, for federal tax purposes "a 'cooperative association' is an organization established by individuals to provide themselves with goods and services or to produce and dispose of the products of their labor. The means of production and distribution are those owned in common and the earnings revert to the members, not on the basis of their investment in the enterprise but in the proportion to their patronage or personal participation in it."[108]

In *Puget Sound Plywood, Inc. v. Commissioner*, the Tax Court noted that cooperatives have three distinct characteristics:[109]

(1) The subordination of capital, both in regard to the control of the cooperative and in regard to the ownership of pecuniary benefit from the cooperative. This means that the amount of capital (i.e., money) contributed to the cooperative does not determine control over the cooperative, nor does it determine the member's financial interest in the cooperative.

(2) Democratic control by the worker-members. This means that all worker-members have equal voting in the cooperative and no proxy voting is permitted.

(3) The vesting of all profits arising from the corporate endeavor to the worker-members. This means that all income made by the cooperative in excess of the operating cost must accrue to the worker-members in proportion not to their capital contribution but rather to their participation in the cooperative enterprise. "Participation" is determined by a combination of statutory guidance and the cooperative's governing documents.

---

107. 26 C.F.R. § 1.522-1(b)(1).
108. Puget Sound Plywood, Inc. v. Comm'r, 44 T.C. 305 (1965).
109. *Id.* at 308.

If these three characteristics are met, then the business enterprise will be classified as a cooperative association under IRC § 521.[110] That section exempts from tax cooperative associations as dictated by Subchapter T of the IRC.[111] As noted in the regulation accompanying IRC § 521, cooperative associations are subject to both normal tax and surtax as normal business corporations, but how that tax is calculated will be determined according to Subchapter T.[112] Subchapter T is very complex, but in sum, unlike for-profit business corporations, cooperative associations are exempt from taxation on all income that is distributed to worker-members.[113] Apart from the requirements of Subchapter T, cooperatives will be considered exempt organizations for any law that refers to organizations exempt from income tax.[114] It is important to note that, while the IRC speaks specifically to agricultural cooperatives, all the rules and regulations apply to all forms of cooperative, such as worker cooperatives considered producer organizations, that have the required characteristics stated above.

Cooperatives—Governance

At their core, cooperatives are still businesslike entities and will, for the most part, be afforded the treatment that the law has given to business entities and their managers. Based on how the cooperative is organized and who it serves, fiduciary duties may be articulated in different ways, but the fundamental duties of loyalty, care, and obedience owed by cooperative managers will remain.[115] The directors and officers of a cooperative enterprise will also be members of the cooperative, and as such, all decisions they make will have a direct impact on their livelihoods.[116] This will present unique problems for cooperative managers.

---

110. 26 C.F.R. § 1.522-1(b)(1); Puget Sound Plywood, Inc. v. Comm'r, 44 T.C. 305. 308 (1965); I.R.C. § 521(b)(1).

111. I.R.C. § 521(a).

112. 26 C.F.R. § 1.522-1(b)(1).

113. I.R.C. § 1382.

114. I.R.C. § 522(a).

115. Ronald L. Perl, *Legal Standards by Which Community Association Boards Are Judged*, N.J. LAWYER, Oct. 2006, at 41, 42; Levandusky v. One Fifth Ave. Apartment Corp., 553 N.E. 2d 1321, 1322 (N.Y. 1990); *see also* Iowa Cooperative v. Schewe, 149 F. Supp. 2d 709 (N.D. Iowa 2001).

116. Suzanne K. Golden, Comment, *Board of Directors' Fiduciary Duties: Are They Compromised in Agricultural Cooperatives?*, 10 SAN JOAQUIN AGRIC. L. REV. 201 (2000).

Cooperative members join a cooperative by contributing capital, also known as membership fees.[117] As noted above, every jurisdiction has its own laws on cooperative formation and what is required in terms of equity contribution and ownership rights among members.[118] Thus, cooperatives may be organized both as stock or non-stock enterprises.[119] The majority of cooperatives in the Unites States are organized on a stock basis.[120] Unlike business corporations, regardless of equity owned, each member receives one vote when asked to vote on cooperative matters and transactions.[121]

Much like business corporations, cooperatives operate on the premise that ownership and management should have some level of separation. Accordingly, a cooperative will have a board of directors that manages day-to-day operations and that may further delegate management powers to officers.[122] Smaller cooperatives resemble small, closely held corporations in which each member will have a larger role in management, while larger cooperatives resemble publicly traded corporations, where there is a more strict separation of management in transacting the day-to-day business.[123] Still, unlike corporations, cooperative board membership is usually restricted by statute to the members of the cooperative.[124] With this corporate form of management, the duties owed by cooperative directors and officers, as well as the protections afforded them, will mirror the duties of their corporate counterparts.[125]

The directors and officers of cooperatives are afforded the protection of the business judgment rule.[126] This is the applicable standard of review when considering the actions of a cooperative board or its officers.[127] Ac-

---

117. *Id.* at 203.

118. *Id.* at 204.

119. *Id.* at 204.

120. *Id.* at 204.

121. *Id.* at 207; Katherine J. Sedo, *The Application of Securities Laws to Cooperatives: A Call for Equal Treatment for Nonagricultural Cooperatives*, 46 DRAKE L. REV. 259, 261 (1997).

122. *General Principles and Problems of Cooperatives: An Introduction*, 1954 WIS. L. REV. 533, 548.

123. Suzanne K. Golden, *supra* note 116 at 201, 207.

134. *General Principles, supra* note 122 at 533, 539.

125. *See infra* Chapter 5.

126. Suzanne K. Golden, *supra* note 116 at 201, 215.

127. Gaillard v. Natomas Co., 256 Cal. Rptr. 702, 711 (Ct. App. 1989); Eldridge v. Tymshare, Inc., 230 Cal. Rptr. 815, 820 (Ct. App. 1986); Nursing Home Building Corp. v. DeHart, 535 P.2d 137 (Wash. Ct. App. 1975).

cordingly, it is presumed that the directors and officers complied with their duties of care, loyalty, and obedience to the mission of the cooperative, all a part of the ultimate duty to operate the cooperative so that each member can increase its profitability.[128]

The duty of loyalty includes acting for the best interest of the cooperative and its members/shareholders in seeking that the members/shareholders receive the greatest benefit. This duty is owed to all members/shareholders and to the entity itself.[129]

The business judgment presumption will not be given with regard to conflicted transactions in which a director or officer has a material interest in the transaction in which he or she is transacting on behalf of the cooperative that is adverse to the interest of the cooperative and other members.[130] Having an interest in a transaction is not enough to cause the individual to lose the benefit of the business judgment rule, as directors and officers will always have an interest in the transaction as members of the cooperative. Rather, the interest must conflict with that of the cooperative and must be material. Additionally, self-dealing—in which a director gains personally at the expense of the cooperative and its member/shareholders—is a particular species of conflicted transaction that must be avoided at all cost in order to maintain business judgment protection.[131] For instance, when an Arkansas cooperative's board accounted for 80 percent of the business done with the cooperative at the expense of the other shareholders, this was found to be impermissible self-dealing.[132] If there is a breach of the duty of loyalty due to a material conflict, the cooperative may void the transaction at its discretion, unless the director or officer can show the intrinsic fairness of the transaction.[133]

The duty of care requires that cooperative directors and officers act with due care when making business decisions. In the execution of the duty of care, the business judgment rule presumes that all business decisions were made with the required care necessary to give the decision valid-

---

128. Suzanne K. Golden, *supra* note 116 at 201, 215–16.
129. *Id.* at 209.
130. *Id.* at 215–16.
131. Douglas Fee & Allan C. Hoberg, *Potential Liability of Directors of Agricultural Cooperatives*, 37 ARK. L. REV. 60 (1983).
132. Driver v. Producers Cooperative Inc., 345 S.W.2d 16 (Ark. 1961).
133. *See infra* Chapter 5.

ity.[134] Much like in the corporate context, the substantive decision making of the cooperative's management will rarely, if ever, come under question, except possibly through claims of waste of cooperative assets. Rather, the duty of care is concerned with process. When making decisions, all fiduciaries must comply with the applicable standard of care. As a general rule, although jurisdictions will differ on what standard of care to use, the majority use a "reasonable person in like position" standard.[135] Consequentially, a director or officer will retain the protection of the business judgment rule if decisions are made on the basis of reasonable information after taking into account such information as a reasonable person in his position would.[136] If business judgment protection is lost and the duty of care is breached, the cooperative may void the transaction at its discretion, unless the director or officer can show the intrinsic fairness of the transaction.[137]

The duty of obedience is one of the central fiduciary duties that managers of a cooperative owe to both the entity and its shareholders/members. This requires fiduciaries to ensure that the cooperative complies with the purposes for which it was organized: namely, to benefit its members/shareholders by providing services to those individuals.[138] Although the duty of obedience does exist for business corporation managers, it rarely is a concern, because most business corporations are organized for any legitimate legal purpose. In any event, an action by the managers of the cooperative that does not comport with the purposes of the cooperative will be considered an ultra vires action and be void, as opposed to voidable.[139]

*   *   *   *

The business forms best suited to the social entrepreneur are the product of imagination and dedication of innovative social entrepreneurs and their attorneys, all committed to increased transparency and accountability, and all seeking to drive positive social change. The next chapter will provide guidance for social enterprises that choose to operate their ventures as nonprofit organizations and will highlight the advantages, disadvantages, and governing issues associated with them.

---

134. Douglas Fee & Allan C. Hoberg, *supra* note 131 at 60, 72–73,
135. *See id.* at 70.
136. Suzanne K. Golden, *supra* note 116 at 201, 215–16.
137. *See infra* Chapter 5.
138. Suzanne K. Golden, *supra* note 116 at 201, 208.
139. *See infra* Chapter 5.

CHAPTER FOUR

Governing the Nonprofit, Tax-Exempt Social Enterprise

In the United States, organizations are broadly divided between those that are for-profit and those that are nonprofit. While social enterprises may be operated by either type of entity or a combination of the two, this chapter discusses the unique opportunities and challenges associated with operating a social enterprise as a nonprofit, tax-exempt organization.

Generally speaking, a tax-exempt organization is organized under a state's nonprofit statute and regulated by the attorney general of the state in which the entity is formed. Qualification for tax exemption is conferred upon the entity by the Internal Revenue Service (IRS). Consequently, forming and operating a tax-exempt social enterprise requires a working knowledge of both federal and state laws.

Advantages to Tax-Exempt Status

The nonprofit form cannot offer the social entrepreneur the prerogatives of ownership available to the for-profit shareholder or member. Moreover, the nonprofit organization can find itself capital-constrained, as it has no shares or other equity securities to sell. But operating a social enterprise as a tax-exempt entity offers numerous benefits.

Of course, the primary advantage is exemption from federal income tax. In some instances, exempt status under federal law will mean comparable or similar status under state and local law, and it may also mean exemption from certain federal excise and employment taxes. In some jurisdictions, these exemptions will also apply to taxes on the sales and use of property and on property purchases.

While funding opportunities are more fully described in Chapter 7, a brief overview of the funding advantages associated with tax-exempt entities is warranted at this point. Tax-exempt social enterprises organized as public charities under IRC § 501(c)(3) are eligible to receive charitable donations from donors who may be sympathetic to, and wish to contribute to, the social enterprise's mission. Many tax-exempt organizations will also qualify to receive grants distributed from private foundations, because a foundation may distribute funds to a public charity in satisfaction of its mandatory distribution requirements, which requires private foundations to distribute annually at least 5 percent of the excess of the aggregate fair market value of all foundation assets, other than those that are used directly for carrying on the foundation's exempt purposes, over any acquisition indebtedness for such assets.[1] Finally, federal and state governments often make grants primarily to tax-exempt organizations.

In addition to the tax savings and multiple sources of revenue that are afforded tax-exempt entities, there are many other advantages that may not be as apparent to social entrepreneurs. Securities issued by an entity organized and operated exclusively for religious, educational, benevolent, fraternal, charitable, or reformatory purposes, and not for pecuniary profit, as long as there is no private inurement, are exempt from registration under the Securities Act of 1933.

Further, charitable organizations are exempt from the Organized Crime Control Act, which otherwise prohibits bingo games, lotteries, and similar games of chance. The proceeds from these activities are exempt from tax as long as no part of the proceeds inures to the benefit of any individual in his or her private capacity.

Finally, a tax-exempt organization may be perceived as having earned the implied endorsement of the federal government as selfless and altruistic, clearly a branding and positioning benefit.

Nonprofit, Tax-Exempt Corporations

The majority of American social enterprises are non-stock corporations organized under a state's nonprofit corporate statute. The nonprofit corpo-

---

1. I.R.C. § 4942(d), (e).

ration must serve public interests and must have a board of directors whose members carry out the day-to-day business of the corporation.

Ownership and Management

No individual or entity owns a non-stock corporation. Still, such entities may be organized to allow for the creation of voting or non-voting membership interests, and individuals or entities may donate to the nonprofit in exchange for such non-monetary interests. Because of the lack of profit motive and the donative nature of contributing to a nonprofit corporation, directors and officers of the nonprofit generally do not owe fiduciary obligations to any member.[2]

Tax-Exempt Status

A tax-exempt nonprofit corporation will generally need to be operated solely for charitable, educational, or other IRC § 170(c)(2)(B) purposes. Assuming tax-exempt status is conferred, the corporation's net income will generally not be subject to income tax. Moreover, it will be eligible to accept tax-deductible contributions or donations from any individual or entity.

To obtain tax-exempt status, the corporation must complete and file Form 1023 (Application for Recognition of Exemption under Section 501(c)(3) of the Internal Revenue Code) with the IRS.

Fiduciary Duties Owed in Nonprofit, Tax-Exempt Corporation Settings

Much like the directors and officers of a for-profit enterprise, directors and officers of a nonprofit corporation owe fiduciary responsibilities to the corporation.[3] While these duties can also be classified in terms of care and loyalty, the ultimate duty to be served by the fiduciary is not one of profit maximization as it is in the for-profit setting. Instead, the ultimate duty to be served is the fulfillment of the social mission, which serves as the basis for the core duties of loyalty and care owed by the directors and officers of

---

2. Terry Lynn Helge, *Policing the Good Guys: Regulation of the Charitable Sector Through a Federal Charity Board*, 19 CORNELL J.L. & PUB. POL'Y 1, 40 (2009).

3. *See generally* MARC J. LANE, LEGAL HANDBOOK FOR NONPROFIT ORGANIZATIONS (Amacom 1981).

nonprofit corporations.[4] Arising from this mission-driven purpose is the additional duty of obedience.[5] Some jurisdictions have classified this duty of obedience as part of the duty of loyalty, but as obedience focuses on keeping the organization's mission uncompromised, many jurisdictions see this duty, in the nonprofit context, as separate and distinct. One of the main differences between for-profit and nonprofit corporations, in the application of fiduciary principles, is that nonprofit directors and officers owe duties only to the corporation.[6]

Accordingly, regardless of the voting power of any members, those members are owed no direct fiduciary duties. The rationale is that members who contribute to a nonprofit corporation do not have a financial stake in the entity.[7] After all, distributions are prohibited. Still, some jurisdictions allow members to bring derivative suits on behalf of the corporation, and all jurisdictions allow the state attorney general to enforce the fiduciary obligations owed to the corporation.[8] Moreover, federal and state tax officials have the power to enforce officers' and directors' duties, in relation to the corporate mission, through IRC § 501(c)(3) and corresponding state tax laws.

The Business Judgment Rule

Although commentators are not in full agreement about the applicability of the "business judgment" rule to decisions by nonprofit directors and officers, courts have generally found the business judgment rule to apply in the nonprofit context.[9] The application of the rule also appears to be supported by the Revised Model Nonprofit Corporation Act (RMNCA).[10]

---

4. *See generally* Harvey J. Goldschmid, *The Fiduciary Duties of Nonprofit Directors and Officers: Paradoxes, Problems, and Proposed Reforms*, 23 J. CORP. L. 631, 640 (1998).

5. *See generally id.* at 640.

6. *See generally* Terry Lynn Helge, *Policing the Good Guys: Regulation of the Charitable Sector Through a Federal Charity Board*, 19 CORNELL J.L. & PUB. POL'Y 1, 40 (2009).

7. *See generally id.* at 40.

8. *See generally id.* at 40; *see also* 760 ILL. COMP. STAT. §§ 11/16.5, 55/16, 55/17.

9. S.H. & Helen R. Scheuer Family Found. v. 61 Assocs., 582 N.Y.S.2d 662 (App. Div. 1992); Summers v. Cherokee Children & Family Servs., 112 S.W.3d 486 (Tenn. Ct. App. 2002); *see generally* MARC J. LANE, LEGAL HANDBOOK FOR NONPROFIT ORGANIZATIONS (Amacom 1981).

10. RMNCA § 8.30 cmt. 3.

The business judgment rule is the presumption that directors and officers have complied with their ultimate duty to advance the corporate mission, complying with the duties of loyalty, care, and obedience owed to the corporation when transacting on its behalf.[11] Unless a specific breach of duty can be proved, the business judgment rule will inoculate nonprofit officers and directors.

The Duty of Loyalty

A nonprofit's directors and officers owe a duty of undivided loyalty to the corporation. They must always act in good faith and in the best interest of the corporate enterprise[12] and may not use corporate resources for their own enrichment or misappropriate corporate resources.[13] (The same rules govern for-profit fiduciaries.)

Breaches of the duty of loyalty that lead to an improper benefit will result in tax penalties for the corporation and the individual who received the improper benefit.[14] If fiduciaries go too far in breaching the duty of loyalty, the result could be the loss of the corporation's tax-exempt status.[15]

Transactions involving material conflicts of interest will result in the loss of the business judgment rule's protection.[16] In most instances, these conflicts mirror those found in the for-profit context, in which directors are on both sides of a transaction involving the nonprofit enterprise. If such a transaction is present, the transaction is voidable, and all conflicted and interested directors may be held personally liable.[17]

(a) Conflicts of Interests

Owing to the specific tax consequences of nonprofit transactions, the IRS has a particular interest in conflicted transactions, as they may lead to im-

---

11. Gantler v. Stephens, 965 A.2d 695 (Del. 2009); see generally MARC J. LANE, LEGAL HANDBOOK FOR NONPROFIT ORGANIZATIONS (Amacom 1981).

12. RMNCA § 8.30 cmt. 3.

13. Id.

14. See I.R.C. § 501(c).

15. Id.; see generally MARC J. LANE, LEGAL HANDBOOK FOR NONPROFIT ORGANIZATIONS (Amacom 1981).

16. RMNCA § 8.30.

17. James J. Fishman, Improving Charitable Accountability, 62 MD. L. REV. 218, 235 (2003).

proper inurement problems.[18] There are questions on the Form 990 (Return of Organization Exempt from Income Tax) that specifically inquire into interested director and officer transactions. Where the IRS determines that a director or officer has improperly gained from an insider transaction, substantial tax penalties may be levied against that person as well as the directors who approved the transaction.[19] To guard against this possibility, the nonprofit should maintain strict conflict-of-interest policies and a method of disclosing and properly authorizing conflicts. The IRS has approved certain policies concerning conflicted transactions, which will avoid any adverse tax consequences.[20] The policies are shown in Exhibit 4-1. It is important for legal counsel to go over these IRS policies and integrate them into the governance instruments of the nonprofit corporation.[21]

(b) Usurping a Corporate Opportunity and Misappropriation of Corporate Information

Irrespective of entity form, directors and officers may not misappropriate a valid corporate opportunity, or misappropriate internal company information in order to enrich themselves.[22] A director may not improperly take an opportunity that rightfully belongs to the corporation.

There are two questions that must be asked. First, did the opportunity belong to the fiduciary or to the corporation?[23] If the opportunity belonged to the corporation, the issue becomes: was the opportunity properly exploited?[24]

When a corporation is still negotiating the purchase or sale of an asset and has not properly rejected the transaction, using inside information and

---

18. I.R.C. § 501(c).

19. I.R.C. § 501(c)(3).

20. *See* Instructions for Form 1023—Additional Material, *available at* http://www.irs.gov/instructions/i1023/ar03.html.

21. *See generally* MARC J. LANE, LEGAL HANDBOOK FOR NONPROFIT ORGANIZATIONS (Amacom 1981).

22. Mile-o-Mo Fishing Club, Inc. v. Noble, 210 N.E.2d 12 (Ill. App. Ct. 1965).

23. Guth v. Loft Inc., 5 A.2d 503 (Del. 1930); Johnston v. Greene, 121 A.2d 919 (Del. Ch. 1956); Mile-o-Mo Fishing Club, Inc. v. Noble, 210 N.E.2d 12 (Ill. App. Ct. 1965).

24. Guth v. Loft Inc., 5 A.2d 503 (Del. 1930); Johnston v. Greene, 121 A.2d 919 (Del. Ch. 1956); Mile-o-Mo Fishing Club, Inc. v. Noble, 210 N.E.2d 12 (Ill. App. Ct. 1965).

Exhibit 4-1

Procedures Recommended by the IRS for Properly Approving Conflicted Transactions

1. **Duty to Disclose**. In connection with any actual or possible conflict of interest, an interested person must disclose the existence of the financial interest and be given the opportunity to disclose all material facts to the directors and members of committees with governing board delegated powers considering the proposed transaction or arrangement.

2. **Determining Whether a Conflict of Interest Exists.** After disclosure of the financial interest and all material facts, and after any discussion with the interested person, he/she shall leave the governing board or committee meeting while the determination of a conflict of interest is discussed and voted upon. The remaining board or committee members shall decide if a conflict of interest exists.

3. **Procedures for Addressing the Conflict of Interest**

   - An interested person may make a presentation at the governing board or committee meeting, but after the presentation, he/she shall leave the meeting during the discussion of, and the vote on, the transaction or arrangement involving the possible conflict of interest.

   - The chairperson of the governing board or committee shall, if appropriate, appoint a disinterested person or committee to investigate alternatives to the proposed transaction or arrangement.

   - After exercising due diligence, the governing board or committee shall determine whether the organization can obtain with reasonable efforts a more advantageous transaction or arrangement from a person or entity that would not give rise to a conflict of interest.

   - If a more advantageous transaction or arrangement is not reasonably possible under circumstances not producing a conflict of interest, the governing board or committee shall determine by a majority vote of the disinterested directors whether the transaction or arrangement is in the organization's best interest, for its own benefit, and whether it is fair and reasonable. In conformity with the above determination it shall make its decision as to whether to enter into the transaction or arrangement.

knowledge to exploit the opportunity without company approval is a clear breach of the duty of loyalty. While exploiting a corporate opportunity and misappropriating inside information are each discrete fiduciary breaches,[25] they often occur during the same instance of fiduciary misconduct.

(c) Bad Faith, Fraud, and Illegality

Nonprofit and for-profit directors and officers alike must act in good faith.[26] Although case law speaking specifically to the duty of good faith in the nonprofit context is rare, courts have uniformly held that for-profit principles, where consistent, may be applied to nonprofit corporations and their fiduciaries.[27] Accordingly, nonprofit directors and officers should be aware that they are charged with managing the corporation in its business affairs and that any failure to do so may constitute a breach of the duty of good faith. As with for-profit corporations, bad faith exists where officers and directors show a conscious disregard for their duty to manage the corporation or where they consciously seek to harm the corporation. In the case of nonprofit organizations, bad faith may include actions that jeopardize the tax-exempt status of the nonprofit corporation.[28]

Not surprisingly, directors and officers will not receive protection for fraudulent or illegal actions taken on behalf of the corporation.[29] These actions, along with *ultra vires* actions (discussed below), are considered classical breaches of the duty of loyalty, which will result in the loss of business judgment protection. In the case of nonprofit organizations, it can also lead to the loss of tax-exempt status.[30]

(d) Duty of Obedience

Although often seen as a discrete duty, the duty of obedience may be con-

---

25. Mile-o-Mo Fishing Club, Inc. v. Noble, 210 N.E.2d 12, 15 (Ill. App. Ct. 1965) (a fiduciary may not, for private gain, employ knowledge obtained by virtue of his position).

26. RMNCA § 8.30; *see generally* MARC J. LANE, LEGAL HANDBOOK FOR NONPROFIT ORGANIZATIONS (Amacom 1981).

27. Mile-o-Mo Fishing Club, Inc. v. Noble, 210 N.E.2d 12, 15 (Ill. App. Ct. 1965).

28. I.R.C. § 501(c)(3), (4).

29. RMNCA § 8.30.

30. I.R.C. § 501(c)(3).

sidered a duty of loyalty owed to the nonprofit corporation. The duty of obedience has become unique to nonprofit corporations because of the limited nature of the corporation's purpose. To qualify for tax exemption under the IRC, a nonprofit must be organized exclusively for charitable, educational, benevolent, religious, or scientific purposes and may not allow distribution of the corporation income to any individual or shareholder.[31] Unlike their for-profit counterparts that are organized for any lawful business purpose, nonprofits are organized to accomplish a specific, mission-driven purpose. It is this specific purpose that makes the duty of obedience, and the responsibilities that follow, unique to nonprofits. Directors and officers are charged with respecting the corporate purpose or they stand to lose business judgment protection for their actions and incur serious tax consequences.[32] This purpose should be clearly expressed in the governance documents of the corporation.[33] If there is any appropriate change in the corporate purpose as allowed by the IRC, this change should also be reflected in the governance documents of the corporation.[34]

(i) Failing to Ensure the Tax-Exempt Status of the Corporation— Pitfalls to Avoid

The duty of obedience includes the duty to ensure that the nonprofit complies with the requirements to maintain its tax exemption.[35] This means not only pursuing the corporate mission, but also seeing to it that all federal and state filing and record-keeping requirements are satisfied.

One of the greatest pitfalls in trying to preserve tax-exempt status is the prohibition against "private inurement."[36] Private inurement occurs when the net earnings or assets of the tax-exempt corporation are transferred to a private individual or shareholder for his or her benefit and not in furtherance of the entity's tax-exempt purpose.[37] The types of conflicted transactions discussed above may be deemed private inurement transactions.[38]

---

31. I.R.C. § 501(c)(3).

32. James J. Fishman, *Improving Charitable Accountability*, 62 MD. L. REV. 218, 235 (2003).

33. *Id.* at 235.

34. *Id.* at 235.

35. *Id.*

36. I.R.C. § 501(c)(3).

37. *Id.*

38. Mosher & Wagenmaker, LLC, Not-for-Profit Directors' and Officers' Responsibilities, *available at* http://www.mosherlaw.com/featuredarticles.htm.

Private inurement may also be found simply because the compensation received by a director or officer is too great in comparison to the services that person performs.

A detailed discussion of private inurement and compensation issues as they relate to nonprofit, tax-exempt organizations is found later in this chapter.

(ii) Loans Between Officers or Directors and the Nonprofit, Tax-Exempt Corporation

Financing transactions involving corporate directors or officers may create a conflict of interest, whether the director or officer is making or receiving the loan. Whenever a fiduciary has a material interest in a transaction that is adverse to the corporation, a conflict of interest arises that will generally cause the business judgment rule presumption to be lost. A loan to a director or officer, or made by a director or officer, is such a conflict. Assuming that the loan is allowed by the applicable state law, such transactions are not void but voidable; the transaction may be saved if it is fair to the corporation or has been approved by a majority of disinterested directors.

A loan transaction may be considered an "excess benefit transaction": under IRC § 4958, a particular form of private inurement, when the value of the compensation received by the director or officer in the transaction exceeds the value of the consideration given by the director or officer for the compensation.[39] Loans made by a fiduciary to the corporation for which the fiduciary collects interest and loans made by the corporation to a fiduciary may be considered excess benefits.

(iii) Ultra Vires Liability

Ultra vires actions are actions taken by a corporation's officers and directors outside of the scope of the corporation's purpose.[40] The duty of obedience calls for strict adherence to that purpose.[41]

Put another way, authorizing ultra vires actions is a violation of the

---

39. Stern v. Lucy Webb Hayes Nat'l Training School, 381 F. Supp. 1003 (D.C. Cir. 1974).

40. James J. Fishman, *Improving Charitable Accountability*, 62 MD. L. REV. 218, 235 (2003).

41. *Id.* at 235.

duty of obedience owed by nonprofit directors and officers.[42] The Revised Model Nonprofit Corporation Act (RMNCA) makes provisions for *ultra vires* liability in cerain circumstances, whereby a current or former director, officer, employee, or other agent of a corporation may be sued for causing the corporation to take actions beyond the scope of its legal powers.[43]

Examples of *Ultra Vires* Actions in the Nonprofit Context

- A nonprofit hospital using corporate assets to fund activities that are not related to health care
- A nonprofit corporation allowing its assets to be controlled by a private person for the benefit of that private person, whether by contract or by forming a new entity with that person[44]
- A nonprofit corporation not utilizing endowments, in furtherance of the corporation's purpose, as specifically directed by donors

The Duty of Care

Directors and officers owe a duty of care to the nonprofit. Like their for-profit counterparts, they must adhere to a particular standard of due care in transacting on behalf of the corporation or lose the protection of the business judgment rule.[45] The duty requires that directors and officers consider all information relevant to a decision before it's made.[46] It applies to the management of corporate funds, overseeing all facets of the corporate function, and any other task germane to the running of the nonprofit corporation.[47] This duty allows for reliance on counsel, employees, and other members of the decision-making body, where that reliance is reasonable.[48]

The duty of care mainly concerns itself not with the substance of a transaction but with the process used to make the decision to enter into the transaction. Each jurisdiction will have its own standard of care, ranging generally from ordinary care to slight care.[49] In every instance, the direc-

---

42. *Id.* at 235.
43. RMNCA § 3.4.
44. *See* Rev. Rul. 98-15, 1998-1 C.B. 718.
45. RMNCA § 8.30(b).
46. *Id.*
47. *Id.*
48. RMNCA § 8.30(d).
49. *See* Ferris Elevator Co, Inc. v. Neffco, Inc., 674 N.E.2d 448 (Ill. App. Ct. 1996); *but see* RMNCA § 8.30(b).

tors and officers of a corporation should incorporate all information into their decision making.[50] Where they choose to rely on the information provided to them, it is imperative that the individuals providing the information are believed to be qualified to provide such information.[51] In any event, whether or not the duty has been breached and the protection of the business judgment lost is a fact-intensive analysis.

Board members, particularly those "insiders" who are employed by the corporation in another capacity, should be involved in every decision that the corporation takes on, except those with respect to which he or she has a personal interest. The same applies to officers in making decisions based on the powers that have been delegated to them.[52] Before making any decision, directors and officers should make sure they are intimately aware of the nonprofit's functional and financial condition.[53] While directors and officers are able to rely on others in the information-gathering process, this does not excuse them from performing the oversight function they owe as fiduciaries.[54] As part of this oversight, directors and officers, should be aware of the various reporting requirements of nonprofits.[55] Failing to properly comply with nonprofit reporting requirements may result in a breach of the common-law duty of care in most jurisdictions. Moreover, many state statutes, which contain state reporting requirements, also create statutory liability for failing to properly report the nature of the company's financial condition.[56]

In one case, directors failed to supervise the management of a nonprofit hospital's assets, abdicating their oversight duty to conflicted directors and allowing money to be deposited in banks with shared directors.[57] Using a gross negligence standard, the court found that some directors

---

50. RMNCA § 8.30(e).

51. *Id.*

52. RMNCA § 8.30(d).

53. Mosher & Wagenmaker, LLC, *Not-for-Profit Directors' and Officers' Responsibilities, available at* http://www.mosherlaw.com/featuredarticles.htm.

54. Stern v. Lucy Webb Hayes Nat'l Training School, 381 F. Supp. 1003 (D.D.C. 1974).

55. Mosher & Wagenmaker, LLC, *supra* note 53.

56. *See* 760 ILL. COMP. STAT. § 55/7.

57. Stern v. Lucy Webb Hayes Nat'l Training School, 381 F. Supp. 1003 (D.D.C. 1974).

breached their duty of loyalty and others their duty of care for paying little or no attention to their supervision duties.[58]

A director or officer may rely on the reports and actions of corporate employees and professionals in making decisions,[59] but that reliance must be warranted. They must reasonably believe the source or report to be reliable.[60] In addition, a director or officer may rely on the advice, opinion, and reports of legal counsel, public accountants, and other persons who the director or officer reasonably believes are competent as to the particular matter in question.[61]

Although these reliance rules are similar to those that apply to for-profit corporations, the RMNCA affords special reliance considerations in the case of an entity that is engaged in religious activity.[62] Directors and officers of such entities may rely on religious authorities and ministers, priests, rabbis, imams, or other persons whose position the director or officer reasonably believes justifies reliance and confidence and who the director or officer reasonably believes is reliable and competent in the matters presented.[63]

Waste and Misappropriation of Charitable Assets

As with for-profit corporations, waste can be classified as a substantive breach of the duty of care and is considered a prohibited act. For example, the Illinois Charitable Trust Act, which applies to nonprofit corporations, explicitly prohibits wasting corporate assets.[64] In the nonprofit corporation context, waste is not defined based so much on return from investment, but rather on how the funds or investment in question was used to forward the mission of the nonprofit organization.[65] In one instance, when the trustee of a nonprofit corporation funneled funds from the corporation into his own personal enterprises, the Illinois Appellate Court found that the investment of the assets into the trustee's personal business signifi-

---

58. *Id.*
59. RMNCA § 8.30(e).
60. RMNCA §§ 8.30(f), 8.42(c).
61. *Id.*
62. *Id.*
63. *Id.*
64. 760 ILL. COMP. STAT. 55/15(a).
65. Eurich v. Korean Found., Inc., 176 N.E.2d 692 (Ill. App. Ct. 1961).

cantly frustrated the corporation from being able to carry out its purpose.[66] This action was tantamount to waste of the nonprofit corporation's assets.[67] Accordingly, mismanaging funds in a way that significantly debilitates a nonprofit corporation in carrying out its function can be considered a waste of assets rather than a simple breach of procedural due care.[68]

Intrinsic Fairness

A fiduciary breach does not necessarily invalidate a transaction if the transaction can be deemed fair to the nonprofit enterprise. There is common-law and statutory support for the intrinsic fairness concept, both of which hinge on the concept of complete disclosure to the decision-making body.[69] Still, because the ultimate goal in a nonprofit enterprise is not the pursuit of profit but mission, the evaluation of intrinsic fairness will take on a different character in the nonprofit context, although the concepts of fair dealing and fair price carry over from the for-profit context.[70] For example, an interested transaction in which a financially weak tax-exempt organization receives credit, supplies, or services from a director may be permissible in the nonprofit context but not in the for-profit context.[71] The reason for this generally lies in the fact that as tax-exempt entities, nonprofit corporations have more limited resources in terms of obtaining funding and allocating services due to the restrictions in IRC § 501(c)(3).[72] What would be unfair to the corporation in the for-profit context may be fair to the corporation in the nonprofit context.[73]

---

66. *Id.*

67. *Id.*; *see also* Stern v. Lucy Webb Hayes Nat'l Training School, 381 F. Supp. 1003 (D.D.C. 1974) (where gross mismanagement of funds led to a misappropriation of corporate assets).

68. Eurich v. Korean Found., Inc., 176 N.E.2d 692 (Ill. App. Ct. 1961); *see also* Stern v. Lucy Webb Hayes Nat'l Training School, 381 F. Supp. 1003 (D.D.C. 1974).

69. *See* 805 ILL. COMP. STAT. § 105/108.60.

70. *See id.*

71. *See id.*

72. I.R.C. § 501(c).

73. James J. Fishman, *Improving Charitable Accountability*, 62 MD. L. REV. 218, 235 (2003).

Sample Conflict of Interest Policy

The Internal Revenue Service requires nonprofit organizations seeking recognition of tax exemption under Internal Revenue Code Section 501(c)(3) to disclose whether they have adopted a conflict of interest policy consistent with a sample conflict of interest policy prescribed by the IRS.[74] While not required, such a conflict of interest policy is strongly recommended. The following is the IRS's sample conflict of interest policy.[75]

(Note: Items marked *Hospital insert—for hospitals that complete Schedule C* are intended to be adopted by hospitals.)

Article I
Purpose

The purpose of the conflict of interest policy is to protect this tax-exempt organization's (Organization) interest when it is contemplating entering into a transaction or arrangement that might benefit the private interest of an officer or director of the Organization or might result in a possible excess benefit transaction. This policy is intended to supplement but not replace any applicable state and federal laws governing conflict of interest applicable to nonprofit and charitable organizations.

Article II
Definitions

1. Interested Person

Any director, principal officer, or member of a committee with governing board delegated powers, who has a direct or indirect financial interest, as defined below, is an interested person.

[*Hospital Insert—for hospitals that complete Schedule C:*

If a person is an interested person with respect to any entity in the health care system of which the organization is a part, he or she is an interested person with respect to all entities in the health care system.]

2. Financial Interest

A person has a financial interest if the person has, directly or indirectly, through business, investment, or family:

---

74. Internal Revenue Service, Form 1023: Application for Recognition of Exemption Under Section 501(c)(3) of the Internal Revenue Code, at 4 (June 2006).

75. Internal Revenue Service, Instructions for Form 1023, at 25–26 (June 2006).

a. An ownership or investment interest in any entity with which the Organization has a transaction or arrangement,

b. A compensation arrangement with the Organization or with any entity or individual with which the Organization has a transaction or arrangement, or

c. A potential ownership or investment interest in, or compensation arrangement with, any entity or individual with which the Organization is negotiating a transaction or arrangement.

Compensation includes direct and indirect remuneration as well as gifts or favors that are not insubstantial.

A financial interest is not necessarily a conflict of interest. Under Article III, Section 2, a person who has a financial interest may have a conflict of interest only if the appropriate governing board or committee decides that a conflict of interest exists.

Article III
Procedures

1. Duty to Disclose

In connection with any actual or possible conflict of interest, an interested person must disclose the existence of the financial interest and be given the opportunity to disclose all material facts to the directors and members of committees with governing board delegated powers considering the proposed transaction or arrangement.

2. Determining Whether a Conflict of Interest Exists

After disclosure of the financial interest and all material facts, and after any discussion with the interested person, he/she shall leave the governing board or committee meeting while the determination of a conflict of interest is discussed and voted upon. The remaining board or committee members shall decide if a conflict of interest exists.

3. Procedures for Addressing the Conflict of Interest

a. An interested person may make a presentation at the governing board or committee meeting, but after the presentation, he/she shall leave the meeting during the discussion of, and the vote on, the transaction or arrangement involving the possible conflict of interest.

b. The chairperson of the governing board or committee shall, if appropriate, appoint a disinterested person or committee to investigate alternatives to the proposed transaction or arrangement.

c. After exercising due diligence, the governing board or committee shall determine whether the Organization can obtain with reasonable efforts a more advantageous transaction or arrangement from a person or entity that would not give rise to a conflict of interest.

d. f a more advantageous transaction or arrangement is not reasonably possible under circumstances not producing a conflict of interest, the governing board or committee shall determine by a majority vote of the disinterested directors whether the transaction or arrangement is in the Organization's best interest, for its own benefit, and whether it is fair and reasonable. In conformity with the above determination it shall make its decision as to whether to enter into the transaction or arrangement.

4. Violations of the Conflict of Interest Policy

a. If the governing board or committee has reasonable cause to believe a member has failed to disclose actual or possible conflicts of interest, it shall inform the member of the basis for such belief and afford the member an opportunity to explain the alleged failure to disclose.

b. If, after hearing the member's response and after making further investigation as warranted by the circumstances, the governing board or committee determines the member has failed to disclose an actual or possible conflict of interest, it shall take appropriate disciplinary and corrective action.

Article IV
Records of Proceedings

The minutes of the governing board and all committees with board-delegated powers shall contain:

a. The names of the persons who disclosed or otherwise were found to have a financial interest in connection with an actual or possible conflict of interest, the nature of the financial interest, any action taken to determine whether a conflict of interest was present, and the governing board's or committee's decision as to whether a conflict of interest in fact existed.

b. The names of the persons who were present for discussions and votes relating to the transaction or arrangement, the content of the discussion, including any alternatives to the proposed transaction or arrangement, and a record of any votes taken in connection with the proceedings.

Article V
Compensation

a. A voting member of the governing board who receives compensation, directly or indirectly, from the Organization for services is precluded from voting on matters pertaining to that member's compensation.

b. A voting member of any committee whose jurisdiction includes compensation matters and who receives compensation, directly or indirectly, from the Organization for services is precluded from voting on matters pertaining to that member's compensation.

c. No voting member of the governing board or any committee whose jurisdiction includes compensation matters and who receives compensation, directly or indirectly, from the Organization, either individually or collectively, is prohibited from providing information to any committee regarding compensation.

[Hospital Insert—for hospitals that complete Schedule C:

d. Physicians who receive compensation from the Organization, whether directly or indirectly or as employees or independent contractors, are precluded from membership on any committee whose jurisdiction includes compensation matters. No physician, either individually or collectively, is prohibited from providing information to any committee regarding physician compensation.]

Article VI
Annual Statements

Each director, principal officer, and member of a committee with governing board delegated powers shall annually sign a statement which affirms such person:

a. Has received a copy of the conflicts of interest policy,

b. Has read and understands the policy,

c. Has agreed to comply with the policy, and

d. Understands the Organization is charitable and in order to maintain its federal tax exemption it must engage primarily in activities which accomplish one or more of its tax-exempt purposes.

Article VII
Periodic Reviews

To ensure the Organization operates in a manner consistent with charitable purposes and does not engage in activities that could jeopardize its tax-exempt status, periodic reviews shall be conducted. The periodic reviews shall, at a minimum, include the following subjects:

a. Whether compensation arrangements and benefits are reasonable, based on competent survey information, and the result of arm's-length bargaining.

b. Whether partnerships, joint ventures, and arrangements with management organizations conform to the Organization's written policies, are properly recorded, reflect reasonable investment or payments for goods and services, further charitable purposes, and do not result in inurement, impermissible private benefit, or in an excess benefit transaction.

Article VIII
Use of Outside Experts

When conducting the periodic reviews as provided for in Article VII, the Organization may, but need not, use outside advisors. If outside experts are used, their use shall not relieve the governing board of its responsibility for ensuring periodic reviews are conducted.

Unincorporated Nonprofit Associations

Although many tax-exempt, nonprofit organizations are organized as corporations, the Internal Revenue Code does not require corporate status for an organization to receive tax exemption under Code Section 501(c)(3). This is implied by the language of the Code itself, which refers to "[c]orporations, and any community chest, fund, or Foundation" as potentially qualifying as tax-exempt.[76] The instructions to IRS Form 1023 (Ap-

---

76. I.R.C. § 501(c)(3).

plication for Recognition of Exemption Under Section 501(c)(3) of the Internal Revenue Code) further clarify this by stating, "Only trusts, unincorporated associations, or corporations (including limited liability companies) are eligible for tax-exempt status under section 501(c)(3) of the Code."[77]

Background

At common law, unincorporated nonprofit associations were not considered separate legal entities in the same way that corporations are. Rather, they were considered to be just the aggregate of their individual members.[78] This meant that it was not possible to make a gift to the association as distinct from a gift to all its members, nor could such an association sue or be sued.[79] The members, on the other hand, were individually liable for claims against the association.[80]

Model Acts

To assist unincorporated nonprofit associations—primarily small, informal ones—in their work to benefit the public the National Conference of Commissioners on Uniform State Laws (NCCUSL) drafted the Uniform Unincorporated Nonprofit Association Act (UUNAA), issued in 1996.[81] The act was drafted to govern "nonprofit associations," which are defined as "unincorporated organization[s], other than one[s] created by a trust, consisting of [two] or more members joined by mutual consent for a common, nonprofit purpose."[82]

This model act provides for unincorporated nonprofit associations to be treated as legal entities for certain purposes, but not necessarily for all purposes.[83] Specifically, the act provides that an unincorporated non-

---

77. Internal Revenue Service, *Instructions to Form 1023*, at 6 (June 2006).

78. Uniform Unincorporated Nonprofit Association Act (UUNAA) pref. note (1996).

79. *Id.*

80. *Id.*

81. *Id.*

82. *Id.* § 1(2). The word "two" appears in brackets in the model act because some states may wish to require a greater minimum number of members or even allow a nonprofit association to be formed with only a single member. *Id.* § 1 cmt. 8.

83. *Id.*

profit association is a legal entity separate from its members for the purposes of acquiring, holding, encumbering, and transferring real and personal property,[84] and for the purposes of determining and enforcing rights, duties, and liabilities in contract and tort.[85] The act also gives an unincorporated nonprofit association the right to sue and be sued and to participate in judicial, administrative, and other governmental proceedings in its own name.[86]

UUNAA has been adopted by 11 states (Alabama, Arkansas, Colorado, Delaware, Hawaii, Idaho, North Carolina, Texas, West Virginia, Wisconsin, and Wyoming) and the District of Columbia.[87]

In 2008, NCCUSL approved a revised model act, the Revised Uniform Unincorporated Nonprofit Association Act (RUUNAA). The revisions were intended to make the act more comprehensive and to harmonize the legal framework for unincorporated nonprofit associations in the United States, Canada, and Mexico.[88]

Under RUUNAA, an unincorporated nonprofit association is defined as "an unincorporated organization consisting of [two] or more members joined under an agreement that is oral, in a record, or implied from conduct, for one or more common, nonprofit purposes."[89] Contrary to UUNAA, the revised act provides that an unincorporated nonprofit association is a legal entity distinct from its members and managers for all purposes, not just for limited purposes.[90]

RUUNAA also provides generally for an unincorporated nonprofit association to be governed in accordance with its "governing principles"—that is, "the agreements, whether oral, in a record, or implied from its established practices, that govern [its] purpose or operation . . . and the rights and obligations of its members and managers."[91] "Established practices," in turn, are

---

84. *Id.* § 4(a).

85. *Id.* § 6(a).

86. *Id.* § 7(a).

87. Peri H. Pakroo, Starting & Building a Nonprofit: A Practical Guide 135 (Nolo 3d ed. 2009).

88. Revised Uniform Unincorporated Nonprofit Association Act (RUULNAA) pref. note (2008).

89. *Id.* § 1(8). As with UUNAA, the revised model ad places the minimum required number of members in brackets to allow states to choose a smaller or larger number. *Id.* § 1 cmt. 8.

90. *Id.* § 5(a).

91. *Id.* § 2(2).

defined as "the practices used by an unincorporated nonprofit association without material change during the most recent five years of its existence, or if it has existed for less than five years, during its entire existence."[92] Hence, an unincorporated nonprofit association's practices may become binding on it in the absence of any oral or written agreement to do otherwise.

RUUNAA requires unincorporated nonprofit associations, unless the association's governing principles provide otherwise, to secure the approval of their members before taking any of the following actions: admitting, suspending, dismissing, or expelling a member; selecting or dismissing a manager; adopting, amending, or repealing the governing principles; selling, leasing, exchanging, or otherwise disposing of all or substantially all of the association's property outside the ordinary course of its activities; dissolving or entering into a merger; undertaking any other act outside the ordinary course of the association's activities; or determining the policy and purposes of the association.[93] Unless the governing principles provide otherwise, approval of a matter by members requires a majority of the votes cast at a meeting of the members, with each member entitled to one vote.[94] Notice and quorum requirements are determined by the association's governing principles.[95]

As of this writing, so far only Iowa[96] has adopted RUUNAA.[97]

Tax-Exempt Status

Although unincorporated nonprofit associations are eligible to apply for recognition of tax-exempt status, the IRS imposes certain restrictions on their doing so. Hence, an unincorporated nonprofit association recognized by state law under UUNAA or RUUNAA may not be eligible for tax-exempt status from the IRS.

Specifically, the IRS requires that an unincorporated association formed under state law must have at least two members who have signed a written

---

92. *Id.* § 2(1).
93. *Id.* § 16(a).
94. *Id.* § 17(a).
95. *Id.* § 17(b).
96. Iowa Acts ch. 1112 (2010).
97. Uniform Law Commission, Unincorporated Nonprofit Association Act (2008) (last visited Jan. 24, 2011), *available at* http://www.nccusl.org/Update/Desktop Default.aspx?tabindex=2&tabid=60 (search for "Unincorporated Nonprofit Association Act (2008)").

document for a specifically defined purpose.[98] Thus, associations formed under UUNAA or RUUNAA by an agreement that is oral or implied from conduct are not eligible for 501(c)(3) status. Nor could an association apply for such status if it had only one member, even if its home state's version of UUNAA or RUUNAA allowed unincorporated nonprofit associations to be formed with only one member.

Duties of Members and Managers

The 1996 version of UUNAA did not address the issue of the duties of the members or managers of a nonprofit association, leaving such issues to be determined by other sources of law.

By contrast, the revised model act does contain such provisions. RUUNAA provides that a member does not have a fiduciary duty to an unincorporated nonprofit association or to another member solely by being a member.[99] However, the revised model act does require that members discharge their duties to the association and the other members and exercise any rights under the act consistent with the association's governing principles and the obligation of good faith and fair dealing.[100] Thus, for example, a member may not disclose to third parties confidential information obtained from the association.[101] The drafters of RUUNAA commented that the obligation of good faith and fair dealing is not a fiduciary duty, but rather a duty derived from the consensual or contract nature of the association.[102]

However, RUUNAA does impose fiduciary duties on the managers of an unincorporated nonprofit association. A manager owes the association and its members the fiduciary duties of loyalty and care.[103] A manager must manage the association in good faith, in a manner he or she reasonably believes to be in the association's best interests, and with such care, including reasonable inquiry, as a prudent person would reasonably exercise in a similar position and under similar circumstances.[104]

---

98. IRS, *Instructions to Form 1023*, at 36 (June 2006).
99. RUUNAA § 18(a).
100. *Id.* § 18(b).
101. *Id.* § 18 cmt. 2.
102. *Id.*
103. *Id.* § 23(a).
104. *Id.* § 23(b).

Distributions and the Threat of Private Inurement for Tax-Exempt Social Enterprises

Each transaction entered into by a nonprofit, tax-exempt organization must be scrutinized to ensure that the tax-exempt mission is of primary concern before proceeding with the transaction. Board members and other management personnel have a duty of obedience that requires them to avoid any transaction that may jeopardize the organization's tax-exempt status.[105]

Private Inurement

Operating a tax-exempt entity presents unique challenges for the organization's directors and officers to ensure that at all times they are using the entity's resources to advance its mission. The IRS has stated that that private inurement is "likely to arise where the financial benefit represents a transfer of the organization's financial resources to an individual solely by virtue of the individual's relationship with the organization, and without regard to accomplishing exempt purposes."[106] These rules serve to ensure that exempt organizations are not organized and operated for the benefit of persons in their private capacity, such as founders, directors, officers, members of their families, entities controlled by these individuals, or any other persons having a personal and private interest in the social enterprise's activities. Any transactions the social enterprise enters into with a person or entity related to it must be scrutinized to ensure that the assets of the social enterprise are not transferred to, or used by, the related person in an unreasonable manner. There should always be a fair exchange of benefits between the parties, similar to the way in which other unrelated organizations would transact their affairs under comparable circumstances. For the purposes of private inurement, the issuing of dividends or distributions to equity holders, because of their position as equity holders, is *per se* private inurement and will never be found reasonable or in the furtherance of the exempt purposes of the organization.

Private inurement transactions are statutorily forbidden under IRC § 501(c) for 13 categories of tax-exempt organizations, including those formed as public charities under that section of the IRC. To retain an organzation's tax-exempt status, the statute mandates that no part of its

---

105. *Id.*
106. Gen. Couns. Mem. 38459 (July 31, 1980).

net earnings may inure to the benefit of any private shareholder or individual.[107] This prohibition applies to all distributions to all individuals with an interest in the organization's activities, but has special application to individuals who have a close relationship with the organization.

Although, at first glance, the restrictions against private inurement may seem to apply to any individual who contracts with or receives any benefits from the organization, those restrictions have been interpreted to mean that "none of the income or assets of an exempt organization subject to the private inurement doctrine may be permitted to directly or indirectly benefit an individual or other person who has a close relationship with the organization, when he, she, or it is in a position to exercise a significant degree of control over it (i.e., insiders)."[108]

Of course, members of the governing board and members of management would be considered to be "insiders" for purposes of interpreting the private inurement implications. However, social enterprises must also consider the implications that result from the use of multi-organizational structures (discussed in Chapter 6) in which related tax-exempt and for-profit organizations contract with one another.

Private Inurement—Multi-Organizational Structures

The doctrine of private inurement prohibits the transfer of income or assets of a tax-exempt organization away from the organization for the use or benefit of a person or entity with a significant relationship to the organization for inappropriate purposes. When tax-exempt entities utilize related for-profit organizations within the organizational structure, the founders of the tax-exempt organization may be direct or indirect owners of the subsidiary or may sit on the subsidiary's board of directors, in which event federal tax laws will consider the person performing functions for both entities to be an insider. Because insiders are in authoritative positions at both the tax-exempt organization and its related for-profit organization, they have the ability to use the tax-exempt entities' assets for private purposes. In order for a social enterprise to protect its tax-exempt status, it must be able to establish that it is not organized and operated for the benefit of any for-profit entity and/or for any personal gain of the owners

---

107. I.R.C. § 501(c)(3).
108. BRUCE R. HOPKINS, PLANNING GUIDE FOR THE LAW OF TAX-EXEMPT ORGANIZATIONS § 20 (John Wiley & Sons 2007).

who have an interest in the activities of both organizations.[109] Because the IRS has stated that "[t]he inurement prohibition serves to prevent anyone in a position to do so from siphoning off any of a charity's income or assets for personal use,"[110] governing boards and management personnel must at all times be mindful that they do not enter into any activity that might endanger the organization's tax-exempt status.

Commercial Reasonableness

Directors, officers, and managers of tax-exempt organizations will often receive compensation, sometimes including benefits and perks, from those organizations. The doctrine of private inurement does not forbid such compensation, but provides that such persons may only receive such compensation as is commercially reasonable. The standard of commercial reasonableness analyzes whether there is an approximately equal exchange of benefits between the parties to a transaction, so as to prevent a "disproportionate share of the benefits of the exchange" flowing to an insider.[111] In short, directors, officers, and managers should not be paid more than the fair market value of their services. Nor are exempt organizations forbidden from having other economic transactions with insiders, such as buying property from them or selling property to them.[112]

In circumstances where it is not easy to determine what would be commercially reasonable, a social enterprise may be counseled to bring in an outside valuation expert to assist in valuing the transaction.

Compensation Considerations

Although social enterprises organized as nonprofit, tax-exempt organizations are driven by a motive other than the generation of profits, running a successful and sustainable social enterprise through such a legal form requires considerable effort by both officers and directors. Nevertheless, the amount of compensation paid to directors or officers for serving in such roles must be determined to be reasonable in relation to the services they provide.[113]

---

109. Treas. Reg. § 1.501(a)-1(c).
110. Gen. Couns. Mem. 39862 (Dec. 2, 1991).
111. Priv. Ltr. Rul. 9130002 (Mar. 19, 1991).
112. *Id.*
113. I.R.C. § 501(c)(3)–(4).

What is considered reasonable compensation is not specifically addressed under the private inurement restrictions. Directors and officers serving nonprofit, tax-exempt corporations are entitled to receive fair compensation for their work in that role and have no legal obligation to receive reduced compensation.[114] Compensation, for the purposes of the private inurement restrictions, includes items such as salary, bonuses, deferred compensation, and pension and other retirement benefits.

The private inurement restrictions require that compensation be reasonable. What is reasonable is a question of fact to be answered based on the surrounding circumstances when analyzed against various factors.[115] The factors look to determine one thing: Is the item of compensation or total compensation under question an amount (or type) that would ordinarily be paid in similar circumstances by a like organization for like services?

Over the years, courts have developed a number of factors to determine whether compensation is reasonable. No single factor is determinative, and each court's interpretation may vary. For example, the factors may include:[116]

- the type and extent of the services rendered;
- the scarcity of qualified employees;
- the qualifications and prior earning capacity of the employee;
- the contributions of the employee to the business venture;
- the net earnings of the employer;
- the prevailing compensation paid to employees with comparable jobs; and
- the peculiar characteristics of the employer's business. For any given position, there will be a range, not unduly narrow, of compensation that could properly be considered "reasonable."

There are no rules of law that mandate particular actions that need to be taken by the board of directors or any other decision-making body when setting compensation. Still, as noted by the presumptions against excess benefit transactions discussed below, the IRS encourages arm's-length, con-

---

114. H. REP. 104-506, 104th Cong., 2d Sess. 56 (1996).
115. Jones Bros. Bakery, Inc. v. United States, 411 F.2d 1282 (Ct. Cl. 1969).
116. Edwin's Inc. v. United States, 501 F.2d 675 (7th Cir. 1974).

flict-free decision making when setting the compensation of key employees whose compensation may trigger the rules against private inurement.[117]

Excess Benefit Transactions

Although the IRS has not provided a clear line that will determine what may or may not constitute a private inurement transaction, it has stated that certain transactions, commonly referred to as "excess benefit transactions," will automatically trigger the private inurement restrictions.[118] Governing members of a tax-exempt social enterprise must understand and adhere to the rules that prohibit excess benefit transactions or else they could personally be subjected to fines and penalties, and/or the organization may endanger its tax-exempt status.

IRC § 4958 defines an excess benefit transaction as any transaction in which an economic benefit is provided by a tax-exempt organization directly or indirectly to or for the use of any "disqualified person" if the value of the economic benefit provided exceeds the value of the consideration (including performance of services) received for providing the benefit.[119]

The IRS has stated that anyone who exercises or has exercised substantial influence over the nonprofit organization within five years before the transaction at issue is a disqualified person.[120] As such, founding members and management of a social enterprise must be acutely aware of the consequences of engaging in a transaction that could be considered an excess benefit transaction.

Determining whether or not a particular benefit will be considered an excess benefit is generally the result of a "facts and circumstances" inquiry. Generally, if the benefit received exceeds what would be objectively reasonable in the circumstance, the amount of the benefit over the reasonable amount will be considered an excess benefit.[121] A rebuttable presumption arises that a benefit is not an excess benefit when certain procedures are followed by the board or other decision-making body that approves the

---

117. BRUCE R. HOPKINS, PLANNING GUIDE FOR THE LAW OF TAX-EXEMPT ORGANIZATIONS § 20.4(e) (John Wiley & Sons 2007).
118. 26 C.F.R. § 53.4958.
119. I.R.C. § 4958.
120. *Id.*
121. *See* 26 C.F.R. § 53.4958.

benefit.[122] A rebuttable presumption will arise that the benefit in question is not an excess benefit where:

(1) an authorized body of disinterested individuals, with no conflicts of interest in the transaction, approved the transaction;

(2) the approval of the transaction is based on appropriate comparability data, which reflects comparable benefits received in exchange for the consideration in question;

(3) there has been documentation reflecting the basis for the decision regarding the transaction, including (a) the terms and date of the transaction, (b) the directors who voted on it, (c) the data relied upon and how it was obtained, and (d) the action of any directors with a conflict of interest in the transaction; and

(4) the documentation in question was prepared before the later of the next board meeting (or meeting of the body that approved the transaction) or 60 days after the transaction and was approved a reasonable time after preparation.[123]

If the transaction in question is determined to be an excess benefit transaction, the individual who receives the excess benefit must pay back the excess benefit to the organization. In addition a tax of 25 percent of the excess benefit will be levied against the individual.[124] Any director, officer, or decision maker who willingly approved the excess benefit transaction and was aware that it is such a transaction will be taxed an amount equal to 10 percent of the excess benefit.[125] Still, if the benefit in question is paid back promptly, there is a high likelihood that further tax penalties will be avoided.[126] Organizations may not pay any penalties related to excess benefit transactions.[127] Repeated excess benefit transactions will lead to revocation of the organization's tax-exempt status.[128] Consequentially,

---

122. *See id.*

123. *See id.*

124. I.R.C. § 4958.

125. *Id.*

126. *Id.*; Mosher & Wagenmaker, LLC, *Not-for-Profit Directors' and Officers' Responsibilities, available at* http://www.mosherlaw.com/featuredarticles.htm.

127. I.R.C. § 4958.

128. *See* Standards for Recognition of Tax-Exempt Status if Private Benefit Exists or if an Applicable Tax-Exempt Organization Has Engaged in Excess Benefit Transaction(s), 73 Fed. Reg. 16,519 (Mar 28, 2008).

apart from and due to the tax consequences, repeated excess benefit transactions will result in breach of the duty of obedience, resulting in the loss of business judgment protection for the most recent transaction.

Excess benefit transactions routinely arise in the context of compensation. Importantly, an economic benefit received will not be treated as consideration for performance of services unless there is clear intent to do so on the part of the organization.[129] As a result, an economic benefit received that is not expressly characterized as compensation for services will most likely be characterized as an excess benefit.[130]

Penalties against Tax-Exempt Organizations

If the IRS determines that an excess benefit transaction has been undertaken, the penalties that result are referred to as "intermediate sanctions." Intermediate sanctions can vary considerably between two extremes: the IRS might decide not to take any action, or it could revoke an entity's tax-exempt status.[131]

Management's Personal Liability

If an excess benefit transaction occurs, the intermediate sanction nature of the rule emphasizes the tax on the individual who engaged in the impermissible private transaction, leading to an excess benefit on that individual's part.[132] This tax is commonly referred to as an excise tax, and the members of the organization who authorized the prohibited transaction could potentially be personally liable for its payment.[133] The excess benefit rules apply to two categories of exempt organizations, public charities (IRC § 501(c)(3) organizations) and social welfare organizations (IRC § 501(c)(4) organizations).[134]

---

129. I.R.C. § 4958.
130. *See* 26 C.F.R. § 53.4958 (for a more in-depth analysis of what is considered an excess benefit).
131. BRUCE R. HOPKINS, *supra* note 108.
132. *See* 26 C.F.R. § 53.4958.
133. I.R.C. § 4958.
134. BRUCE R. HOPKINS, *supra* note 108.

Exempt Organization Checklist

It is recommended that the following questions be addressed and that the answers be kept with the books and records of the tax-exempt organization. These questions were proposed by the IRS to determine whether compensation leads to private inurement.

A tax-exempt organization should be prepared to answer the following questions about the compensation of insiders:

(1) Is there a written compensation policy or guideline that the governing body of the tax-exempt organization must follow?

(2) Does this policy establish how the compensation for each individual is to be set based on the services that the individual provides to the organization, and how is reasonableness calculated?

(3) Does this policy establish how the compensation for each individual is to be reported to the IRS?

(4) Is the governing body that sets the compensation independent from the insider?

(5) What are the general duties of this governing body with respect to the organization?

(6) If there is a conflict or potential conflict of interest in setting the compensation, how does the governing body resolve that conflict of interest?

(7) Are the amounts of compensation paid to insiders from year to year internally recorded?

Political and Legislative Activities

Social enterprises qualifying as tax-exempt under IRC § 501(c)(3) are constrained when they engage in political activities, subjecting them to standards that do not apply to for-profit entities. The IRS differentiates between "political activities" (campaigning, promoting candidates, etc.) and "legislative activities" (lobbying). As a result, the activities that fall into these two broad categories must be considered as two separate acts, each subject to its own rules.

Political Activities

A social enterprise may wish to promote certain political issues that advance its cause and mission. Such promotion may be accomplished in person, through mailings, or over the Internet. The question then arises—to what level may a social enterprise promote political issues and take positions on public policy issues when it is organized as a tax-exempt entity under IRC § 501(c)(3)?

IRC § 501(c)(3) organizations must avoid any issue advocacy that functions as "political campaign intervention."[135] This means that tax-exempt entities are required to refrain from promoting certain candidates for public office, even if such candidates support their missions or purpose. The IRS has made clear that a social enterprise should not expressly encourage an audience to vote for or against specific candidates, or it may endanger its tax exemption.

This prohibition extends to both direct and indirect communication. If an organization posts something on its website that favors or opposes a candidate for public office, the organization will be treated as if it distributed printed material, oral statements, or broadcasts that favored or opposed a candidate.[136]

That said, under IRS guidance, tax-exempt organizations are not prohibited from simply identifying candidates for office as long as it is done in a non-partisan manner. Tax-exempt organizations may issue statements that identify a candidate's name, or they may show a picture of a candidate and refer to the candidate's political party affiliations or other distinctive features or a candidate's platform or biography.[137] However, when doing so, the organization must take into account all the facts and circumstances and determine if, in doing so, they are engaging in political campaign intervention.[138]

The IRS has stated that the following key factors are to be considered in determining whether a communication results in political campaign intervention:[139]

- Whether the statement identifies one or more candidates for a given public office;

---

135. I.R.S., ELECTION YEAR ACTIVITIES AND THE PROHIBITION ON POLITICAL CAMPAIGN INTERVENTION FOR SECTION 501(c)(3) ORGANIZATIONS, FS-2006-17 (February 2006), *available at* http://www.irs.gov/newsroom/article/0,,id=154712,00.html.

136. *Id.*

137. *Id.*

138. *Id.*

139. *Id.*

- Whether the statement expresses approval or disapproval for one or more candidates' positions and/or actions;
- Whether the statement is delivered close in time to the election;
- Whether the statement makes reference to voting or an election;
- Whether the issue addressed in the communication has been raised as an issue distinguishing candidates for a given office;
- Whether the communication is part of an ongoing series of communications by the organization on the same issue that are made independent of the timing of any election; and
- Whether the timing of the communication and identification of the candidate are related to a non-electoral event, such as a scheduled vote on specific legislation by an officeholder who also happens to be a candidate for public office.

Campaigning and Promoting Certain Candidates

In addition, the IRS strictly prohibits tax-exempt organizations from directly or indirectly participating in any political campaign for a candidate for elective public office.[140] This prohibition applies to campaigns at the federal, state, and local levels.[141] Social enterprises that wish to engage in political campaign activity should be counseled on what types of activities are permissible so that they do not run afoul of the prohibition and thereby endanger their tax exemption.

Prohibited political campaign intervention includes any and all activities that favor or oppose one or more candidates for public office.[142] The prohibition includes candidate endorsements,[143] contributions to political campaign funds, and public statements of position made by or on behalf of an organization in favor of or in opposition to any candidate for public office.[144]

140. I.R.C. § 501(c)(3).

141. Treas. Reg. § 1.501(c)(3)–1(c)(3)(iii).

142. I.R.S., Election Year Activities and the Prohibition on Political Campaign Intervention for Section 501(c)(3) Organizations, FS-2006-17 (February 2006), available at http://www.irs.gov/newsroom/article/0,,id=154712,00.html.

143. Id.

144. Id.

Business Activities and Use of Assets or Facilities

In addition, tax-exempt social enterprises may not participate or intervene in a political campaign indirectly through their business activities. For that reason, they should not allow candidates to use assets or facilities unless all other candidates are given an equivalent opportunity.[145]

The IRS may consider the following factors to determine whether a tax-exempt organization is engaging in political campaign activity through its business activities:[146]

- Whether the good, service, or facility is available to candidates in the same election on an equal basis,
- Whether the good, service, or facility is available only to candidates and not to the general public,
- Whether the fees charged to candidates are at the organization's customary and usual rates, and
- Whether the activity is an ongoing activity of the organization or whether it is conducted only for a particular candidate.

The IRS has published extensive guidance regarding the political campaign activities of organizations exempt under IRC § 501(c)(3). Counsel for the social enterprises that seek additional information and examples can turn to resources listed in Exhibit 4-2 for guidance.[147]

Lobbying Activities

The IRS views "political activities," as discussed above, and "legislative activities" differently. As a result, the rules and regulations pertaining to each type of activity are different. When advising social enterprises, it is important to distinguish between the two categories of activities.

The IRS has stated that "legislation" includes action by Congress, any state legislature, any local council, or similar governing body with respect to acts, bills, resolutions, or similar items (such as legislative confirmation of appointive office), or by the public in referendum, ballot, initiative, constitutional amendment, or similar procedure.[148] It does not include actions

---

145. *Id.*
146. *Id.*
147. http://www.irs.gov/charities/charitable/article/0,,id=163395,00.html.
148. http://www.irs.gov/charities/article/0,,id=163392,00.html.

Exhibit 4-2

Activities or Organizations Exempt under IRC § 501(c)(3)

IR-2008-61 (April 17, 2008): Announcing steps the IRS is taking to secure compliance with the ban on political campaign activity by IRC § 501(c)(3) organizations during the 2008 election cycle.

IR-2007-190 (Nov. 19, 2007): Reminding charities and churches of the political activity ban.

IR-2006-87 (June 1, 2006): Reminding charities to avoid political campaign activities during election season.

Fact Sheet 2006-17 (Feb. 2006): Explaining how the IRS interprets the federal tax law provisions on political campaign intervention by IRC § 501(c)(3) organizations; the fact sheet provides 21 examples of possible campaign intervention and explains how the law applies in each.

IR-2006-36 (Feb. 24, 2006): Announcing the release of a report on the IRS's examination of political activity by tax-exempt organizations during the 2004 election campaign.

Fact Sheet 2004-14 (Oct. 2004): Explaining rules on political campaign activities of IRC § 501(c)(3) organizations.

IR-2004-79 (June 10, 2004): Issuing a letter to national political parties confirming guidance regarding political activities by tax-exempt organizations, including churches.

IR-2004-59 (Apr. 28, 2004): Stating that charities may not engage in political campaign activities.

---

by executive, judicial, or administrative bodies.[149] A social enterprise will be regarded as attempting to influence legislation if it contacts, or urges the public to contact, members or employees of a legislative body for the purpose of proposing, supporting, or opposing legislation, or if the organization advocates the adoption or rejection of legislation.[150]

The IRS has laid out two tests to aid in this determination: the Substantial Part Test and the Expenditure Test.

---

149. *Id.*
150. *Id.*

Substantial Part Test

Under the Substantial Part Test, the IRS will examine the facts and circumstances of each particular social enterprise's lobbying activity to determine if it is attempting to influence legislation. The IRS will consider a variety of factors, including the time devoted (by both compensated and volunteer workers) and the expenditures devoted by the organization to the activity, when determining if the lobbying activity is substantial.[151]

Expenditure Test

As an alternative to measuring lobbying expenditures under the Substantial Part Test, tax-exempt organizations may elect the expenditure test under IRC § 501(h) to measure lobbying activity. The election is made by filing Form 5768 (Election/Revocation of Election by an Eligible IRC § 501(c)(3) Organization to Make Expenditures to Influence Legislation).

Generally speaking, under the expenditure test, lobbying expenditures will not jeopardize an organization's tax-exempt status as long as expenditures do not exceed certain dollar limits contained in IRC § 4911. The limits of that section are based on the size of the tax-exempt organization and may not exceed $1 million.[152] A tax of 25 percent is levied on expenditures in excess of the limits contained in IRC § 4911 in addition to the risk of loss of tax exemption. If, over a four-year period, a tax-exempt organization electing the expenditure test for measuring lobbying expenditures has expenditures that exceed 150 percent of either limitation above, it will lose its tax exemption.[153]

Finally, if a tax-exempt social enterprise engages in lobbying activities that ultimately endanger the tax exemption of the social enterprise, a tax equal to 5 percent of the lobbying expenditures for the year may be imposed against the organization's managers, jointly and severally, if such managers agreed to and made such expenditures knowing that they would endanger the tax-exempt status of the organization.

---

151. *Id.*
152. I.R.C. § 4911(c)(2).
153. Treas. Reg. § 1.501(h)-3.

Volunteer Labor—Unrelated Business Income Exception

Social enterprises using volunteers should be aware that an exception exists to the unrelated business taxable income (UBTI) rules for income earned by an entity using a volunteer workforce. Generally speaking, under IRS-provided guidance, any activity in which substantially all of the work is performed by unpaid volunteers is not considered an unrelated trade or business under the UBTI rules.[154] For example, suppose a public charity operates a thrift store that sells items on consignment. The store is open during normal business hours and sells items regularly throughout the year. Before an item is sold, the charitable organization and consignor agree on the retail price of the item, determine the charity's share of the profits from the sale, and plan for the disposition of the item if it is not sold within a certain period of time. The operation of the store is considered an unrelated trade or business; therefore, as a result, if the store were staffed by paid employees, most likely the proceeds from the sale of the items would be considered UBTI. However, if the charity staffed the store with volunteers, and substantially all the work at the store was performed by volunteers, the income earned would be specifically excluded from the calculation of UBTI.[155]

State Laws Dealing with Charitable Organizations

Most jurisdictions have laws in place that apply specifically to charitable organizations that solicit and hold property for charitable purposes. These laws impose additional duties on managers of these organizations as well as create continuing reporting obligations. Failure to comply with these laws could lead to sanctions and other liability for the organization. The managers who fail to comply with these laws, in addition to statutory liability, will also be in breach of their fiduciaries duties owed to the organization. As an example, the following subsections will look at laws from Illinois, Maryland, and New York. Maryland and Illinois are pioneering new laws in the realm of social enterprise, with the statutory creation of the L³C (Illinois) and the benefit corporation (Maryland). New York presents an example from a state with well-developed charitable solicitation laws.

---

154. I.R.C. § 513(a)(1).
155. Rev. Rul. 80-106, 1980-1 C.B. 113.

The following laws apply to any entity with charitable purposes, not just nonprofit, tax-exempt organizations. Still, they almost always apply to nonprofit organizations. A summary of exceptions from the charitable registration requirement, including the statutory citations, is also located in this subsection.

Illinois' Approach

In Illinois, the duties and obligations of managers and directors who engage in charitable operations throughout the state are detailed in two separate pieces of legislation, the Illinois Charitable Trust Act and the Illinois Solicitation for Charity Act. Both acts are detailed below.

The Illinois Charitable Trust Act

All charitable nonprofit, tax-exempt organizations holding property in Illinois will be subject to the Illinois Charitable Trust Act (Trust Act). Additionally, all social enterprises, regardless of how they are organized, may fall under the jurisdiction of the Trust Act.

The Trust Act adds a layer of obligation to all organizations (charitable or otherwise) that hold property for a charitable purpose in Illinois.[156] For the purposes of the Trust Act, any person, individual, organization, company, or nonprofit corporation holding property for or solicited for charitable purposes will be considered a "trustee."[157] Additionally, any chief operating officer, director, executive director, or owner of a corporation who is soliciting or holding property for a charitable purpose will be considered a "trustee."[158] This does not mean that that such entities or their managers will be treated according to trust principles, but only that the obligations of the Trust Act apply to them, along with the continuing obligations and rights afforded to them by the statutes that govern their particular entity, located elsewhere in the Illinois Code.[159] The main thrust of the Trust Act deals with certain registration requirements related to holding and distributing property for charitable purposes.

---

156. 760 ILL. COMP. STAT. § 55/3.
157. *Id.*
158. *Id.*
159. *Id.*

(a) The Registration and Reporting Requirements under the Trust Act
The Trust Act applies to any trustees who hold property in excess of
$4,000.[160] Under this law, the attorney general shall establish and main-
tain a register of trustees subject to the Trust Act, which tracks the relationship to the property held or solicited by the charitable organization.
Every trustee who has received property for a charitable purpose shall file
within six months after the property is received, but prior to disbursement, a copy of any governance documents that provides for the trustee's
powers or duties with respect to the property.[161] After this initial filing,
each trustee will be required to file annual periodic reports about the
nature of the assets held for charitable purposes, based on rules proscribed
by the attorney general.[162] Regardless of the rules proscribed by the attorney general, the first annual report shall be filed no later than one year
after any part of the charitable assets are applied to charitable use. Thereafter, an annual financial report shall be filed within six months of the
close of the trustee's fiscal year.[163] If the trustee has received less than
$25,000 in revenue or holds less than $25,000 in assets during a fiscal
year, then only a simplified summary financial statement will be required.[164] The attorney general may acquire whatever records are needed
from the trustee to maintain this register.[165]

(b) Trustee Duties under the Trust Act
As stated above, the Trust Act applies across all organizations (charitable or
otherwise), as long as the organization or its managers meets the definition
of trustee. Accordingly, depending on how an organization is organized,
i.e., nonprofit corporation, L3C, for-profit corporation, etc., different fiduciary standards will apply to the managers of that organization. Still, the
Trust Act prescribes certain duties that apply to all trustees. Under the
Trust Act, the trustee shall:

  (1)   avoid self-dealing or impermissible conflicts of interest;
  (2)   avoid wasting charitable assets;

---

160. 760 ILL. COMP. STAT. § 55/2.
161. 760 ILL. COMP. STAT. § 55/6.
162. 760 ILL. COMP. STAT. § 55/7.
163. *Id.*
164. *Id.*
165. 760 ILL. COMP. STAT. § 55/4.

(3) avoid incurring penalties, fines, and unnecessary taxes;

(4) adhere and conform the charitable organization to its chari-
     table purpose;

(5) not make non-program loans, gifts, or advances to any person,
     except as allowed by the General Not for Profit Corporation
     Act;

(6) utilize the trust (corporate assets) in conformity with its pur-
     poses for the best interest of the beneficiaries (members);

(7) timely file registration and financial reports required by the
     Trust Act; and

(8) comply and cause to comply the charitable organization with
     the Trust Act and, if incorporated, the General Not for Profit
     Corporation Act.[166]

*(c) Self-Dealing and Conflicts of Interest under the Trust Act for Social
Enterprises*

In defining self-dealing by, and conflicts of interest with, trustees of charitable assets under the Trust Act, Illinois' nonprofit corporation law serves
as a guide. In general, self-dealing occurs when a manager of an organization receives a pecuniary benefit at the expense of the company due to the
fact that he or she is on both sides of a transaction into which the company
enters. Under the Trust Act, trustees have a duty to avoid such transactions.
Still, self-dealing is considered a form of conflict of interest that results
from a breach of fiduciary duties when two different interests clash. That
being said, conflicts of interest, including self-dealing, can be cured if the
transaction in question is shown to be fair to the organization or if it was
ratified or approved by a disinterested body.[167] The ratification or approval
must proceed by ensuring that (1) the material facts and the trustee's conflict were disclosed or known by a governing body, and the transaction was
authorized by the affirmative votes of the majority of disinterested members of that governing body; or (2) the material facts and the trustee's conflict were disclosed or known to the individuals entitled to vote, such as
shareholders or members, and they authorized the transaction without count-
ing the vote of the conflicted trustee.[168] Unless this process takes places,

---

166. 760 ILL. COMP. STAT. § 55/15.
167. 805 ILL. COMP. STAT. § 805.
168. *Id.*

the burden of proving the fairness of the transactions will be placed on the party looking to validate the transaction.[169]

The Illinois Solicitation for Charity Act

The registration requirements of the Trust Act work in conjunction with the Solicitation for Charity Act (Solicitation Act), which prescribes a different set of registration requirements before any solicitation for charitable purposes can proceed.[170] While most states do not have an equivalent of the Illinois Charitable Trust Act, most states have a version of the Solicitation Act. Unlike the Trust Act, the Solicitation Act only applies to charitable organizations, meaning any benevolent, philanthropic, patriotic, or eleemosynary person or one purporting to be such, which solicits and collects funds for charitable purposes.[171] "Person" means any individual, organization, group, association, partnership, corporation, trust, or any combination of the preceding.[172] Accordingly, in Illinois, if the social enterprise is formed as a tax-exempt charitable organization, it will fall under the requirements of the Solicitation Act. Additionally, all social enterprises, regardless of how organized, may fall under the jurisdiction of the Solicitation Act.

(a) The Registration Requirement under the Solicitation Act
Under the Solicitation Act, every charitable organization, except those specifically exempted by the act (see the chart below), which solicits or intends to solicit contributions from persons within the state of Illinois, by any means whatsoever, shall, prior to any such solicitation, file with the attorney general a registration statement.[173]

(b) The Reporting Requirement under the Solicitation Act
Once registered, the reporting requirements under the Solicitation Act are determined by two independent factors: a) the amount of charitable contributions received in a fiscal or calendar year, and b) the nature of the person or persons doing the soliciting.[174] Where the amount received in

---

169. *Id.*
170. 225 ILL. COMP. STAT. § 460/1.
171. *Id.*
172. *Id.*
173. 225 ILL. COMP. STAT. § 460/2.
174. 225 ILL. COMP. STAT. § 460/4.

any 12-month period ending on the fiscal or calendar year is in excess of $150,000, an extended annual report in required.[175] Where the amount received is in excess of $25,000 in any 12-month period ending on the fiscal or calendar year and was solicited by persons other than unpaid employees and volunteers, an extended annual report must be filed.[176] If the amount solicited in the given 12-month period ending on the fiscal or calendar year exceeds $25,000 but is not in excess of $150,000 and is solicited by unpaid volunteers or employees, a simplified financial report can be filed.[177] If the amount solicited in the given 12-month period exceeds $15,000 but not $25,000, regardless of who solicits the funds, a simplified report can be filed.[178] If contributions are not solicited or received during the reporting period, no annual report is required.

Maryland's Approach

The Maryland Solicitation Act

Maryland, like Illinois, imposes special duties and restrictions on organizations operating charitable enterprises or engaging in charitable activities within the state. Maryland has a registration and reporting requirement for all charitable organizations that solicit charitable contributions in the state of Maryland.[179] Under the Maryland Solicitation Act (Maryland Act), a charitable organization is defined as a person (including any entity) that is or holds itself out to be a benevolent, educational, eleemosynary, humane, philanthropic, or religious organization and solicits charitable contributions from the public.[180] A charitable organization also includes any area, branch, chapter, office, or similar affiliate that solicits charitable contributions from the public within Maryland that is organized or has its principal place of business outside the state.[181]

(a) The Registration Requirement under the Maryland Act
Under the Maryland Act, unless exempt from the registration require-

---

175. *Id.*
176. *Id.*
177. *Id.*
178. *Id.*
179. MD. CODE ANN. BUS. REG. § 6-401.
180. MD. CODE ANN. BUS. REG. § 6-101.
181. MD. CODE ANN. BUS. REG. § 6-401.

ment (see chart below), a charitable organization will have to register with the secretary of state, prior to soliciting charitable contributions in Maryland, if it has charitable contributions solicited on its behalf in Maryland or if it solicits charitable contributions outside Maryland, if the charitable organization is located in Maryland.[182] A parent charitable organization must file a consolidated registration statement for any affiliated charitable organizations that solicit in Maryland.[183]

(b) The Reporting Requirement under the Maryland Act

Once registered, a charitable organization will have to submit annual reports to the secretary of state.[184] These reports must be submitted after registration, within six months after the end of each fiscal year.[185] The secretary of state, by rule, may change the reporting periods; as such, the careful practitioner should check all the rules and regulations that accompany this statute.[186] The report must contain financial statements, including such audit or review information as the secretary of state may require.[187] If no contributions are solicited or received during the reporting period, no annual report is required.

New York's Approach

New York's Charitable Solicitation Laws

Under New York's law, much like Maryland's and Illinois', charitable organizations that solicit charitable contributions within the state must register with New York's attorney general and provide continuing financial reports. Under New York law, a charitable organization is defined as any benevolent, philanthropic, patriotic, or eleemosynary person (including any entity) or one purporting to be such, or certain law enforcement organizations.[188]

---

182. *Id.*
183. *Id.*
184. MD. CODE ANN. BUS. REG. § 6-408.
185. *Id.*
186. *Id.*
187. *Id.*
188. N.Y. EXEC. LAW § 171-a.

(a) The Registration Requirement under New York Law

Unless exempt (see chart below), every charitable organization, prior to soliciting charitable contributions within the state, must register with the Attorney General of New York if it intends to solicit charitable contributions from
persons in the state of New York or from any state governmental agency.[189]

(b) The Reporting Requirement under New York Law

Every charitable organization that has registered under New York statutes
must file financial reports with the attorney general after registration. Similar to Illinois, the amount of charitable contributions received and how the
charitable contributions are collected will trigger different filing requirements. In any fiscal year in which the registered charitable organization grosses
over $250,000, it must file a full annual report containing a financial state-
ment that has been audited by a certified public accountant.[190] In any fiscal
year in which the registered charitable organization grosses between $100,000
and $250,000, the organization must file an annual report that contains a
financial statement that itself contains a certified public account's review
report.[191] In this second instance, the financial statements need not go through
a full audit.[192] Finally, if the registered charitable organization receives in
any fiscal year charitable contributions that do not exceed $100,000, the
organization will have to file an annual report that contains a financial statement.[193] This statement need not be audited or reviewed by a certified public account.[194] Additionally, regardless of the amount of contribution, if the
organization has fundraising activities carried on by individuals who are not
unpaid for such services, it must file a full annual report with an audited
financial statement.[195]

All annual reports must be signed by the president or other authorized officer certifying that all information in accurate, to the best of his
or her knowledge.[196] All annual reports must be filed by the 15th day of
the fifth calendar month after the close of the fiscal year.[197] If no contri-

---

189. N.Y. EXEC. LAW § 172.
190. N.Y. EXEC. LAW § 172-b.
191. *Id.*
192. *Id.*
193. *Id.*
194. *Id.*
195. *Id.*
196. *Id.*
197. *Id.*

butions are solicited or received during the reporting period, no annual report is required.[198]

The Unified Registration Statement (URS)

Many jurisdictions allow charitable organizations to fulfill their registration requirements through the filing of a unified registration statement, or URS. This registration statement, which has been created through the efforts of the National Association of State Charity Officials (NASCO, at www.nasconet.org), is accepted in all jurisdictions that require charitable registration, with the exception of three states: Colorado, Florida, and Oklahoma. While these three states require registration prior to charitable solicitation, they do not accept the URS. In the other jurisdictions that do accept the URS, the URS must be filled out and filed separately for each state and sent to each jurisdiction's administering agency.[199] A copy of the URS can found at http://www.multistatefiling.org/urs_webv401.pdf. Several jurisdictions have supplemental forms that are required to be filed with the URS if the charitable organization chooses to use the URS to fulfill the registration requirements. Those jurisdictions are:

- Arkansas
- California
- District of Columbia
- Georgia
- Maine
- Minnesota
- Mississippi
- North Carolina
- North Dakota
- Tennessee
- Utah
- Washington
- West Virginia
- Wisconsin

---

198. *Id.*
199. *See* http://www.multistatefiling.org/.

State-Specific Registration Requirements

A charitable organization's solicitation of funds in a particular jurisdiction will trigger jurisdiction-specific registration and reporting requirements. If an organization is exempt from registration, it will not need to fulfill any continuing reporting requirements. If, after registration, the organization falls within an exemption from registration, it will no longer have to file any annual reports, assuming the exemption remains current. However, some jurisdictions provide for exemptions from the reporting requirement but not from the initial registration requirement. Exhibit 4-3 lists a jurisdiction-by-jurisdiction list of the statutes that detail the registration requirements (and exemptions from registration) and/or reporting for all U.S. jurisdictions.

*   *   *   *

Nonprofit, tax-exempt organizations are venturing more and more into the realm of social enterprise, in which pursing a social mission is coupled with business operations that engage and facilitate that mission. Accordingly, the nonprofit, tax-exempt sector remains as one of the most fertile areas in which a social enterprise may choose to establish itself and operate.

Operating a social enterprise through a nonprofit, tax-exempt organization has many advantages but also presents a number of unique management challenges. Alternatively, social enterprises may be operated as for-profit organizations. Operating as such also presents challenges, unique to the for-profit sector, which must be addressed. The next chapter provides insight into the unique issues faced in managing a social enterprise as a for-profit organization and provides strategies for achieving success.

Exhibit 4-3
Statutes that Detail Registration Requirements/Reporting for U.S. Jurisdictions

State	Registration Requirement	Exemptions from Registration and/or Reporting	State Charity Office's Website (where available)
Alabama	Ala. Code § 13A-9-71	Ala. Code § 13A-9-71	http://www.ago.state. al.us/consumer_ charities.cfm
Alaska	Alaska Stat. § 45.68.010	Alaska Stat. § 45.68.120	http://www.law.state. ak.us/department/ civil/consumer/ cpindex.html
Arizona	Ariz. Rev. Stat. § 44-6552	Ariz. Rev. Stat. § 44-6553	http://www.azsos. gov/business_ services/Charities/ Default.htm
Arkansas	Ark. Code Ann. § 4-28-401	Ark. Code. Ann. § 4-28-404	http://www. arkansasag. gov/ consumers_ protection_charitable_ registration.html
California	Cal. Gov't Code § 12585	Cal. Gov't Code § 12583	http://ag.ca.gov/ charities.php
Colorado	Colo. Rev. Stat. § 6-16-104	Colo. Rev. Stat. § 6-16-104	http://www.sos.state. co.us/pubs/charities/ charitable.htm
Connecticut	Conn. Gen. Stat. § 21a-190b	Conn. Gen. Stat. § 21a-190d	http://www.ct.gov/ag/ cwp/browse.asp? a=2074
Delaware	No registration requirement	No registration requirement	No registration requirement
District of Columbia	D.C. Code § 44-1703	D.C. Code § 44-1703	http://dc.gov/DC/ DCRA/For+ Business/Apply+ for+a+Business+ License/General+ Business+and +Charitable+Solicitation +License+Information

State	Registration Requirement	Exemptions from Registration and/or Reporting	State Charity Office's Website (where available)
Florida	Fla. Stat. § 496.405	Fla. Stat. § 496.406	http://www.800helpfla.com/soc.html
Georgia	Ga. Code Ann. § 43-17-5	Ga. Code Ann. § 43-17-9	http://sos.georgia.gov/securities/charitable_organization.htm
Hawaii	Haw. Rev. Stat. § 467B-2.1	Haw. Rev. Stat. § 467B-11.5	http://hawaii.gov/ag/charities
Idaho	No registration requirement	No registration requirement	No registration requirement
Illinois	225 Ill. Comp. Stat. Ann. § 460/2	225 Ill. Comp. Stat. Ann. § 460/3	http://www.ag.state.il.us/charities/index.html
Indiana	No registration requirement	No registration requirement	No registration requirement
Iowa	No registration requirement	No registration requirement	No registration requirement
Kansas	Kan. Stat. Ann. § 17-1761	Kan. Stat. Ann. § 17-1762	http://www.kscharitycheck.org/register.html
Kentucky	Ky. Rev. Stat. Ann. § 367.657	Ky. Rev. Stat. Ann. § 367.660	http://ag.ky.gov/civil/consumerprotection/charity/registration.htm
Louisiana	La. Rev. Stat. Ann. §§ 51: 1901-1909	La. Rev. Stat. Ann. §§ 51: 1901-1909	http://www.ag.state.la.us/Article.aspx?articleID=3&catID=18
Maine	Me. Rev. Stat. Ann. tit. 385 § 5004	Me. Rev. Stat. Ann. tit. 385 § 5006	http://www.state.me.us/pfr/professionallicensing/professions/charitable/organization.htm

State	Registration Requirement	Exemptions from Registration and/or Reporting	State Charity Office's Website (where available)
Maryland	Md. Code Ann., Bus. Reg. § 6-101	Md. Code Ann., Bus. Reg. § 6-102	http://www.sos.state.md.us/Charity/RegisterCharity.aspx
Massachu-setts	Mass. Gen. Laws ch. 68, § 19	Mass. Gen. Laws ch. 68, § 20	http://www.mass.gov/?pageID=cagosubtopic&L=3&L0=Home&L1=Non-Profits+%26+Charities&L2=Charitable+Organizations&sid=Cago
Michigan	Mich. Comp. Laws Ann. § 400.273	Mich. Comp. Laws Ann. § 400.283	http://www.michigan.gov/ag/0,1607,7-164-17334_18095—,00.html
Minnesota	Minn. Stat. § 309.52. subd. 1	Minn. Stat. § 309.515	http://www.ag.state.mn.us/Charities/
Mississippi	Miss. Code Ann. § 79-11-503	Miss. Code Ann. § 79-11-505	http://www.sos.ms.gov/securities_and_charities_charities.aspx
Missouri	Mo. Rev. Stat. § 407.456	Mo. Rev. Stat. § 407.456	http://ago.mo.gov/consumer-programs.htm
Montana	No registration requirement	No registration requirement	No registration requirement
Nebraska	No registration requirement	No registration requirement	No registration requirement
Nevada	No registration requirement	No registration requirement	No registration requirement
New Hampshire	N.H. Rev. Stat. Ann. § 7:19-7:31-1	N.H. Rev. Stat. Ann. § 7:19-7:30	http://www.doj.nh.gov/charitable/
New Jersey	N.J. Stat. Ann. § 45:17A-23	N.J. Stat. Ann. § 45:17A-26	http://www.njconsumeraffairs.gov/charity/charfrm.htm

State	Registration Requirement	Exemptions from Registration and/or Reporting	State Charity Office's Website (where available)
New Mexico	N.M. Stat. Ann. § 57-22-6	N.M. Stat. Ann. § 57-22-4	http://www.nmag. gov/office/Divisions/ Civ/charity/ default.aspx
New York	N.Y. Executive Law § 172	N.Y. Executive Law § 172-A	http://www. charitiesnys.com/
North Carolina	N.C. Gen. Stat. Ann. § 131F-5	N.C. Gen. Stat. Ann. § 131F-3	http://www. secretary.state.nc.us/ csl/ThePage.aspx
North Dakota	N.D. Century Code § 50-22-02	N.D. Century Code § 50-22-01	http://www.nd.gov/ sos/ nonprofit/ charitableorg/ index.html
Ohio	Ohio Rev. Code Ann. § 1716.02	Ohio Rev. Code Ann. § 1716.03	http://www. ohioattorneygeneral. gov/Services/Non-Profits/Charitable-Registration
Oklahoma	Okla. Stat. tit. 18 § 552 .3	Okla. Stat. tit. 18 § 552.4	https://www. sos.ok.gov/forms/ FM0101.PDF
Oregon	Ore. Rev. Stat. § 128.670	Ore. Rev. Stat. § 128.640	http://www. doj.state. or.us/charigroup/ howtoreg.shtml
Pennsyl-vania	10 Pa. Stat. Ann. tit. § 162.5	10 Pa. Stat. Ann. tit. § 162.6	http://www. recovery. pa.gov/portal/ server.pt/community/ charities/12444
Rhode Island	R.I. Gen. Laws § 5-53.1-2	R.I. Gen. Laws § 5-53.1-3	http://www. dbr. state.ri.us/divisions/ banking_securities/ charitable.php
South Carolina	S.C. Code Ann. § 33-56-30	S.C. Code Ann. § 33-56-40 - 33-56-55	http://www.scsos. com/Public_ Charities
South Dakota	No registration requirement	No registration requirement	No registration requirement

State	Registration Requirement	Exemptions from Registration and/or Reporting	State Charity Office's Website (where available)
Tennessee	Tenn. Code Ann. § 48-101-504	Tenn. Code Ann. § 48-101-502	http://www.state. tn.us/sos/charity/
Texas	No registration requirement	No registration requirement	No registration requirement
Utah	Utah Code Ann. § 13-22-5	Utah Code Ann. § 13-22-8	http://www. consumer protection.utah.gov/ consumerinfo/ charities.html
Vermont	No registration requirement	No registration requirement	No registration requirement
Virginia	Va. Code Ann. § 57-49	Va. Code Ann. § 57-60	http://www. vdacs.virginia.gov/ consumers/ registrations.shtml
Washing-ton	Wash. Rev. Code § 19.09.075	Wash. Rev. Code § 19.09.076	http://www.sos. wa.gov/charities/ charities.aspx
West Virginia	W. Va. Code § 29-19-5	W. Va. Code § 29-19-6	http://www.sos.wv. gov/business-licensing/charities/ Pages/default.aspx
Wisconsin	Wis. Stat. Ann. § 440.42	Wis. Stat. Ann. § 440.42	http://ww2. wisconsin.gov/state/ license/app; jsessionid=0001 HnEvk-DKRREh6s ZeSmqkESp:-L1IAJ? COMMAND =gov. wi.state.cpp. license. command. Show PermitTypes &selectedLicense =2001101609094 12872058
Wyoming	No registration requirement	No registration requirement	No registration requirement

Governing the For-Profit Social Enterprise

Operating the social enterprise through a for-profit legal form will allow the social enterprise to ameliorate social problems while, at the same time, generating a profit and attracting outside investment capital that would not be available if the social enterprise were operated as a nonprofit.

There are various for-profit legal forms from which to choose, and each presents its own unique tax, business, and governance considerations.[1] An organization will be considered a "for-profit" entity from a tax perspective if that entity has any substantial part of its operations dedicated to the production and accrual of profit, even if that profit motive is secondary. From a governance perspective, an entity will be considered "for-profit" if it is run primarily for the production of income.

Driving positive social change in a for-profit setting has become increasingly important for companies of all shapes and sizes. While the traditional forms of doing business have been embraced by social entrepreneurs and continue to be utilized, new forms of "hybrid entities" have recently emerged on the social enterprise scene. Hybrid entities such as the low-profit limited liability company (L³C) and the benefit corporation—classified as for-profit entities under state and federal laws—are designed to drive positive social change as their primary purpose, with profit motivation as a dual or secondary purpose. Operating in a hybrid business form

---

1. *See generally* MARC J. LANE, LEGAL HANDBOOK FOR SMALL BUSINESS, rev. ed. (Amacom 1989).

117

allows social enterprises to pursue greater private-sector funding opportunities and to capitalize on positive consumer sentiment.

The Greyston Foundation (www.greyston.org) is one example of a social enterprise that is achieving both mission-driven and profit-driven objectives. Operating out of New York, this foundation operates various interlocked and interconnected for-profit and nonprofit businesses, each organized as a different legal entity. One of its for-profit businesses, the Greyston Bakery, has been organized as a way of providing job and vocational training to the members of the underemployed population of Yonkers, New York. While profits and income are a motive of the bakery, this is secondary to the goal of providing assistance to the underprivileged population that the foundation as a whole serves.[2]

Another example can be found in Stonyfield Farms (www.stonyfield.com), which is committed to selling and producing organic yogurt.[3] This social enterprise is run as a for-profit entity that operates out of the state of New Hampshire. The enterprise purchases products only from farmers who meet their organic production standards, thus accomplishing two ends. First, it promotes and sustains the family farm.[4] Second, it ensures that farming practices do not harm the environment. Stonyfield Farms pursues both profit-driven and mission-driven goals and has managed to find a common link between the two without compromising either goal. For the social entrepreneur running a for-profit business, finding a common link between profit production and social purposes can be good way of avoiding liability that may otherwise accrue when management fails to maximize profits for the enterprise's equity owners.

The following is an in-depth discussion of the major for-profit business forms and the specific governance concerns that will be encountered when a social enterprise is operated in each form. The business form possibilities range from the classical business corporation to newly created hybrid entities.

---

2. *See* http://www.greyston.org/index.php?what_we_do.

3. *See* http://www.stonyfield.com/about_us/making_a_difference_since_1983/index.jsp

4. *See id.*

The Business Corporation

The business corporation is one of the most widely used business forms in the United States. Ownership and management are separated, and profit maximization is the chief concern of the directors and officers of the enterprise. The business corporation has the most stable and widely accepted body of governance law.[5] In addition, this entity form enjoys the greatest potential to generate the most revenue through investment and unrestricted business activity. Despite its many advantages, the business corporation may present serious governance concerns for the social entrepreneur, whose goal is not profit maximization but doing social good.[6] Directors and officers of a business corporation who do not treat profit maximization as their chief concern may incur personal liability to their shareholders.[7] The "business judgment rule" (described below) will protect corporate managers only if their decisions are tied to driving shareholder value. Accordingly, running a business corporation in a socially beneficial manner may prove challenging.

Notwithstanding the corporation's profit-driven motive, the social entrepreneur may be able to run the corporation with an eye toward all stakeholder concerns, as opposed to shareholder concerns alone, in pursuit of socially beneficial purposes. The business judgment rule will offer the presumption of validity to any decision made by a corporate manager as long as there is some attenuated connection to making profit.[8] For example, many financial models have shown that promoting social good through the adoption of environmentally safe production standards actually increases profitability.[9] Additionally, as discussed in the subsection below, certain states have constituency statutes that provide statutory protection for socially conscious decisions made by the managers of a corporation.[10]

---

5. *See generally* MARC J. LANE, REPRESENTING CORPORATE OFFICERS, DIRECTORS, MANAGERS, AND TRUSTEES, 2d ed. (Aspen Publishers 2010).

6. *See supra* Chapter 1.

7. Gantler v. Stephens, 965 A.2d 695 (Del. 2009); DEL. ANN. CODE tit. 8; Model Business Corporation Act § 8.

8. Alissa Mickels, *Beyond Corporate Social Responsibility Reconciling the Ideals of a For-Benefit Corporation with Director Fiduciary Duties in the U.S. and Europe,* 32 HASTINGS INT'L COMP. L. REV. 271 (2009).

9. *Id.*

10. *Id.*

Ownership and Management

In the classical business corporation form, ownership and management of the company are divided. Ownership is represented by shares, of which there may be several classes held by shareholders,[11] and management is generally carried out by directors and officers.

Tax Status

Corporations are taxed on all income. There are two types of corporations for tax purposes: the S corporation and the C corporation. The S corporation affords flow-through taxation in which income will only be taxed once, on the ownership level. There are special requirements (outside the scope of this publication) that need to be met in order to obtain and retain S corporation status. C corporations have a traditional corporate tax status, in that all corporate income is taxed at two levels—first as income to the corporation and then as income to the owners of the corporation when such income is distributed. While there are a number of permissible deductions that a corporate business enterprise can claim, the profitable business corporation will not be able to escape income tax.

Fiduciary Duties Owed in Traditional For-Profit Corporate Settings

As a general principle of corporate law, the managers, directors, and officers of a for-profit corporation owe fiduciary responsibilities and duties to both the corporation and its shareholders.[12] Although these duties have evolved over the decades and have subtle differences from jurisdiction to jurisdiction, they can be boiled down to one concept: profit maximization. The ultimate duty of any corporate director or officer is to ensure that the shareholders of the company have their potential returns maximized.[13] This mandatory profit-driven directive creates several core duties that are owed to both the corporation and directly to the shareholders, including primarily the duties of care and loyalty.[14] Any inap-

---

11. DEL. CODE ANN. tit. 8, § 151.
12. Gantler v. Stephens, 965 A.2d 695 (Del. 2009); DEL. ANN. CODE tit. 8; Model Business Corporation Act § 8.
13. Guth v. Loft, Inc. 5 A.2d 503 (Del. 1939).
14. *Id.*

propriate corporate action can always be associated with a breach of one of these core corporate duties.[15]

Nevertheless, corporate actions are generally given the protection of the business judgment rule, which, absent specific instances of breach, presumes that a director or officer has complied with his or her duties of care and loyalty.[16] As long as the business judgment presumption stands, a court will not and cannot interfere with corporate decision making. Accordingly, anyone seeking to challenge a corporate decision in court must find a method of pleading past the business judgment rule.

It is critical to understand that the managers' fiduciary duties are also owed by anyone who may control the corporate concern.[17] As a consequence, a controlling shareholder will always owe the same fiduciary responsibilities to the corporation and the minority shareholders.

The Duty of Loyalty

Officers and directors of a corporation owe an undivided duty of loyalty to the corporation and shareholders and must do what they reasonably believe is in the best interests of both.[18] Generally, this means that they may not deal with the corporate property in order to enrich themselves at the expense of the corporation and its shareholders.[19] It also means that a fiduciary may not hinder or harm the corporate enterprise.[20] In certain instances, a breach of the duty of loyalty will lead to the loss of business judgment protection, opening up the corporate decision to scrutiny. There are certain traditional instances where business judgment protection will be lost. These are touched on below.

---

15. Smith v. Van Gorkom, 488 A.2d 858 (Del. 1985); Levien v. Sinclair Oil, 261 A.2d 911 (Del. Ch. 1966).

16. Gantler v. Stephens, 965 A.2d 695 (Del. 2009).

17. Levien v. Sinclair Oil, 261 A.2d 911 (Del. Ch. 1966).

18. Guth v. Loft Inc., 5 A.2d 503 (Del. 1939); DEL. ANN. CODE tit. 8; Model Business Corporation Act § 8.

19. Guth v. Loft Inc., 5 A.2d 503 (Del. 1939); DEL. ANN. CODE tit. 8; Model Business Corporation Act § 8.

20. Guth v. Loft Inc., 5 A.2d 503 (Del. 1939); DEL. ANN. CODE tit. 8; Model Business Corporation Act § 8.

(a) Usurping a Corporate Opportunity

A director or officer of the corporation may not exploit an opportunity that rightfully belongs to the corporation.[21] Courts generally handle the usurping of a corporate opportunity through a two-part approach that takes into account two considerations. First, did the opportunity belong to the fiduciary or the corporation?[22] Second, if the opportunity did belong to the corporation, did the fiduciary properly exploit the opportunity or was it improperly misappropriated?[23] Although the test will vary from jurisdiction to jurisdiction, a corporate opportunity is said to exist when the opportunity in question is within the corporation's line of business, the corporation has an expectancy in the opportunity, and the corporation is financially capable of taking advantage of the opportunity.[24] A fiduciary can properly appropriate an opportunity if an independent majority of the board approves the appropriation.[25] If misappropriation of a corporate opportunity is found, the director in question will be in breach of his or her duty of loyalty and will not be able to claim protection under the business judgment rule. The transaction involving the opportunity is voidable, and an accounting may be owed to the corporation.

Type of Opportunity	Independent Board Approval of Appropriation?	Breach of Duty?
Corporate	No	Yes
Corporate	Yes	No
Individual	Not Needed	No

---

21. Guth v. Loft Inc., 5 A.2d 503 (Del. 1939); DEL. ANN. CODE tit. 8; Model Business Corporation Act § 8.

22. Guth v. Loft Inc., 5 A.2d 503 (Del. 1939); Johnston v. Greene, 121 A.2d 919 (Del. Ch. 1956).

23. Guth v. Loft Inc., 5 A.2d 503 (Del. 1939); Johnston v. Greene, 121 A.2d 919 (Del. Ch. 1956).

24. Guth v. Loft Inc., 5 A.2d 503 (Del. 1939); Johnston v. Greene, 121 A.2d 919 (Del. Ch. 1956).

25. Guth v. Loft Inc., 5 A.2d 503 (Del. 1939); Johnston v. Greene, 121 A.2d 919 (Del. Ch. 1956).

(b) Fraud, Illegality, Ultra Vires

The business judgment rule will not provide protection to directors or officers who engage in illegal acts. For instance, the Third Circuit did not provide protection to director action where the directors caused the corporation to contribute funds to a political campaign illegally.[26] In line with this concept, fraudulent actions, such as stock option backdating, will not receive protection from shareholder action through the business judgment rule. Finally, if management causes the corporation to act outside of the scope of its charter or bylaws, the act will be deemed *ultra vires* in that the corporation is not authorized to take the action.[27] Such an action will not receive business judgment protection and the transaction will be considered void, in that the shareholders will not be able to ratify it. However, in modern corporate America, *ultra vires* actions are rarely seen because, unlike their nonprofit counterparts, most for-profit corporations are organized to pursue any lawful business purposes.

Examples of Fraud, Illegality, and *Ultra Vires*

- Backdating stock options
- Violating state or federal (SEC, FCC, EPA, CFTC, etc.) regulations
- Entering into an agreement that involves any kind of criminal activity
- Intentionally lying to investors or shareholders

(c) Conflicts of Interest

A director or officer having a material conflict of interest during a corporate transaction is the kind of breach of loyalty that most commonly leads to loss of business judgment protection for the officer or director.[28] If a director or officer has a material financial interest in the transaction that affects the decision-making process of the board, the board will lose the protection of business judgment review.[29] When a director or officer contracts with the corporation or is a director or officer of a corporation on the

---

26. Miller v. Am. Tel. & Tel. Co, 507 F.2d 759 (3d Cir. 1974).
27. Kamin v. Am. Express Co., 383 N.Y.S.2d 807 (Sup. Ct. 1976).
28. Cede & Co. v. Technicolor, 663 A.2d 1156 (Del. 1995).
29. *Id.*

other side of a transaction, materiality is generally found.[30] For there to be a material conflict, it must affect the decision-making process of the entire board, such as when the conflicted director or officer dominates a majority of the board or fails to disclose his or her conflict when a disclosure of that conflict would be significant to the decision making of the reasonable independent director.[31]

Examples of Conflicts of Interest Involving a Director or Officer

- Being on interlocking boards when both are involved in the same deal
- Having a family member on an opposing board during a transaction
- Directly contracting with the corporation
- Having a family member be the beneficiary of a contract with the corporation

---

(d) Bad Faith

Bad faith, in many instances, has been classified as a particular type of loyalty breach which results in the loss of business judgment protection.[32] Bad faith involves a director's or officer's conscious disregard of his or her obligation to manage the corporation, i.e., a director or officer who fails to act.[33] It can also be classified as a director or officer purposely harming the corporation. In either event, the conduct must be egregious, and it will result in the loss of business judgment protection.

Examples of Bad Faith

- Having no corporate system in place to monitor employees in the performance of their duties
- Failing to attend board meetings
- Failing to secure an independent valuation of the business during an asset sale or merger
- Failing to conduct annual performance reviews for employees and board members

---

30. *Id.*
31. *Id.*
32. *In re* Caremark Derivative Litig., 698 A.2d 959 (Del. Ch. 1996).
33. *Id.*

The Duty of Care

All corporate directors and officers are charged with seeing that they attend to their responsibilities with the appropriate level of care that is required by law.[34] This means taking account of all information and analyzing the relevant data before making a decision. It also means that, in circumstances where the reliance on the reports of employees and the other members of the decision-making body is allowed, such reliance must be reasonable and in good faith.[35] Failure to meet the required standard of care will result in the loss of business judgment protection.

(a) Procedural Due Care

The duty of care is generally not concerned with the substantive decision making of the board or the officers of a corporation.[36] Instead, the duty is focused on the process that is used to make the corporation's business decisions.[37] Every jurisdiction has its own prescribed standard of care. In jurisdictions that follow the Model Business Corporation Act, the reasonable person standard, or ordinary negligence, is the order of the day.[38] In jurisdictions that follow the Delaware conception of care, a fiduciary's actions will be measured against a gross negligence standard.[39] Before the groundbreaking decision of *Smith v. Van Gorkom*, procedural attacks on the duty of care were rarely successful.[40] After *Van Gorkom*, in which a board considered and approved a merger after only a two-hour presentation from the company's financial officers, Delaware enacted a statutory exculpation provision that can insulate directors and officers from liability associated with due care breaches.[41] Many jurisdictions have enacted similar legislation. By any analysis, whether or not there has been a breach of the duty of care is a fact-intensive analysis.

---

34. Model Business Corporation Act § 8.
35. DEL. CODE ANN. tit. 8, § 141.
36. Smith v. Van Gorkom, 488 A.2d 858 (Del. 1985).
37. Id.
38. Model Business Corporation Act § 8.
39. Smith v. Van Gorkom, 488 A.2d 858 (Del. 1985).
40. Id.
41. DEL. CODE ANN. tit. 8, § 102(b)(7).

How to Avoid Procedural Due Care Issues

- Always take accurate and detailed notes at board and committee meetings.
- Always use legal and financial professionals when transacting on behalf of the corporation.
- Carefully read all reports presented before making any business decisions based on those reports.
- Always check and carefully consider the professional credentials of any individual to which responsibilities have been delegated.

(b) Waste

Engaging in waste can arguably be classified as a breach of the substantive due care standard. At times it has been classified as its own discrete breach of fiduciary duty. In the for-profit setting, waste is defined as a corporate transaction in which the corporation makes a gift of corporate assets in giving away such assets and receiving little or no consideration in return.[42] As noted by Delaware Chancery Judge William Allen:

> The judicial standard for determination of corporate waste is well developed. Roughly, a waste entails an exchange of corporate assets for consideration so disproportionately small as to lie beyond a range at which any reasonable person might be willing to trade. Most often the claim is associated with a transfer of corporate assets that serves no corporate purpose; or for which no consideration at all is received. Such a transfer is in effect a gift. If, however, there is any substantial consideration received by the corporation, and if there is a good faith judgment that in the circumstances the transaction is worthwhile, there should be no finding of waste, even if the fact finder would conclude ex post that the transaction was unreasonably risky.[43]

Accordingly, waste claims are linked primarily to loss of monetary value. However, in the social enterprise setting, finding a waste of corporate assets will not be inextricably tied to loss of monetary value due to the social mission of the enterprise.

---

42. Lewis v. Vogelstein, 699 A.2d 327 (Del. Ch. 1997).
43. *Id.* at 336 (citations omitted).

Examples of Waste

- Compensation (including stock options) to an employee at a rate that materially exceeds the consideration received in return
- Gratuitously transferring corporate assets to another entity without receiving an adequate interest in that entity

---

Intrinsic Fairness Test

As noted above, particular breaches of the duty of loyalty and care will result in the loss of business judgment protection, which will open up the transaction to judicial scrutiny and avoidance. But if a transaction is subject to a material conflict or lack of due care, it is only voidable, and not necessarily void. In the majority of U.S. jurisdictions, most notably Delaware, where the breaching party can show the intrinsic fairness of a transaction, the transaction may be upheld.[44]

The intrinsic fairness test is statutory law in many states. Generally, the two components of the intrinsic fairness test are fair dealing and fair price.[45] Fair dealing generally requires a showing of disinterested director approval or shareholder ratification of the transaction, while fair price requires an objective evaluation of the economic terms of the transaction.[46] The effect of showing intrinsic fairness may reinstall business judgment protection or it may simply shift the burden of showing unfairness to the complaining party. How intrinsic fairness will be evaluated and applied is heavily jurisdictional.

The Benefit Corporation

The benefit corporation is a new form of corporate entity. So far, only two jurisdictions, Maryland and Vermont, allow the formation of benefit corporations. Unlike the business corporation, the directors and officers of the benefit corporation are expected to consider socially beneficial factors in their decision making.[47] Profit motive is not their only concern. Accord-

---

44. *Id.*

45. Cede v. Technicolor, 634 A.3d 345 (Del. 1993).

46. *Id.*

47. MD. CODE ANN. CORPS. & ASS'NS § 5-6C-07(a)(1); 11A VT. STAT. ANN. § 21.09(a)(1).

ingly, the fiduciary duties of loyalty and care are informed by the social motives of the corporate enterprise without the fear of shareholder liability. From a governance standpoint, this business form is attractive for running a social enterprise. Still, from a funding standpoint, the entity may not draw as many traditional investors because of its socially beneficial purposes, which must be accounted for in the corporation's governing documents in order to gain benefit corporation status.[48]

Ownership and Management

Much like the business corporation, the benefit corporation will have a split between ownership and management. The managers of the corporation are the directors and officers. Statutorily, the directors are tasked with the management of the corporation and may delegate those duties to officers of the corporation.

Tax Status

The benefit corporation is taxed as any other for-profit corporate concern would be taxed, meaning it will be taxed on all income. If the corporation is classified as an S corporation, the income will only be taxed once—to the shareholders. If the corporation is classified as a C corporation, the income will be taxed at both the corporate level and the shareholder level.

Fiduciary Duties Owed in Benefit Corporate Settings

The body of law governing fiduciary duties in the benefit corporate setting is scant. The concepts of loyalty and care have not yet been judicially defined for benefit corporations as they have been in the business corporation setting. Still, the core duty of the benefit corporation can be defined as the duty to secure profits for the shareholders while considering the socially beneficial purposes of the corporation.

Under the statute, the directors and officers of beneficial corporations are statutorily allowed to consider the following when making any decision: (1) the corporation's stockholders; (2) the corporation's employees, workforce, subsidiaries, and suppliers; (3) the interests of consumers as beneficiaries of the corporation's general or specific public benefit purposes;

---

48. MD. CODE ANN. CORPS. & ASS'NS § 5-6C-07(a)(1); 11A VT. STAT. ANN. § 21.09(a)(1).

(4) community and societal considerations, including those of any community where the corporation, its subsidiaries, or its suppliers have offices or facilities; and (5) the local and global environment.[49]

The Duty of Loyalty

The duty of loyalty still calls for a general prohibition against illegal actions, fraudulent actions, or actions that would subvert the beneficial purposes of the corporation. There is also the general prohibition on entering into conflicted transactions and usurping or taking a corporate opportunity away from the corporation.

The Duty of Care

It is safe to assume that the corporate standards of care that have developed in the jurisdiction will be applicable to benefit corporations. Thus, it would be wise for all benefit corporation managers to make business decisions in a manner in which a reasonable person, in his or her position, would do so.

The Limited Liability Company

Limited liability companies (LLCs) and corporations share much in common. Both the corporation and the manager-managed LLC offer a business structure in which management and ownership are divided. If litigation is contemplated against the managers of an LLC, issues concerning the derivative nature of the litigation must be considered, much as in the case of litigation against a corporation. Like the directors and officers of a corporation, the managers of an LLC are afforded business judgment protection. Additionally, both offer limited liability from claims made against the business. Yet there are critical differences between the two entities. One of these differences is that the LLC affords its owners pass-through taxation, similar to that of a partnership. As a consequence, distributions are generally taxed at the ownership level, and not at the company level. Additionally, LLCs, unlike their corporate counterparts, are creatures of contract, with few statutorily or judicially created mandatory fiduciary duties. The call to profit maximization need not be absolute in the LLC setting.[50] For social enterprises looking to take on a social purpose, this makes the LLC a more attrac-

---

49. MD. CODE ANN. CORPS. & ASS'NS § 5-6C-07(a)(1); 11A VT. STAT. ANN. § 21.09(a)(1).

50. 805 ILL. COMP. STAT. § 180/15-3.

tive option than the business corporation. LLCs, like corporations, have a well-developed body of law that a social enterprise may draw from when developing its business plan and devising its legal structure.

Ownership and Management

An LLC may be member-managed, in which there is little or no separation between the member owners and management, or manager-managed, which is more along the lines of a corporate split in ownership and management. As noted below, how the LLC is organized will determine who owes fiduciary duties to the organization. Even if an LLC is organized as member-managed, the members can still elect to designate the management duties to a particular member or group of members, which would have an impact on how the fiduciary duties are allocated among them.

Tax Status

The LLC's taxable income, regardless of how the LLC is managed, will be taxed at either the entity level or the ownership level. As with corporations, there are many exemptions and deductions from taxation that are available to the LLC.

While most LLCs are formed for profit, it should be noted that the IRS expressly provides for the possibility of an LLC being recognized as a tax-exempt charitable organization. This is possible because an LLC may elect to be taxed as a corporation and thus fit within the description in Code Section 501(c)(3) identifying charitable organizations as "[c]orporations, and any community chest, fund, or foundation." Hence, by electing to be treated as a corporation, an LLC, if organized and operated for exempt charitable purposes, may become tax-exempt.[51] Special requirements apply to such LLCs, particularly a requirement that only 501(c)(3) organizations and governmental units or instrumentalities may be members of such an LLC, and the organizational language of the LLC must prohibit any transfer of any membership interest to any other type of entity.[52]

---

51. Robert R. Keatinge, *LLCs and Nonprofit Organizations—For-Profits, Nonprofits and Hybrids*, 42 SUFFOLK U. L. REV. 553, 572 (2009).

52. *Id.* at 574.

Fiduciary Duties Owed by Managers and Members

The fiduciary obligations in LLCs are generally created by contract. This chapter will look at the LLC statute in Illinois, which was amended as of January 4, 2010, to authorize the L³C (low-profit limited liability company). Since Illinois has adopted the Uniform Limited Liability Company Act, its provisions (apart from those relating to the LLC) will generally apply to most other states.

The statute prescribes the default fiduciary obligations of members and managers. How fiduciary obligations are distributed will depend, in large measure, on the management structure of the LLC.

Duty of Loyalty

By virtue of its articles of organization, an LLC may be member-managed or manager-managed.[53] Member-managed LLCs have no firm split between ownership and management; thus, fiduciary duties are charged to all the members.[54] Manager-managed LLCs maintain a division between ownership and management, with managers being elected by a majority of the members.[55] In a manager-managed LLC, fiduciary duties are charged only to the managers and to members that decide to take on managerial functions.[56] Much like in the corporate setting, failing to meet the required fiduciary standards as set by the statute or organizational documents will result in the loss of business judgment protection.

(a) Member-Managed LLC

A member's duty of loyalty to a member-managed company and to the other members includes the following:

(1) to account to the company and to hold as trustee for it any property, profit, or benefit derived by the member in conduct or winding up of the company's business or derived from a use by the member of the company's property, including the appropriation of a company's opportunity;

---

53. *Id.*
54. *Id.*
55. *Id.*
56. 805 ILL. COMP. STAT. § 180/15-3(g)(3).

(2) to act fairly when a member deals with the company in the con-
     duct or winding up of the company's business as or on behalf of a
     party having an interest adverse to the company; and

(3) to refrain from competing with the company in the conduct of the
     company's business before the dissolution of the company.[57]

(b) Manager-Managed LLC

A manager in a manager-managed LLC is held to same standards of conduct, in terms of loyalty obligations, as a member in a member-managed
LLC.[58] As stated above, where the LLC is manager-managed, the members do not have fiduciary obligations. Still, even if the LLC is organized
as manager-managed, members may be charged with fiduciary responsibilities, pursuant to the operating agreement, to the extent that the member exercises management authority over any aspect of the company's
business.[59] Along these lines, a manager is relieved of fiduciary responsibilities to the extent that those responsibilities have been delegated, through
the operating agreement, to the members.[60]

The Duty of Care

Managers in a manager-managed LLC and members in a member-managed
LLC owe the company and its members a duty of care in the conduct or
winding up of the company's business.[61] This duty is limited to refraining
from engaging in grossly negligent conduct, intentional misconduct, or a
knowing violation of law during the winding-up process.[62] This is the only
statutory duty that is prescribed in Illinois, and many states are similarly
sparse on care requirements. Still, breaching this duty will lead to the loss of
business judgment protection for the manager's or member's actions.

Good Faith

As in the corporate setting, there is a standing duty of good faith owed by
managers in a manager-managed business and members in a member-man-

---

57. 805 ILL. COMP. STAT. § 180/15-3(b).
58. 805 ILL. COMP. STAT. § 180/15-3(g)
59. 805 ILL. COMP. STAT. § 180/15-3(g)(3).
60. 805 ILL. COMP. STAT. § 180/15-3(g)(4).
61. 805 ILL. COMP. STAT. § 180/15-3(c).
62. Id.

aged business.[63] However, unlike the corporate setting, where good faith can be properly classified as part of the duty of loyalty, good faith in the LLC context is more akin to the contractual duty of good faith.[64] The duty of good faith governs the exercise of all duties that are owed under the operating agreement or statute.[65] All duties must be performed in good faith and in accordance with the governing documents of the LLC.

Contracting Around Fiduciary Obligations

Although it has been debated in academic circles for decades, black-letter law notes that fiduciary duties in a profit-driven corporate setting cannot be contracted around, contracted away, or significantly altered by contract.[66] This is not the case in LLCs. In the LLC setting, although fiduciary duties can never be eliminated, they can be freely altered and tailored to fit the purpose of the business. In the social enterprise setting, this characteristic is what makes the L³C—a specialized, mission-driven LLC—so appealing. The fiduciary duties can be tailored to match the mission-driven motive of the L³C, including seeing that profit maximization is not the primary responsibility of the managers or members. The Illinois LLC statute states:

> (a) All members of a limited liability company may enter into an operating agreement to regulate the affairs of the company and the conduct of its business and to govern relations among the members, managers, and company. . . . Except as provided in subsection (b), an operating agreement may modify the provisions of this Act governing relations among the members, managers, and company.[67]
>
> (b) The operating agreement many not . . .
>
> > (6) eliminate or reduce a member's fiduciary duties, but may:
> >
> > > (A) identify specific types or categories of activities that do not violate these duties, if not manifestly unreasonable; and

---

63. 805 ILL. COMP. STAT. § 180/15-3(d).

64. Wood v. Baum, 953 A.2d 136 (Del. 2008).

65. 805 ILL. COMP. STAT. § 180/15-3(d).

66. Daniel Fischel & Frank Easterbrook, *Corporate Control Transactions*, 91 YALE L.J. 698 (1982).

67. 805 ILL. COMP. STAT. § 180/15-5(a).

(B) specify the number or percentage of members or disinterested managers that may authorize or ratify, after full
disclosure of all material facts, a specific act or transaction
that otherwise would violate these duties; or

(7) eliminate or reduce the obligation of good faith and fair
dealing under subsection (d) of Section 15-3, but the operating agreement may determine the standards by which the performance of the obligation is to be measured, if the standards
are not manifestly unreasonable.[68]

In some jurisdictions, where neither the articles of organization, the
operating agreement, nor the statute speaks to a particular fiduciary obligation, such as the standard of care in ordinary business transactions, such
duties can be supplemented by concepts from corporation or partnership
law. The body of law is used for this purpose is dependent on whether or
not the LLC is manager-managed, which leans towards corporate form, or
member-managed, which indicates a partnership form. This exercise is ju-
risdictionally particular.

"L³C": The Low-Profit Limited Liability Company

The Low-Profit Limited Liability Company, or "L³C" as it is commonly
called, is a new hybrid business form that combines aspects of the traditional
for-profit LLC and socially beneficial aspects of nonprofit organizations.

The L³C is a subset of the LLC, in which the governing documents
must specifically identify governance objectives that are geared toward charitable or educational purposes. The jurisdictions authorizing the organization of L³Cs require their purpose to track the charitable and benevolent
purposes of IRC § 170(c)(2)(B). Such purposes must be represented in
the governing documents of the L³C. The L³C may blend these purposes
with secondary profit-driven motives. Accordingly, the L³C will typically
have both mission-driven and profit-driven motives.

Much like the benefit corporation, the L³C must have a charitable or
educational purpose. The social entrepreneur may be counseled to choose
this form over the LLC. Unlike the traditional LLC, the L³C is statutorily

---

68. 805 ILL. COMP. STAT. § 180/15-5(b).

required to have primarily social purposes. Many commentators believe this contrast may mitigate the governance risk in running the enterprise for a socially beneficial purpose. Yet, because of its profit-driven purpose, the L³C retains the ability to attract traditional investors seeking market-rate returns. Because of the statutorily required social purpose, the L³C may also be able to attract foundations' program-related investments as well as socially responsible investment from individuals and others (including mission-related investments from foundations and charities). However, as with any new business entity, the law surrounding the L³C is evolving, something social entrepreneurs and their attorneys should keep in mind.

Ownership and Management

Like any other LLC, the L³C may be member-managed or manager-managed. Accordingly, there can be a split between ownership and management, or the company can elect to be run by its owners. Also as with any other LLC, the organizational structure of the L³C will dictate how the fiduciary obligations are applied.

Tax Status

Since the L³C is a for-profit enterprise for tax purposes, its net income is subject to tax. The L³C will be disregarded for tax purposes (in which event its income will be taxed at the ownership level) unless it elects to be taxed as a corporation. The same exemptions and deductions available to other LLCs are available to the L³C.

Fiduciary Duties of Loyalty and Care Owed in the L³C Setting

Because L³Cs are specialized LLCs, the fiduciary obligations prescribed by the LLC statute will apply, as discussed above.[69] In short, because the fiduciary duties in the L³C are creatures of contract, its managers and members have the ability to tailor their fiduciary obligations to specifically match the mission of their company.[70] This ability is what makes the L³C attractive for the social entrepreneur who seeks to combine mission and profit-driven goals.

---

69. *See supra* Chapter 5.
70. 805 ILL. COMP. STAT. § 180/15-3.

*The following statutory duties are based on the Illinois LLC stat-
ute, which is similar to the statute in most jurisdictions. The duties
mentioned apply to managers of manager-managed L³Cs and members of member-managed L³Cs.*

The Duty of Loyalty:
The duty of loyalty requires all fiduciaries of the L³C:
- to account to the company and to hold as trustee for it any
  property, profit, or benefit derived by the member in conduct
  or winding up of the company's business or derived from a use
  by the member of the company's property, including the appropriation of a company's opportunity;
- to act fairly when a member deals with the company in the
  conduct or winding up of the company's business as or on behalf of a party having an interest adverse to the company; and
- to refrain from competing with the company in the conduct of
  the company's business before the dissolution of the company.

The Duty of Care:
The duty of care requires all fiduciaries of an L³C:
- to refrain from engaging in grossly negligent conduct, intentional misconduct, or a knowing violation of law during the
  winding-up process.

The Duty of Good Faith:
- A fiduciary shall discharge his or her duties to the L³C and its
  members under this Act or under the operating agreement and
  exercise any rights consistent with the obligation of good faith
  and fair dealing.

**Contracting Around and Altering Fiduciary Obligations to
Match the Mission:**
- All members of a limited liability company may enter into an
  operating agreement to regulate the affairs of the company and
  the conduct of its business and to govern relations among the
  members, managers, and company. . . . An operating agreement
  may modify the provisions of this Act governing relations among
  the members, managers, and company.

- The operating agreement many not eliminate or reduce a member's fiduciary duties, but may:
  (A) identify specific types or categories of activities that do not violate these duties, if not manifestly unreasonable; and
  (B) specify the number or percentage of members or disinterested managers that may authorize or ratify, after full disclosure of all material facts, a specific act or transaction that otherwise would violate these duties.
- A fiduciary many not eliminate or reduce the obligation of good faith and fair dealing, but the operating agreement may determine the standards by which the performance of the obligation is to be measured, if the standards are not manifestly unreasonable.

Constituency Statutes

Constituency statutes came into vogue in the early 1980s and were enacted, in part, as a statutory tool to be used by corporations and other for-profit entities, depending on jurisdiction, to protect themselves during takeovers and change-of-control transactions.[71] The scope of the statutes' application varies from state to state. Some statutes provide only the tools necessary to fend off takeovers, while others arguably allow directors, officers, and managers to consider stakeholder interests when making day-to-day decisions.[72] Although there have been few judicial decisions on how these statutes should be interpreted, some courts have had occasion to speak to the issue. Generally, how these statutes are interpreted will be limited by the definition of "stakeholder" and in what context the statute may apply.[73]

The first state to enact a constituency statute was Pennsylvania. The statute in Pennsylvania states:

---

71. Eric Otis, *Beyond Shareholders: Interpreting Corporate Constituency Statutes*, 61 GEO. WASH. L. REV. 14 (1996).

72. Alissa Mickels, *Beyond Corporate Social Responsibility: Reconciling the Ideals of a For-Benefit Corporation with Director Fiduciary Duties in the U.S. and Europe*, 32 HASTINGS INT'L COMP. L. REV. 271 (2009).

73. *Id.*

(a) In discharging the duties of their respective positions, the board of directors, committees of the board and individual directors of a business corporation may, in considering the best interests of the corporation, consider to the extent they deem appropriate:

>(1) The effects of any action upon any or all groups affected by such action, including shareholders, employees, suppliers, customers and creditors of the corporation, and upon communities in which offices or other establishments of the corporation are located;

>(2) The short-term and long-term interests of the corporation, including the benefits that may accrue to the corporation from its long-term plans and the possibility that these interests may be best served by the continued independence of the corporation.

>(3) The resources, intent and conduct (past, stated and potential) of any person seeking to acquire control of the corporation.

>(4) All other pertinent factors.[74]

*   *   *

(d) Absent breach of fiduciary duty, lack of good faith or self-dealing, any act as the board of directors, a committee of the board or an individual director shall be presumed to be in the best interests of the corporation. In assessing whether the standard set forth in section 1712 [concerning proper corporate conduct] has been satisfied, there shall not be any greater obligation to justify, or higher burden of proof with respect to, any act as the board of directors, any committee of the board or any individual director relating to or affecting an acquisition or potential or proposed acquisition of control of the corporation than is applied to any other act as a board of directors, any committee of the board or any individual director.[75]

The Pennsylvania statute prompts several legal issues worth noting. First, the statute was clearly aimed at director actions during mergers, acquisitions, and attempted hostile takeovers, all of which trigger enhanced

---

74. 15 PA. CONS. STAT. § 1715(a).
75. 15 PA. CONS. STAT. § 1715(d).

judicial security in certain jurisdictions.[76] Second, a wide variety of constituencies can have their interests taken into consideration as stakeholders, including the community surrounding the business's offices. Finally, although the statute is geared toward end-term transactions, it arguably can apply to day-to-day business decisions, particularly in light of interpretive judicial decisions.

As an example of the application of this statute, the district court for the Eastern District of Pennsylvania decided a case involving a defensive stock reclassification plan in response to a hostile tender offer.[77] Citing the constituency statute, the court noted that in taking corporate action, the long-term consequences on non-shareholder constituencies may be considered in lieu of the short-term financial interests of shareholders.[78] Although this statement was made in the context of a takeover defense, it may be applicable to other business decisions.

Most of the other 30 jurisdictions with constituency statutes employ language similar to that of Pennsylvania's statute. Although the Pennsylvania statute addresses only corporate directors, most other statutes also specifically address officers,[79] and many apply to for-profit non-corporate entities as well. For the social enterprise, the effect of all of these statutes on all the business entities to which they apply is that they appear to give directors, officers, and managers room to pursue benevolent interests, as they will be able to look to interests other than maximizing shareholder profits. (Most constituency statutes are permissive in terms of allowing directors to take into account interests other than those of the shareholders. In states with mandatory constituency statutes, such as Connecticut[80] and Arizona,[81] the statute typically applies only in the context of a corporate takeover or similar situation.)

Outside of organizing in Maryland and Vermont, which authorize benefit corporations, the best way to run a traditional for-profit corporation with a socially beneficial purpose may be to organize in a state with

---

76. *See* Unocal Corp. v. Mesa Petrol. Co., 493 A.2d 946 (Del. 1985); Revlon, Inc. v. MacAndrews and Forbes Holdings, Inc., 506 A.2d 173 (Del. 1985).

77. Baron v. Strawbridge & Clothier, 646 F. Supp. 690 (E.D. Pa. 1986).

78. *Id.*

79. *See* 805 ILL. COMP. STAT. 5/8.85.

80. CONN. GEN. STAT. § 33-756(d).

81. ARIZ. REV. STAT. § 10-2702.

one of these statutes. Still, based on how each jurisdiction's statute is interpreted, there may be significant limitations.

Some commentators have suggested that the ultimate legal effect of constituency laws may be to insulate directors, officers, and corporate managers from liability, based on day-to-day transactions, when they fail to maximize shareholder profits.[82] However, other commentators have indicated more recently that this has not been the case. Instead, courts have been found to treat constituency statutes as adding essentially nothing to the existing law.[83] This may be due in part to the fact that constituency statutes were originally created as an anti-takeover device, rather than as a means of promoting corporate social responsibility.[84] It has been suggested that constituency statutes are "either misguided or just a subterfuge for allowing management to block takeovers that [are] contrary to managerial interests."[85] In a takeover context, courts may tend to resort to common-law principles of shareholder primacy in judging the actions of a board of directors. Thus, in the case of a shareholder lawsuit against a board of directors where a constituency statute is used as a defense, a court may perceive the board's resort to a constituency statute as an excuse to avoid a takeover. By contrast, the benefit corporation laws that have been enacted in Maryland and Vermont are grounded in a clear policy in favor of corporate social responsibility and thus may be taken into account more effectively by the courts in the future.

As a consequence, directors or officers of a corporation or management of another for-profit entity relying on constituency statutes must be very careful when making decisions based on larger global or humanitarian concerns, because the threat of a shareholder derivative suit for waste or lack of due care may loom.[86]

---

82. Lawrence E. Mitchell, *A Theoretical and Practical Framework for Enforcing Corporate Constituency Statutes*, 70 TEX. L. REV. 579 (1992).

83. Anthony Bisconti, Note, *The Double Bottom Line: Can Constituency Statutes Protect Socially Responsible Corporations Stuck in* Revlon Land?, 42 LOY. L.A. LAW REV. 765, 790 (2009).

84. *Id.* at 765, 793 n.203 (2009).

85. This is described as "the canonical law and economics account on corporate social responsibility" in Einer Elhauge, *Sacrificing Corporate Profits in the Public Interest*, 80 N.Y.U. L. REV. 733, 736–37 (2005).

86. Alissa Mickels, *Beyond Corporate Social Responsibility: Reconciling the Ideals of a For-Benefit Corporation with Director Fiduciary Duties in the U.S. and Europe*, 32 HASTINGS INT'L COMP. L. REV. 271 (2009).

Compensation and Benefits in the For-Profit Social Enterprise

The managers of for-profit enterprises have great discretion in setting the compensation and benefits of officers, directors, and/or managers. Unless a specific instance of breach of fiduciary duty, violation of any applicable statute, or violation of any governing document, such as the bylaws or the operating agreement, is shown, their business decision in setting compensation will be protected by the business judgment rule.[87] This is a premise that applies equally to all for-profit entities.

Business Judgment Protection

Board members and managers empowered to make decisions concerning compensation will receive the protection of the business judgment rule, which generally presumes that management decisions are made in good faith.[88] Successfully pleading waste is one of the only methods of voiding a compensation decision of the board members or managers, outside a clear violation of statutory law or acting contrary to the organization's governing documents.[89] To avoid a waste claim, directors must set managers' compensation with due care, must not enter into conflicted transactions, and must exercise good faith or risk falling outside the protection of the business judgment rule.

Due Care in Setting Compensation

As with any business decision, those who owe fiduciary obligations to their principals must make decisions regarding compensation with the required standard of care. That standard will differ from jurisdiction to jurisdiction. In Delaware, when dealing with corporate actors, the standard of care for all business decisions is called "slight care."[90] That is, directors and officers will be liable for actions and decisions made in a grossly negligent manner and will not receive business judgment protection.[91] In most other juris-

---

87. Brehm v. Eisner, 746 A.2d 244, 263 (Del. 2000).
88. *See generally id.*
89. *See generally id.*
90. Smith v. Van Gorkom, 488 A.2d 858 (Del. 1985).
91. *Id.*

dictions, the standard of care for corporate actors is ordinary care.[92] That is, directors and officers in these jurisdictions will be liable for actions and decisions made in a negligent manner in which they did not exercise the ordinary care a reasonable person in similar situation would have.[93] These corporate principles will generally be applied to other for-profit entities. Of note, the members of an LLC may choose to limit what constitutes a breach of the duty of care in the operating agreement.[94] Still, where there is no such limitation, corporate principles will generally be applied to manager-managed LLCs and partnership principles will be applied to member-managed LLCs.

As a consequence, any decision about the amount of management compensation must be made in a procedurally correct manner.[95] This means that regardless of jurisdiction, the managers of the organization should consider all information before setting compensation, including but not limited to the following:

- whether the manager's compensation package comprises appropriate compensation vehicles;
- whether the manager's performance in prior years correlates with any incentive portion of the overall compensation package;
- levels of compensation as compared to similar companies; and
- overall performance of the company during the time the manager served the company.[96]

Avoiding Conflicts of Interest when Setting Compensation

LLC managers, corporate officers, corporate directors, and any other fiduciaries owe an undivided duty of loyalty to their principals as well as to the entities in which their principals have an ownership interest.[97] As such,

---

92. Revised Model Corporation Act § 8.

93. *Id.*

94. *See* 805 ILL. COMP. STAT. § 180/15-5(a).

95. *See generally* Smith v. Van Gorkom, 488 A.2d 858 (Del. 1985).

96. *See* R. William Ide, *Post-Enron Corporate Governance Opportunities: Creating a Culture of Greater Board Collaboration and Oversight*, 54 MERCER L. REV. 829, 862 (2003).

97. Guth v. Loft Inc., 5 A.2d 503 (Del. 1939); DEL. ANN. CODE tit. 8; Revised Model Business Corporation Act § 8.

managers of for-profit enterprises are prohibited from causing the company to enter into a transaction in which they have any material conflict of interest that affects the entire decision-making body involved in approving the transaction.[98] Where such a material conflict exists, the transaction in question will not be protected by the business judgment rule, and the conflicted manager may be liable for breach of the fiduciary duty of loyalty.[99] Whenever a manager stands on both sides of a transaction, there is enough of a financial interest to create a material conflict. Accordingly, a basic premise of the law dictates that a manager can in no way be involved with setting his or her own salary or any other form of compensation, or this decision will be voidable. A group of other disinterested and independent managers must make the decision regarding compensation.

Federal Law and Executive Compensation

There is a large body of federal law that speaks to methods of compensation, setting levels of compensation, and disclosure of compensation, but these laws affect only publicly traded issuers of securities and certain financial institutions that pose a large systemic risk to the U.S. economy. The laws are administered by a host of federal agencies, including, but not limited to, the Securities and Exchange Commission, the Federal Deposit Insurance Company, the Commodity Futures Trading Commission, and the Office of the Comptroller of the Currency. These laws and the rules under which they are administered are outside the scope of this publication. For reference, some of the laws that deal with executive compensation on the federal level are:

- The Securities Exchange Act of 1934
- The Sarbanes-Oxley Act of 2002
- The Investment Company Act of 1940
- The Emergency Economic Stabilization Act of 2008
- The American Recovery and Reinvention Act of 2009
- The Dodd-Frank Wall Street Reform and Consumer Protection Act of 2010.

* * * *

---

98. Cede & Co. v. Technicolor, 663 A.2d 1156 (Del. 1995).

99. Guth v. Loft Inc., 5 A.2d 503 (Del. 1939); Del. Ann. Code tit. 8; Revised Model Business Corporation Act § 8; Cede & Co. v. Technicolor, 663 A.2d 1156 (Del. 1995).

For-profit business entities, because of their ability to generate funding and well-developed bodies of law, can be extremely attractive organizational options for the social entrepreneur. Still, they present a minefield of governance issues that must be navigated carefully. As the next chapter will point out, additional considerations need to be addressed should for-profit and nonprofit organizations collaborate.

Multi-Organizational Structures

Operating a social enterprise through a multi-organizational structure is increasingly common and can be beneficial for social entrepreneurs who wish to combine the best aspects of tax-exempt organizations and for-profit businesses. Although operating a social enterprise as a tax-exempt organization has many advantages for the social entrepreneur, federal tax laws impose stringent standards on the operation of tax-exempt entities in exchange for permitting them to operate tax-free. These rules and regulations often have the effect of prohibiting certain activities that could help the social enterprise accomplish its mission. The use of a related for-profit entity by a tax-exempt organization (whether as a partly or wholly owned subsidiary or through a joint venture) may allow multiple objectives to be accomplished that otherwise might not have been possible through the use of a single tax-exempt entity.

The benefits of forming a for-profit subsidiary are many and varied. Most obviously, they can be used to generate additional revenue. In fact, a relatively common reason for the use of a for-profit subsidiary is to permit a tax-exempt entity to develop and operate a business that may or may not be related to the tax-exempt entity's exempt purposes. Operation of a business through a subsidiary may allow the tax-exempt organization to generate alternative revenue streams outside of the contributions and donations usually relied on to cover operational expenses.

Forming a for-profit subsidiary might also allow a tax-exempt social enterprise to gain access to investors from a wide range of outside sources, including individuals, private foundations, institutional investors, and others. Tax-exempt organizations have traditionally been disadvantaged (compared to for-profit enterprises) in raising capital from outside sources. This disadvantage stems from the fact that tax-exempt entities, typically organized as non-stock corporations, will generally not be able to issue equity.[1] Creating a for-profit subsidiary will allow the tax-exempt entity to attract equity investment from outside players. Further, the subsidiary may have fewer limits on its operational capabilities and have greater flexibility than a tax-exempt entity might have on its own. Both factors may contribute to the venture's potential to achieve scale.

In addition to the financial benefits that can be obtained through the operation of a for-profit subsidiary, there are significant non-financial reasons for their use. For one thing, certain assets can be held in a subsidiary for asset protection purposes. For another, the tax-exempt entity can be insulated from activities that may trigger liabilities.

While there are many advantages to using a related for-profit subsidiary, there are also important rules in place to ensure that the tax-exempt organization is not employed as a device to further the interests of private investors. The doctrine of private inurement, discussed below, requires that a tax-exempt organization be organized and operated so that no part of its earnings inures to the benefit of any private shareholder or individual. If a tax-exempt organization also has for-profit investors in its subsidiary, compliance with this doctrine is of primary importance.

This chapter highlights how tax-exempt entities may interact with related for-profit entities (through common ownership and other joint venture/partnership arrangements) and highlights the key issues that should be addressed to ensure that the enterprise works as intended without incurring adverse tax consequences.

Unrelated Business Taxable Income (UBTI) Considerations

In exchange for its income tax exemption, tax-exempt organizations have traditionally been restricted from competing with for-profit organizations in the marketplace. To eliminate the harmful effects of such unfair compe-

---

1. *See* VA. CODE ANN. § 13.1-804 (providing an example of a non-stock corporation statute, similar to such statutes in all relevant jurisdictions).

tition, the IRC imposes a tax on the unrelated business taxable income (UBTI) of tax-exempt organizations. Essentially, all income earned from unrelated trades or businesses is required to be segregated from income that is related to the tax-exempt function and taxed separately at the prevailing corporate income tax rates.

The tax consequences to a tax-exempt investor are usually favorable when an investment made by the tax-exempt investor is considered to be substantially related to the purposes for which tax exemption has been granted. When the investment is substantially related to the tax-exempt purpose, the income thereby generated is usually tax-free. If the income generated by an investment is not substantially related to the tax-exempt investor's purpose, the income may constitute UBTI. Excessive UBTI could potentially endanger a tax-exempt investor's tax-exemption.

By taxing UBTI, Congress has attempted to eliminate a source of unfair competition by placing the unrelated business activities of tax-exempt organizations on the same tax basis as the non-exempt business endeavors with which they compete.[2] The rules are designed to put tax-exempt entities and for-profit entities competing in the same marketplace on equal footing so that neither has an unfair tax advantage over the other.

Determining whether activities of a tax-exempt social enterprise are "unrelated" to the organization's tax-exempt purposes or whether they are a "regularly carried on" trade or business has been a topic of considerable consideration by the IRS and the courts. Indeed, this area of the law is well documented and well critiqued. While a discussion of whether income earned by a tax-exempt social enterprise will be considered to be UBTI is outside of the scope of this book, this section will provide guidance to social enterprises operating in a tax-exempt form and their attorneys on how best to approach multi-organizational structures so as to minimize and, where possible, eliminate UBTI.

Corporation or Flow-Through Entity?

Tax-exempt social enterprises that utilize a for-profit subsidiary must determine what legal form the subsidiary should take. In this regard, the for-profit subsidiary can either be a flow-through entity (e.g., a partnership, LLC, L3C, S corporation, etc.) or a corporation (e.g., a C corporation,

---

2. Treas. Reg. § 1.513-1(b).

benefit corporation, etc.). The determination of the appropriate legal form that a for-profit subsidiary should take is of extreme importance. This is especially true when activities undertaken by the for-profit will be unrelated to the tax-exempt mission of its exempt parent.

The major difference between corporate subsidiaries and pass-through subsidiaries centers on the revenue recognition effects at the parent level and how those effects are implicated by unrelated business income considerations. Income generated by corporate subsidiaries does not "flow through" to a tax-exempt parent. Rather, income generated by corporate subsidiaries will be taxable at the subsidiary level directly. As a result, the tax-exempt parent does not report a subsidiary's income and expense on its own income statement. Although dividend payments may be made to the parent on earnings at the subsidiary level, dividends are specifically excluded from the definition of UBTI.[3] Therefore, if a corporate subsidiary of a tax-exempt parent generates income from the conduct of activities unrelated to the parent's exempt purposes, that income would not adversely affect the parent.

In contrast, if a flow-through subsidiary is utilized by a tax-exempt parent, income and expenses generated at the subsidiary level will "flow through" to the tax-exempt parent and be reported on the parent's income statement (retaining the character such income had at the subsidiary level). As a result, if the revenue-generating activity at the subsidiary level is determined to be unrelated to the parent's tax-exempt purpose, there may be UBTI at the parent level if a flow-through subsidiary were utilized.

This distinction between corporate and flow-through subsidiaries is of paramount importance to tax-exempt parent organizations. Care should be taken in planning parent-subsidiary designs.

Corporate Considerations

Operating a subsidiary in a corporate form will provide social enterprises with two main benefits. First, a corporation provides a shield against liability for its shareholder because the corporation is a separate legal being operating independently of the tax-exempt parent. Second, because dividends are specifically excluded from the definition of UBTI, a corporation creates the opportunity to avoid UBTI on earned income that is unrelated to

---

3. I.R.C. § 512(b)(1).

the tax-exempt purposes of the social enterprise. Of course, the downside to operating a corporate subsidiary is that income earned may be subject to double taxation, first at the corporate level and again at the shareholder level.

Regardless of the ownership stake that the nonprofit, tax-exempt entity may have in the corporate enterprise in relation to the ownership stake of any for-profit co-owner, the nonprofit generally need not fear losing its tax exemption, even if the for-profit subsidiary's business is wholly unrelated to the charitable purposes of the exempt organization.[4]

If the subsidiary is formed as a regular corporation, the revenue flow to the social enterprise can be structured as a dividend. The classification of such revenue as a dividend is advantageous because, under Treasury regulations, dividends and other passive income paid to tax-exempt organizations are generally not taxable as unrelated business income.[5] By contrast, if the subsidiary were formed as a pass-through entity (as discussed below), revenue generated at the subsidiary level would flow through to the parent, retaining its character.

So, if the activities undertaken by the subsidiary are unrelated to the tax-exempt social enterprise's purpose, the corporate form will overcome the adverse impact that an IRS determination of the income as unrelated business income could have on the parent's tax-exempt status.

If a corporate form is selected, the nonprofit parent should ensure that the subsidiary is organized and operated as a separate entity for tax purposes and not as an extension of the tax-exempt parent. The IRS has stated that where a corporate subsidiary is organized for a *bona fide* business purpose, the taxable subsidiary was not a mere instrumentality of the parent, and the exempt parent is not involved in the day-to-day management of the subsidiary, the activities of the subsidiary cannot be attributed to the parent for purposes of determining the parent's exempt status.[6] Therefore, if structured properly, the tax-exempt parent and the corporate subsidiary will be respected as separate entities as long as the

---

4. BRUCE R. HOPKINS, PLANNING GUIDE FOR THE LAW OF TAX-EXEMPT ORGANIZATIONS § 29.1 (John Wiley & Sons 2007).

5. I.R.C. § 512(b)(1).

6. Gen. Couns. Mem. 39326 (Jan. 17, 1985)

purposes for which the subsidiary is formed are reflected in authentic business activities.[7]

To achieve the required separation between the tax-exempt parent and its subsidiary, the subsidiary must be independent and not act as a mere instrumentality of the parent.[8] To the extent practicable, the following guidelines should be followed:

(1) There should be minimal overlap between officers, directors, and key employees;

(2) The locations of the entities should be separated (or separately situated offices within the same location), and ideally the entities should have separate lease agreements;

(3) Utilities, office equipment, and furniture should be separately accounted for (if dual use is contemplated);

(4) The entities should enter into a formal agreement allocating costs and expenses; and

(5) There should be separate books, records, and bank accounts for the two entities.

A tax-exempt organization and its corporate subsidiary may have interlocking boards of directors. However, the extent to which the boards of directors interlock should be carefully examined in light of IRS guidance. In an often-cited General Counsel Memorandum, the IRS stated that a tax-exempt parent may appoint a taxable corporate subsidiary's board of directors as long as restrictions are in place providing that a majority of the taxable subsidiary's board did not consist of directors, officers, or employees of the tax-exempt organization.[9] In providing this guidance, the IRS also stated that the taxable subsidiary's chief executive officer could not have any affiliation with the tax-exempt parent.[10] Keep in mind that in this situation, each board member with an interlocking directorship will owe fiduciary obligations to both the tax-exempt parent and the for-profit subsidiary corporation.

---

7. Comm'r v. Bollinger, 485 U.S. 340 (1988).
8. Gen. Couns. Mem. 39598 (Feb. 4, 1987).
9. Gen. Couns. Mem. 39326 (Jan. 17, 1985).
10. *Id.*

When this occurs, the profit maximization directive of the for-profit organization is placed directly at odds with the mission-driven directive of the nonprofit. For that reason, both organizations should be run as separate entities, keeping the assets and activities of each separate and distinct. All board members should be sure to operate under the fiduciary principles of for-profits when wearing that hat and under the fiduciary principles for nonprofits when wearing that hat.

Keeping the two roles separate and distinct is the key to avoiding a breach of fiduciary duty. If the interlocking boards are seeking to enter into a transaction, directors who serve on both boards must recuse themselves completely from the transaction and both organizations must build "Chinese walls" around the individual.[11]

Even if these requirements are satisfied, the IRS may determine that there is potential for the unrelated activities of the for-profit subsidiary corporation to be attributed to the tax-exempt parent if, given the facts and circumstances, the parent is simply using the subsidiary as an alter ego.[12] Only when the subsidiary has actual and substantial business functions and has a *bona fide* business purpose will its existence be respected for tax purposes.[13] For that reason, the subsidiary must not be an extension of the business or operations of the parent.[14] Nor should the parent organization be so involved in, or so in control of, the day-to-day activities of the subsidiary as to make the subsidiary ita instrumentality or agent.[15]

The parent's control through the ownership of stock, and the parent's ability to appoint the board of the subsidiary, or even the complete interlocking of boards in certain circumstances will not necessarily cause the two organizations to be treated as one.[16] Respect for each separate entity will be afforded or withheld on a case-by-case basis. The guiding principle is that "where the parent organization so controls the affairs of the subsidiary that it is merely an extension of the parent, the subsidiary may not be

---

11. Weinberger v. UOP, Inc., 457 A.2d 701 (Del. 1983).

12. BRUCE R. HOPKINS, PLANNING GUIDE FOR THE LAW OF TAX-EXEMPT ORGANIZATIONS § 29.2 (John Wiley & Sons 2007).

13. Britt v. United States, 431 F.2d 227 (5th Cir. 1970).

14. Gen. Couns. Mem. 39326 (Jan. 17, 1985).

15. Gen. Couns. Mem. 39598 (Feb. 4, 1987).

16. *Id.*; Priv. Ltr. Rul. 200132040 (Aug. 13, 2001).

regarded as a separate entity."[17] Should the subsidiary be regarded as a separate legal entity, it may be treated as a pass-through entity, which, as noted above, can have severe tax consequences.

Flow-Through Considerations

As an alternative to the corporate form, a nonprofit may operate a social enterprise through a related flow-through entity, such as an LLC, L³C,[18] or partnership.[19] The activities of a flow-through entity—treated as a partnership for federal income tax purposes—will be considered the activities of the tax-exempt parent when evaluating whether the tax-exempt organization is operated exclusively for exempt purposes within the meaning of the IRC.[20] Although a tax-exempt organization is permitted to form and participate in a flow-through business enterprise while still meeting the operational test required of tax-exempt organizations, participation in the partnership must at all times further the tax-exempt purposes of the tax-exempt organization, and the partnership arrangement must explicitly allow the tax-exempt organization to act exclusively in furtherance of its exempt purposes at all times and only incidentally for the benefit of the for-profit partners.[21]

The IRS explicitly permits tax-exempt organizations to be either the sole owner of the flow-through organization or to be a co-investor with other outside private investors seeking a profit. If the tax-exempt organization is the sole owner, the wholly owned subsidiary will be considered a disregarded entity for tax-purposes, and all activities undertaken by the wholly owned flow-through entity will be attributable to the tax-exempt parent.

While a flow-through entity can provide the same shield against personal liability that corporations provide, the downside to their use is that income earned "flows through" to the owner, retaining its character. As a

17. BRUCE R. HOPKINS, PLANNING GUIDE FOR THE LAW OF TAX-EXEMPT ORGANIZATIONS § 29.2 (John Wiley & Sons 2007) (citing Krivo Indus. Supply Co. v. Nat'l Distillers & Chem. Corp., 483 F.2d 1098 (5th Cir. 1970)).

18. An L³C (low-profit limited liability company) is a kind of limited liability company organized under a specific state statute. L³Cs are organized primarily for charitable purposes but still have a for-profit component, which means that they do not qualify for tax-exempt status under federal tax law. *See supra* Chapter 3.

19. Rev. Rul. 98-15, 1998-1 C.B. 718.

20. *Id.*

21. *Id.*

result, if the activities undertaken in the related flow-through entity are anticipated to be unrelated to the exempt purposes of the social enterprise, such income will generate UBTI, which will flow through to the tax-exempt organizational owner. If a tax-exempt organization operates a related enterprise through a flow-through organization which has a purpose that is not in furtherance of its tax-exempt purpose, the nonprofit entity may ultimately lose its exemption.[22] Therefore, if a nonprofit wishes to engage in business activity that will generate significant UBTI, the corporate form is recommended over a flow-through entity.

Flow-through organizations must also adhere to the tax rules concerning private inurement. As we stated above, where a for-profit entity or private person is allowed control over the assets or activities of the nonprofit and directs those activities or assets for its benefit, the tax-exemption for the nonprofit may be lost.[23] To steer clear of the adverse tax implications, the tax-exempt entity must at all times be unhindered from fulfilling its tax-exempt purpose and must ensure that at all times it is operated to provide some type of public and not private benefit.[24] If a co-investor is permitted to control or use the nonprofit social enterprise's assets for the benefit of a private party, and such benefit is not incidental to the accomplishment of tax-exempt purposes, the organization will fail to be organized and operated exclusively for tax-exempt purposes—which could ultimately jeopardize the social enterprise's tax exemption.[25] The regulations specifically provide that an organization is not organized or operated exclusively for tax-exempt purposes unless it serves a public rather than private interest.[26]

The IRS is particularly concerned with the internal operational characteristics where a tax-exempt organization and an unrelated for-profit investor are co-owners of a pass-through business enterprise. In this scenario, the tax-exempt organization should be given actual or effective control over the business enterprise in order to ensure the organization's continued tax-exempt status.[27] The primary concern of the IRS is that the

---

22. Bus. Bureau of Wash., D.C. v. United States, 326 U.S. 279 (1945).
23. Rev. Rul. 98-51, 1998-1 C.B. 718.
24. *Id.*
25. *Id.*
26. Treas. Reg. § 1.501(c)(3)-1(d)(1)(ii).
27. Rev. Rul. 98-15, 1998-1 C.B. 718.

tax-exempt entity will be used in a manner that furthers the private interests of the other co-investors.

In an effort to provide guidance to tax-exempt organizations that desire to invest in a flow-through organization with private investors, the IRS has issued several rulings regarding participation of a tax-exempt organization in flow-through investments.

In one ruling, the IRS analyzed two separate but similar scenarios involving a tax-exempt entity that forms a limited liability company (taxed as a partnership for federal tax purposes) with other outside for-profit investors. The primary concern of the IRS in this ruling focuses on the element of "control." The ruling sets forth two alternative scenarios:

In Scenario 1, a tax-exempt hospital and an unrelated for-profit entity contribute assets to an LLC and, in return, receive ownership interests proportional and equal in value to their respective contributions (i.e., returns of capital and distributions of earnings proportional to ownership).[28] The Articles of Organization and Operating Agreement (governing documents) provide that the venture is to be governed by a board of which the majority is to be appointed by the tax-exempt partner, and the tax-exempt partner intends to appoint to the board only persons with no business relationship to itself. The governing documents further state that a majority vote is needed for major decisions, including decisions relating to the following: (1) annual capital and operating budgets, (2) distributions of earnings, (3) selection of key executives, (4) acquisition or disposition of health-care facilities, (5) contracts in excess of a specified amount per year, (6) changes to the types of services offered by the hospital, and (7) renewal or termination of management agreements. In addition, the governing documents contain a charitable purpose that is explicitly given priority when it conflicts with the business interests of the venture. By including this provision, the LLC ensures that the charitable purpose will override any duty that the governing board may have to operate the LLC for the financial benefit of its owners. As a result, in the event of a conflict between operation in accordance with the charitable purpose and duty to maximize profits, the members of the governing board are to satisfy the charitable purpose without regard to maximizing profitability. Finally, the terms of the governing documents are legal, binding, and enforceable under applicable state law. Under this scenario and fact pattern, the IRS concluded that the hos-

---

28. *Id.*

pital organization's principal activity continues to be the provision of hospital care (its charitable purpose), even when such activities are conducted through an LLC that has an unrelated for-profit member, because the tax-exempt hospital retains control over the LLC and the LLC serves its charitable purposes.

In Scenario 2, the IRS again analyzed the formation of an LLC with both a tax-exempt and a for-profit member.[29] However, in this scenario, there is no provision in the operating agreement requiring that the hospital be operated for community benefit or that the tax-exempt purposes should supersede any profitable motivation. Under this second scenario, the LLC lacks many of the features that will allow the exempt organization to control the venture and thereby ensure that its charitable purpose will be furthered and that any benefit to private parties will be incidental to the charitable purpose. In particular, the tax-exempt organization does not have a majority voice on the board of directors of the LLC, and there is no explicit charitable purpose contained in the governing instruments. In such a scenario, the IRS concluded that the hospital organization would lose its tax-exempt status because it would have failed to establish that it will be operated exclusively for exempt purposes.

Thus, the IRS has clearly indicated that when a tax-exempt organization participates as a co-investor in a flow-through investment, the tax-exempt purposes must at all times be furthered by participation in the enterprise. The partnership agreement, articles of organization, operating agreement, or other governing documents must explicitly permit the tax-exempt organization to act exclusively in furtherance of its exempt purposes and only incidentally for the benefit of the for-profit partners.[30] Social enterprises seeking to co-invest in a flow-through entity with an outside investor must adhere to the constructs of this revenue ruling when entering into an investment of this nature.

Sharing Personnel

When a tax-exempt entity utilizes a for-profit subsidiary, the two entities may have overlapping employees who perform functions for each entity. As long as certain conditions are adhered to, the IRS permits tax-exempt or-

---

29. *Id.*

30. *Id.; see also* Bus. Bureau of Wash., D.C. v. United States, 326 U.S. 279 (1945).

ganizations to share personnel and function in close operational conjunction with their for-profit subsidiaries without adversely endangering the organization's tax-exempt status.

The employees can either be employed by both entities independently or one entity may be the primary employer and subsequently lease the employees to the other. In either event, the entities must be sure to properly withhold certain tax payments and adhere to reporting obligations.

For instance, the entities must determine the following:

1. When employees are performing services for more than one entity, which employer must meet tax obligations for the Federal Insurance Contributions Act (FICA), the Federal Unemployment Tax Act (FUTA, together with FICA often referred to as employment taxes) and the collection of income at source on wages (tax withholding)?

2. Which employer will be required to comply with reporting obligations, such as issuing Form W-2 to employees and filing IRS Forms 940 (annual return for FUTA tax) and 941 (quarterly return for FICA and income taxes)?

3. How should the relevant transactions be structured to avoid onerous administrative requirements?

For purposes of federal employment taxes (FICA and FUTA), common-law rules ordinarily apply in determining whether an employer-employee relationship exists, and if so, who is the employer.[31] The regulations generally identify "employers" as persons who employ employees[32] and as any person for whom services are performed as an employee.[33]

Treasury regulations define who is considered an employee. The IRC specifically states that, with respect to the relationship of employer and employee:

1. Every individual is an employee if, under the usual common-law rules, the relationship between the individual and the person for whom the individual performs services is the legal relationship of employer and employee.

---

31. Rev. Rul. 69-316, 1969-1 C.B. 263.
32. Treas. Reg. §§ 31.3121(d)-2, 31.3306(a)-1.
33. Treas. Reg. § 31.3401(d)-1.

2. Generally, such a relationship exists when the person for whom services are performed has the right to control and direct the individual who performs the services, not only as to the result to be accomplished by the work but also as to the details and means by which that result is accomplished. That is, an employee is subject to the will and control of the employer not only as to what shall be done but how it will be done.

An officer of a corporation is presumed to be an employee of the corporation. However, an officer of a corporation who as such does not perform any services or performs only minor services, and who neither receives nor is entitled to receive, directly or indirectly, any remuneration, is considered not to be an employee of the corporation.[34] Accordingly, whether or not an individual is an employee of the tax-exempt entity or the subsidiary will be a facts and circumstances determination.

While employment tax regulations appear to be concerned with whom the services are performed, income tax withholding regulations look to whether the person for whom the individual performs or performed the services has control over the payment for such services. If the person does not have control of the payment of the wages for such services, the employer is the person having control of the payment of such wages.[35] The rules and regulations thus differ when determining withholding and reporting obligations for employment taxes (FICA and FUTA) on one hand and income tax withholding on the other. This conflict was addressed in the IRS's Revenue Ruling 69-316.[36]

---

34. Rev. Rul. 74-390, 1974-2 C.B. 331, states: "In determining whether services act10ually performed by a corporate officer in that capacity may be considered to be of a minor or nominal nature the character of the services, the frequency and duration of their performance, and the actual or potential importance or necessity of the services in relation to the conduct of the corporation's business, are the primary elements to be considered. Thus, occasional, routine signing of documents, presiding over or attendance at infrequent meetings, and similar isolated or noncontinuous acts having no significant bearing or effect on the day-to-day functioning of the corporation in the conduct of its business, will be considered, as a general rule, to be services of a minor or nominal nature."

35. I.R.C. § 3401(d).

36. Rev. Rul. 69-316, 1969-1 C.B. 263.

IRS Revenue Ruling 69-316 deals with whether a corporation, or its subsidiaries, or both, are the employers of certain individuals with respect to employment taxes and income tax withholding. The revenue ruling describes circumstances (outlined below as Groups 1 through 3) in which the individuals (employees and officers) perform services for a parent corporation, its subsidiaries, or both and are paid by the parent corporation.

In **Group 1**, certain individuals are engaged by a subsidiary of Y to perform services solely for the subsidiary under its direction and control. The wages of the employees are paid initially by Y and the amounts thereof are billed to the subsidiary.

Under common-law rules, the IRS held that the individuals who are engaged by and perform services solely for a subsidiary of Y under the direction and control of the subsidiary are employees of the subsidiary for which they render services even though the wages are paid initially by Y, the particular subsidiary involved being billed by Y corporation for the amount thereof. Although Y pays the wages of the employees, the subsidiary is responsible for the reporting and payment of the taxes imposed by the FICA and FUTA.

In **Group 2**, certain individuals are engaged by Y to handle such matters as accounting, auditing, purchasing, etc., for Y and also for a number of its subsidiaries. The individuals in this group perform their services under the direction and control of Y and are paid by Y. The premises on which they work and the equipment used by them are furnished by Y.

The individuals in Group 2 who perform services for both Y and its subsidiaries, who are engaged and paid by Y, and who are subject to the direction and control of Y in the performance of their services, are employees only of Y and are not of a subsidiary. Y alone is responsible for reporting and payment of the taxes imposed by FICA and FUTA with respect to their wages.

In **Group 3**, certain executives, in addition to being officers of Y, are also officers of one or more of the subsidiaries. They perform substantial services as officers for each corporation and are paid for those services by Y. In some cases Y charges the subsidiaries a flat rate for services rendered to them by the officers, and in other cases a charge for those services is based on the normal production of the subsidiaries. In still other cases, Y makes no charge for the services.

The executives in Group 3, who are officers of Y and of one or more of its subsidiary corporations, perform "substantial" services in their official capacities for each such corporation and are remunerated for their services. Accordingly, the officers of each corporation are employees thereof. This relationship is not affected by the fact that in some cases the subsidiaries are not charged with any portion of the total remuneration paid by Y to the officers. Since each corporation is the employer of the individuals who are its officers, any payment made by Y to an individual that represents remuneration as an officer of the subsidiary is remuneration paid by the subsidiary for purposes of FICA and FUTA employment taxes.

It is important to note that, for income tax withholding purposes, with respect to Groups 1, 2, and 3 above, IRC § 3401(d), in defining the term "employer," provides in part that if the person for whom the individual performs or performed the services does not have control of the payment of the wages for such services, the term "employer" means the person having control of the payment of such wages. Thus, when Y has control of the payment of wages for services performed by an employee or officer of a subsidiary, Y is the employer of that employee for purposes of income tax withholding, even though the subsidiary is the employer with respect to the wages for purposes of FICA and FUTA.

To summarize the cited revenue ruling, as between a parent and a subsidiary:

Employment Taxes (FICA & FUTA)

- If an individual is hired to perform services for a subsidiary under its direction and control, the individual is the subsidiary's employee for employment tax purposes, even though the parent initially pays his or her wages, and then bills the subsidiary for them.
- Where the same individual performs services for both parent and subsidiary but performs under the direction of the parent and is paid by the parent, the parent is the employer for employment tax purposes.
- If the same individual is an officer in both corporations, performing substantial services for both, any payment made by the parent to an individual that represents remuneration of the individual as an officer of the subsidiary is remuneration paid by the subsidiary for employment tax purposes.

Income Tax Withholding

- If the employer for whom services are performed doesn't have control of payment of the wages to the employee, the person having control of the payment is treated as the employer for income tax withholding purposes.

Employee Benefit Plan Considerations

If two or more businesses are found to be under common control, tax rules generally treat all employees of the group as employed by a single employer for purposes of 401(k) and other employee benefit plans.

For purposes of determining whether two businesses are considered to be under common control, a parent-subsidiary group of businesses under "common control" means the businesses must be connected through ownership constituting a "controlling interest," which has been interpreted to mean, in the case of an LLC/L^{3}C/partnership, ownership of at least 80 percent of the profits interest or capital interest of such LLC/L^{3}C/partnership.[37]

Sharing of Office Space/Furniture/Equipment

In addition to sharing employees, it is common for tax-exempt entities to share office space, equipment, furniture, and other fixed assets with a related for-profit entity.

This sharing arrangement can be accomplished through a commercially reasonable allocation of the expenses associated with the use of the office space and equipment. It is important that the amount paid for use of such space and equipment be determined to be commercially reasonable and at all times negotiated at arm's length.

Often, an independent appraiser can assist in determining the price that is commercially reasonable. If the IRS should inquire about the commercial reasonableness of an intercompany transaction, an independent appraisal would help to persuade the IRS that the entities have structured intercompany payments in a reasonable manner.

---

37. Treas. Reg. § 1.414(c)-2(b).

*   *   *   *

Multi-organizational, hybrid structuring models present an opportunity for social enterprises to take advantage of the beneficial aspects of both for-profit and nonprofit business; however, care should be taken when entering into such arrangements. In the next chapter, there is a discussion of the various alternatives to capitalizing the social enterprise as well as useful strategies for obtaining such funding.

Capitalizing the Social Enterprise

Both initial capital and ongoing operational funding may be required for the social enterprise to be successful. Because a social enterprise can be operated as a nonprofit, a for-profit, or a combination of the two, a broad spectrum of funding possibilities exists to fund the venture's initial and continuing operations.

This chapter will look at the tools available to social entrepreneurs in generating funding and will provide practical examples of funding models. The purpose of this chapter is to help social entrepreneurs and their attorneys navigate the maze of funding possibilities that exist and provide insight and pragmatic strategies involved in securing and maintaining capital.

Access to Capital

Access to capital for growth and development remains one of the greatest challenges that social enterprises face because many will never yield financial returns that attract traditional, market-rate investors. Nevertheless, because potential investors may consider the social benefits along with the financial benefits of their investments, creative deal-making remains available to launch and support a successful social enterprise.

Three primary sources of capital should be considered: philanthropic, governmental, and commercial. Accordingly, potential investments in a social enterprise should be viewed along a continuum of expected financial returns to be generated. At one end of the continuum lies philanthropic capital in the form of grants and donations that require no financial returns, although some type of social return or impact is required. At the other end lie commercial investments in the social enterprise, requiring market-rate financial returns, where the social return or impact may not be a concern. Somewhere in the middle lies governmental support. All three sources of capital are discussed below.

Grants and Contributions

Grant and contribution funding is available from a wide variety of sources, including individuals, foundations, corporations, and state and local governments; and each donor may have a different motive for giving. Traditionally, grant and contribution revenue generated by foundations has been a major source of funding for social enterprises and other charitable organizations. Grant and contribution funding for social enterprises is especially attractive, as it represents a capital source that does not require repayment or financial return. Although donated funds need not be repaid, social enterprises should consider from whom the funds may be solicited, the potential restrictions on use of the funds received, and the reporting requirements that ensue should they obtain such funding.

The typical grant is made in the form of a single- or multi-year pledge of support used to provide project-specific funds, or start-up financing, as opposed to providing support for administrative expenses. Many foundations have been disinclined to support "proof of concept" or even capacity building. Depending on the financial requirements and needs of the social enterprise, donors may agree to provide partial support contingent upon the obtainment of other funding from outside sources.

When courting public donations, it is important for social enterprises to understand exactly what potential donors expect in exchange for their donations. Some donors will be interested in the recognition that comes with making a donation, as they may be motivated by the desire to be publicly recognized for making a grant or contribution. Such public recognition may range from mere name recognition in social circles to providing the donor with the ability to name a building or program operated by the social enterprise.

Other donors may desire some direct personal involvement in the social enterprise. This may be accomplished to some extent by providing such donors with a seat on the board of directors or, if the social enterprise is organized as a non-stock corporation, giving donors membership interests with voting rights. The social enterprise should critically evaluate the possibility of a donor's participation in the venture's governance or management before accepting a donation.

Restrictions on the Use of Grants and Donations

Grants and contributions generally fall into one of three categories—unrestricted, temporarily restricted, or permanently restricted. Social enterprises should be mindful of the restrictions placed on all funds received so as not to use the funds in a manner that is not permitted by the donor.

The determination of what the funds may be used for is dependent upon any restriction placed on the funding by the donor. Social enterprises will not only be obligated to the donor to adhere to the restriction imposed, but also legally bound to do so.

- Unrestricted: Grants and contributions that are free from all external restrictions and available to the organization for general use.
- Temporarily Restricted: Grants and contributions that have specific donor restrictions placed on their use. There are two ways in which temporary restrictions are imposed by a donor: (1) use for a specific purpose, or (2) the passage of a certain amount of time. Typically, temporarily restricted grants and donations will be given with the intention that they support a particular program or project of the social enterprise.
- Permanently Restricted: These grants and contributions are similar to temporarily restricted funds, as they also have purpose and time restrictions imposed by the donor. The key difference is that the restrictions will never expire. These donated funds are permanently restricted in the sense that the principal balance (the amount contributed) will remain forever intact, with the recipient organization utilizing the investment income (interest or dividends) for operations.

Substantiation Required for Charities Receiving Donations

Social enterprises that are exempt from taxation under IRC § 501(c)(3) should be informed of their obligation under the Internal Revenue Code to provide substantiation to the donors in order for them to receive a tax deduction. Because tax-deductible charitable donations may only be made to organizations exempt from taxation under IRC § 501(c)(3), social enterprises organized as for-profit companies will not be able to attract such funding.

IRC § 170(f)(8)(A) states that no deduction shall be allowed for any contribution of $250 or more unless the taxpayer provides the required substantiation for the contribution with a contemporaneous written acknowledgment of the contribution from the donee organization that meets the requirements of IRC § 170(f)(8)(B).[1] IRC § 170(f)(8)(B) states that such acknowledgment must contain the following information:

1. the amount of cash received and a description (but not value) of any property other than cash contributed;
2. whether the donee organization provided any goods or services in consideration, in whole or part, for the cash or property; and
3. a description and good faith estimate of the value of any goods or services provided by the donee organization or, if such goods or services consist solely of intangible religious benefits, a statement to that effect.[2]

The acknowledgment must be sent according to specific timing requirements. IRC § 170(f)(8)(C) provides that for the acknowledgment to be considered contemporaneous, the taxpayer must obtain the acknowledgment on or before the earlier of (1) the date on which the taxpayer files a return for the taxable year in which the contribution was made, or (2) the due date (including extensions) for filing such return.[3]

Attracting Private Foundation Investments

Program-Related Investments

In addition to grants and contribution funding, social enterprises are often capitalized through debt and/or equity investments made by outside investors. Increasingly in recent years, many social enterprises have looked to private foundations as a source of this capital.

Private foundations, defined under IRC § 509, are statutorily created organizations formed for the primary purpose of making charitable gifts

---

1. I.R.C. § 170(f)(8)(A).
2. I.R.C. § 170(f)(8)(B).
3. I.R.C. § 170(f)(18)(B).

from contributed funds. In exchange for the tax breaks granted to private foundations, IRC § 4942 requires such organizations to distribute at least 5 percent of its asset value each year in "qualifying distributions." If this amount is not distributed, a 30 percent penalty tax is imposed. Most foundations have traditionally satisfied their distribution requirements through the issuance of grants, but they also have the option to satisfy these requirements through direct debt and/or equity investments known as program-related investments (PRIs).

If a foundation chooses to satisfy its distribution requirement by making a PRI, it must be certain not to run afoul of the "jeopardizing investment" rules contained in IRC § 4944. That Code section penalizes private foundations if they make an investment that might "jeopardize" the carrying out of their tax-exempt purpose. If a private foundation's investment is determined to be a jeopardizing investment that endangers the ability of the foundation to carry out its exempt purpose, IRC § 4944 will impose an excise tax on the private foundation as well as on its managers.[4]

An investment is considered to jeopardize the carrying out of the exempt purposes of a private foundation if it is determined that the foundation managers, in making such investment, have failed to exercise ordinary business care and prudence, under the facts and circumstances prevailing at the time of making the investment, in providing for the long-term and short-term financial needs of the foundation to carry out its exempt purposes.[5] In the exercise of the requisite standard of care and prudence, the foundation managers may take into account the expected return (including both income and appreciation of capital), the investment portfolio (for example, with respect to the type of security, type of industry, maturity of company, degree of risk, and potential for return).[6] The determination of whether the investment of a particular amount jeopardizes the carrying out of the exempt purposes of a foundation is made on an investment-by-investment basis, in each case taking into account the foundation's portfolio as a whole.[7]

PRIs are a specific exception, in that if a distribution qualifies as a PRI it will not be considered to jeopardize a private foundation's exempt purpose. Under IRC § 4944(c) and the regulations issued thereunder, a PRI must meet the following requirements:

---

4. I.R.C. § 4944(a)(1), (2).
5. Treas. Reg. § 53.4944-1(a)(2)(i).
6. *Id.*
7. *Id.*

- The primary purpose of the investment is to accomplish religious, charitable, scientific, literary, or educational purposes, or to foster national or international amateur sports competition (but only if no part of the activities involve the provision of athletic facilities or equipment), or for the prevention of cruelty to children or animals, all within the meaning of IRC § 170(c)(2)(B). The regulations clarify that that the investment must not have been made but for the relationship between the investment and the accomplishment of the foundation's exempt purpose.
- No significant purpose of the investment shall be the production of income or the appreciation of property; however, the fact that such investment actually does produce income or appreciation will not disqualify it from being a PRI.
- The investment shall not be used to attempt to influence legislation, or participate or intervene in any political campaign on behalf of any candidate for public office, all within the meaning of IRC § 170(c)(2)(D).[8]

Contained within the regulations under IRC § 4944 are examples of investments that will and will not qualify as PRIs. Each of the examples describes certain loan and investment scenarios, which, under the specific facts and circumstances described, may or may not qualify as a PRI. Unfortunately, these examples are outdated and do not reflect the wide variety of PRIs that are made by private foundations in today's world. In fact, the examples in the Code have not been revised since 1972, when the regulations were finalized. Although private foundations can turn to the examples for useful guidance on certain issues, updated regulations on PRI examples would be quite welcome.

On March 3, 2010, the American Bar Association's Section of Taxation proposed 17 additional PRI examples to the Commissioner of the Internal Revenue Service for possible inclusion in updated regulations. The significant points addressed by the examples are as follows:

1. If an activity is charitable when conducted in the U.S., it is likewise charitable if conducted in a foreign country;
2. Efforts to preserve and protect the natural environment and endangered species serve a charitable purpose;

---

8. Treas. Reg. § 53.4944-3(a)(1).

3. Raising the living standards of needy families in underdeveloped or developing countries serves a charitable purpose;

4. The recipients of loans and working capital need not themselves qualify for charitable assistance because they are "merely the instruments" by which the charitable purposes are served;

5. The presence of a seemingly high projected rate of return should not, alone, prevent an investment from qualifying as a program-related investment because determination of the significant purposes for an investment requires facts and circumstances analysis that takes into account all of the objective facts and circumstances of an investment, including evidence of the motive behind the investment, and the potential production of income or property appreciation is merely a factor in the analysis;

6. Program-related investments may be properly accomplished by or through loans to individuals, tax-exempt organizations, or for-profit domestic or foreign organizations, as well as by or through equity investments in for-profit domestic or foreign organizations, including limited liability companies;

7. Providing credit enhancement, whether in the form of a guarantee, letter of credit, or otherwise, for a borrowing by a third party that accomplishes a charitable purpose may qualify as a program-related investment; and

8. The existence of an "equity kicker" as part of the overall return does not prevent an investment from qualifying as a program-related investment.[9]

From the private foundation's perspective, making a grant will result in an expense on the foundation's income statement. An expense has no chance of being repaid or earning an investment return. However, if the private foundation were to make a PRI, it would debit an asset account on its balance sheet, thus creating the opportunity for repayment and return on investment. Those funds can then be recycled over and over again, creating a financial—and social—multiplier effect.

---

9. ABA Section of Taxation, *Comments on Proposed Additional Examples of Program-Related Investments* (Mar. 3, 2010), *available at* http://www.abanet.org/tax/pubpolicy/2010/Comments_Concerning_Proposed_Additional_Examples_on_Program_Related_Investments.pdf.

Why, then, would a private foundation choose to make a grant over a PRI? Most likely, the complexity involved in making a PRI has discouraged some private foundations. Making a PRI involves an analysis of sophisticated legal and accounting rules and regulations, which can be prohibitive. While private foundations could obtain a private letter ruling from the IRS, securing a private letter ruling can be expensive and time-consuming. In fact, by the time a ruling is issued, an entrepreneurial opportunity may have evaporated. For that reason, most foundations that make PRIs rely on private legal opinions instead of private letter rulings.

Private foundations are required to exert "expenditure responsibility" over their grants or PRIs to ensure that they are used for proper purposes. Under IRC § 4945(h), expenditure responsibility requires that the private foundation exert all reasonable efforts and establish adequate procedures to ensure that the funds it distributes are used for the purpose for which a grant or investment was made, to obtain records and reports detailing how the funds were utilized, and to make such reports available to the IRS. If the grant or PRI is disqualified, the private foundation and its managers may be subject to excise taxes under the jeopardizing investment rules, as noted above. Only grants to, or PRIs in, public charities, will escape the expenditure responsibility rules.

Despite these statutory obstacles to program-related investing, a trend has recently emerged favoring PRIs. Until relatively recently, only a few large foundations, such as the Ford Foundation and the John D. and Catherine T. MacArthur Foundation, publicly promoted and engaged in making PRIs. Recently, however, the world's largest private foundation, the Bill and Melinda Gates Foundation, announced that it would begin extensive use of program-related investments as a way to leverage the Gates Foundation's resources and to encourage broader financial support for its mission.[10] The Gates Foundation has initiated a $400 million commitment to PRIs, which may spur other private foundations to follow suit.

Furthermore, over the past few years, legislation in several states has allowed for the creation of low-profit limited liability companies ("L³Cs"). The L³C was developed in an effort to create a for-profit entity that would more easily access—and leverage—PRIs. As a result, formation of a social

---

10. BILL & MELINDA GATES FOUNDATION, PROGRAM-RELATED INVESTMENTS: LEVERAGING OUR RESOURCES TO CATALYZE BROADER SUPPORT FOR OUR MISSION (Oct. 8, 2009), *available at* http://www.gatesfoundation.org/about/Pages/program-related-investments-faq.aspx.

enterprise as an L³C may enable the social enterprise to access equity and debt investments from private foundations that otherwise might not be as readily available or attractive if the entity were formed as a regular limited liability company. (Chapter 3 on entity formation provides detailed information about the L³C.)

Overall, the trend toward promotion of PRIs holds promise for social enterprises that wish to tap into private foundation investment as a potential funding source. In fact, the IRS appears to have determined that the trend toward PRIs is forthcoming, as it has announced that providing guidance under IRC § 4944 is a regulatory priority.[11]

As a final note, although private foundations are permitted to invest in for-profit business enterprises, those that do should be mindful not to violate the "excess business holdings" rules articulated in IRC § 4943. The "excess business holding rules" derive from the belief that foundational ownership of large interests in business enterprises may tempt foundation managers to subordinate the foundation's charitable purposes to the needs of the businesses.[12]

Generally speaking, under IRC § 4943, prIvate foundations are permitted to hold up to 20 percent of the voting stock of a corporation or other business type (i.e., partnership, LLC, etc.).[13] If a third party has effective control over the business enterprise, the limits may increase to 35 percent.[14] Private foundations should be mindful of these limits when investing in for-profit social enterprises.

Mission-Related Investments

A mission-related investment (MRI) is another form of investment made by philanthropic foundations, designed to pursue both financial and societal returns. MRIs align a foundation's philanthropic mission with its investment portfolio by promoting investments that advance both financial as well as societal returns. Any foundation may make an MRI and earn a similar finan-

---

11. U.S. DEP'T OF THE TREASURY, FIRST PERIODIC UPDATE OF THE 2009-2010 PRIORITY GUIDANCE PLAN, at 13 (Mar. 16, 2010), *available at* http://www.irs.gov/pub/irs-utl/2009_-_2010_priority_guidance_plan.pdf.

12. Boris I. Bittker & Lawrence Lokken, *Private Foundations, in* FEDERAL TAXATION OF INCOME, ESTATES, AND GIFTS, ch. 101 .

13. I.R.C. § 4943(c)(2)(A).

14. I.R.C. § 4943(c)(2)(B).

cial return as would be expected from a mainstream investment. As a result, social enterprises are uniquely suited to be viable recipients of such funding.

MRIs are not to be confused with PRIs, which, as noted above, come from private foundations' distribution requirements. Rather, MRI s are made from the remaining 95 percent of the foundation's corpus. While PRIs have as a primary purpose the achievement of the foundation's charitable or educational objectives, with no specific purpose of the investment to generate income or capital, an MRI's primary purpose is to generate a return on capital while investing in ventures that promote social purposes.

The trustees of a philanthropic foundation are subject to fiduciary standards established by law: the duties of care, loyalty, and obedience.[15] The duty of care, as described in the Revised Model Nonprofit Corporation Act (RMNCA), requires the trustees to exercise their duties as such in good faith, with the care an ordinarily prudent person in a like position would exercise under similar circumstances, and in a manner that they reasonably believe to be in the best interests of the corporation.[16] The duty of loyalty for such trustees has been described as the duty of "pursuing or ensuring pursuit of the charitable purpose or public benefit which is the mission of the corporation . . . rather than his or her own financial or other interests, or those of another person or organization."[17] The duty of obedience has been described as including "the obligation . . . to act within the organization's purposes and ensure that the corporation's mission is pursued"[18] as well as the requirement that the trustees comply with applicable federal, stale, and local laws.[19]

A key aspect of the duties of care and obedience that affects a foundation's ability to make MRIs is the fact that the Internal Revenue Code imposes a tax on any "foundation manager" (officer, director, or trustee) who participates in the foundation's making of any investment that would jeopardize the foundation's carrying out of any of its exempt purposes, knowing the investment to be a jeopardizing one.[20]

---

15. BOARDSOURCE, THE HANDBOOK OF NONPROFIT GOVERNANCE 130 (2010).

16. RMNCA § 8.30(a).

17. Summers v. Cherokee Children & Family Serv., 112 S.W.3d 486, 504 (Tenn. Ct. App. 2002).

18. N.Y. State Attorney General Charities Bureau, *The Regulatory Role of the Attorney General's Charities Bureau* 4 (July 15, 2003), *available at* http://www.courts.state.ny.us/reporter/webdocs/role.pdf.

19. BOARD SOURCE, THE HANDBOOK OF NONPROFIT GOVERNANCE 132 (2010).

20. I.R.C. § 4944(a).

However, even purchases of common stocks may be classified by the IRS as jeopardizing investments, as indicated by an example in Treasury Regulations where an investment in a corporation that "has been in business a short period of time and manufactures a product that is new, is not sold by others, and must compete with a well-established alternative product that serves the same purpose" is so classified.[21] Consequently, MRIs, if not prudently made, may be subject to excise taxes imposed under IRC § 4944 on jeopardizing investments (as described above in the PRI section).

Socially Responsible Investments

Similar to mission-related investing, socially responsible investing (SRI) is another broad-based investment strategy that takes into account not only financial returns generated, but also non-financial and societal benefits that may be achieved. Essentially, while typically SRI seeks to maximize financial results, positive social returns generated by such an investment are also considered as part of the overall return on the investment.

The difference between mission-related investments and socially responsible investing is that socially responsible investments may take into account a "screening" procedure designed to ensure that investments are made in companies that engage in socially beneficial endeavors. Screening permits the socially responsible foundation to evaluate investments based on social, environmental, and such other criteria as a company's governance practices.

Socially responsible investments constitute a valuable source of capital for social enterprises owing to their pursuit of both financial and social returns. When the attorney advises a social enterprise on potential capital sources, the socially responsible investor certainly should be part of the conversation.

Cause-Related Marketing

Cause-related marketing is defined as the process of formulating and implementing marketing activities that are characterized by contributing a specific amount to a designated nonprofit effort that, in turn, causes customers to engage in revenue-providing exchanges.[22] Cause-related marketing provides an ideal opportunity for nonprofit social enterprises to align themselves with

---

21. Treas. Reg. § 53.4944-1(c) ex. 1.

22. Jennifer Mullen, *Performance-based Corporate Philanthropy: How "Giving Smart" Can Further Corporate Goals*, PUBLIC RELATIONS QUARTERLY (June 1997), 42–48.

for-profit businesses in an effort to promote socially beneficial missions. In addition, social enterprises will be in a position to increase awareness of their social cause.

Cause-related marketing may come in many forms. Typically, a nonprofit organization and a business will enter into an agreement to raise money to promote a certain cause. Entering into such an arrangement usually increases sales or revenue for the business while increasing awareness of the cause promoted by the nonprofit organization.

The Better Business Bureau recommends that, in such arrangements, the parties "clearly disclose how the charity benefits from the sale of products or services (i.e., cause-related marketing) that state or imply that a charity will benefit from a consumer sale or transaction. Such promotions should disclose, at the point of solicitation:

a. the actual or anticipated portion of the purchase price that will benefit the charity (e.g., 5 cents will be contributed to ABC charity for every XYZ company product sold),

b. the duration of the campaign (e.g., the month of October),

c. any maximum or guaranteed minimum contribution amount (e.g., up to a maximum of $200,000)."[23]

An excellent illustration of a successful cause-related marketing campaign is the "(RED)" campaign formed to promote the social mission of preventing and eliminating HIV/AIDS in Africa. (RED) is not a charity, but rather a business model designed to create awareness and a sustainable flow of money from the private sector into the "Global Fund" to help eliminate AIDS in Africa. (RED) works with the world's most iconic brands, including American Express, Apple, Nike, Armani, Gap, and others, to make unique (RED) products. When these products are sold, up to 50 percent of the profits are invested in the Global Fund to fight HIV/AIDS in Africa. Since its launch in 2006, (RED) has generated more than $150 million for the Global Fund, and over 5 million people have been helped by HIV and AIDS programs supported by (RED) purchases.[24]

As illustrated by the (RED) campaign, participating nonprofit organizations do not have to be tax-exempt to take advantage of a cause-related

---

23. The BBB Wise Giving Alliance Standards for Charitable Accountability are available at www.bbb.org/us/charity-standards/.

24. *See* http://www.joinred.com.

marketing opportunity. Although cause-related marketing entails the use of a nonprofit organization, the collaboration with a for-profit company will be quite different from philanthropic efforts discussed above, where charitable donations are solicited. The main difference is that donations toward a cause-related marketing campaign are not considered tax-deductible, as a grant or charitable donation would usually be treated.

Advising a social enterprise on the benefits of cause-related marketing is a way in which practitioners can add value to a client's business model by generating additional capital and increasing awareness of the mission advanced by the social enterprise.

Opportunities exist for a wide range of social enterprises to enter such arrangements as a way to strategically align support of a mutual cause and achieve tailored and specific business objectives. Cause-related marketing should not be confused with sponsorship (discussed later in this chapter), but should be viewed as an alliance between the two organizations designed to achieve mutual benefits. Social enterprises should carefully research past corporate giving history from a wide variety of businesses to determine funding sources that are available and to concentrate on corporations that share a sense of responsibility for the cause that the social enterprise is engaged in. If the social enterprise's mission and purpose fits in line with a profit-driven corporation's business line or marketing structure, there is often an opportunity for both entities to benefit from a positive relationship.

Sponsorships

As the strength and reach of the social enterprise field increases, entities may find it advantageous to be aligned with certain ventures that promote their objectives. One way in which a business may team up with a social enterprise is through a sponsorship arrangement.

Sponsorship income is generated when a payment is made by a company, the sponsor of an activity or event, to a social enterprise that represents a potential source of revenue for both parties. Of course, if the payment is made to a social enterprise formed as a for-profit organization, it will constitute ordinary taxable income. Similarly, if the social enterprise is set up as a nonprofit, tax-exempt organization, the payment may be taxable as unrelated business taxable income (UBTI). UBTI in excess of IRS guidelines may ultimately jeopardize the social enterprise's tax-exempt status.

Although advertising revenue is generally taxed as unrelated business income, the IRC includes a "safe harbor" rule for sponsorships in stating that the activity of soliciting and receiving "qualified sponsorship payments"[25] is not UBTI. "Qualified sponsorship payments" are payments to a tax-exempt organization by a person engaged in a trade or business when there is no arrangement or expectation that the payer will receive a "substantial return benefit" in exchange other than the use or acknowledgment of the name or logo (or product lines) of the payer's trade or business in connection with the tax-exempt organization's activities.[26] The term "substantial return benefit" means any benefit other than (1) goods, services, or other benefits of insubstantial value that are disregarded under Reg. § 1.513-4(c)(2)(ii), or (2) certain use or acknowledgment of the sponsor's name and/or logo as described in Reg. § 1.513-4(c)(2)(iv).

Under Reg. § 1.513-4(c)(2)(ii), benefits are not treated as "substantial return benefits" if the aggregate fair market value of all the benefits provided to the payer in connection with the payment does not exceed 2 percent of the amount of the payment.[27] If the aggregate fair market value of the benefits exceeds 2 percent of the amount of the payment, then the entire fair market value of such benefits, not merely the excess amount, is a substantial return benefit.[28]

Acceptable and permitted uses or acknowledgments that do not constitute substantial return benefits to payers include:

1. logos and slogans that do not contain qualitative or comparative descriptions of the payer's products, services, facilities, or company;
2. a list of payer locations, telephone numbers, or Internet addresses;
3. value-neutral descriptions, including displays or visual depictions, of the payer's product-line or services; or
4. the payer's brand or trade names and product or service listings.[29]

Treasury regulations provide an example of a permitted use that is useful in explaining this concept. In the example, a symphony orchestra maintains a website containing pertinent information and a concert schedule. A store (the Music Shop) makes a payment to the orchestra to fund a concert series. The orchestra posts a list of sponsors on its website, including the Music

---

25. I.R.C. § 513(i)(1).
26. I.R.C. § 513(i)(2)(A).
27. Treas. Reg. § 1.513-4(c)(2)(ii).
28. *Id.*
29. Treas. Reg. § 1.513-4(c)(2)(iv).

Shop's name and Internet address, which appears as a hyperlink from the orchestra's website to the Music Shop's. The site does not promote the Music Shop or advertise its products. The orchestra's posting of the Music Shop's name and address constitutes acknowledgment of the sponsorship. In this case, the entire payment is treated as a qualified sponsorship payment.[30]

Listing a sponsor's logo on a tax-exempt social enterprise's website with a hyperlink to the sponsor's website in exchange for a payment from the sponsor should not have any adverse UBTI effects. However, it is important not to make reference to the sponsor's products or services (including messages containing qualitative or comparative language), price information, or other indications of savings or value, or an endorsement or other inducement to purchase, sell, or use the products or services.

Endorsements

A tax-exempt social enterprise may also wish to promote its own brand on companies' websites or merchandise by soliciting and negotiating licensing agreements with various businesses to authorize them to use the social enterprise's intellectual property (name, logos, etc.) in connection with the distribution, sale, advertising, and/or promotion of merchandise or services offered by those businesses. In exchange for entering into such a licensing agreement, the social enterprise will receive compensation from those businesses that will help to defray its operating expenses.

The fact that revenue generated from such licensing agreements may not have a causal relationship to the performance of a tax-exempt social enterprise's tax-exempt purposes (and most likely therefore does not contribute importantly to the accomplishment of such purposes) will cause such income to be gross income from unrelated trade or business within the meaning of IRC § 513. However, because the payments are for the use of intellectual property, they should be considered royalties within the meaning of IRC § 512(b)(2). Under the Code, payments for the use of trademarks, trade names, service marks, or copyrights, whether or not payment is based on the use made of such property, are ordinarily classified as royalties for federal tax purposes.[31] This is significant because, under IRC § 512(b), royalties and directly connected deductions are not taken into

---

30. Treas. Reg. § 1.513-4(f) ex. 11.

31. Comm'r v. Affiliated Enters., Inc., 123 F.2d 665 (10th Cir. 1941).

account in determining an organization's UBTI.[32] As a consequence, neither the receipts received from nor the expenses incurred in connection with the licensing endorsement activities will be taken into account in computing UBTI.

But payments for administrative, marketing, or other services provided in connection with granting the right to use the organization's name and logo are not royalties and, for that reason, are generally taxable as unrelated business income.

It is important to stress that when entering into sponsorship and endorsement relationships, a tax-exempt social enterprise must at all times ensure that it is serving only exempt purposes rather than private interests so as not to violate the "private inurement" rules contained in the Code.

Fiscal Sponsorship

Nonprofit social enterprises may benefit from entering into a fiscal sponsorship arrangement with a tax-exempt sponsoring organization either initially, during the start-up phase as it awaits its tax exemption, or on a continuing basis moving forward as a way to leverage economies of scale. Fiscal sponsorship is a broad term that refers to a contractual arrangement, whereby a nonprofit, tax-exempt IRC § 501(c)(3) organization "sponsors" another taxable organization or its project. Through this sponsorship arrangement, the taxable organization itself becomes able to solicit tax-deductible grants and contributions from outside funding sources, and is also able to leverage off the tax-exempt organization's existing infrastructure to manage the project more efficiently.

According to the Trust for Conservation Innovation (TCI), a San Francisco–based IRC § 501(c)(3) organization which conducted an in-depth study of fiscal sponsorships and services,[33] the services provided under sponsorship service models generally fall into two broad categories. The first area includes fiscal sponsors that focus primarily on providing financial management and administrative support services, with minimal training, promotion, or other services. The second category includes fiscal sponsors that provide significant amounts of project incubation by providing direct capacity-building and technical assistance to projects through training workshops, fundraising

---

32. I.R.C. § 512(b).

33. *See* http://www.trustforconservationinnovation.org/Fiscal_Sponsorship_Report.pdf for a full view of the study conducted.

assistance, project management and support, and extensive promotion. A social enterprise wishing to advance its mission could benefit greatly by contracting with an existing fiscal sponsor that can provide the key services noted above with greater efficiency, thus advancing the mission of the social enterprise more effectively.

A typical fiscal sponsorship arrangement is effectuated through a contractual agreement executed between the tax-exempt organization and the project. The contract should define in detail the responsibilities of both parties regarding the receipt and disbursement of funds, filing taxes, covering expenses, purchasing insurance, payment of administrative costs, record-keeping, reporting, and control over termination of the project or the results of the project.[34] In addition, the contract should be drafted in a manner that asserts the fiscal sponsor's control over the funds received. To be compliance with tax-exempt laws, the charitable organization must at all times be in control over the funds received to ensure that the project advances the tax-exempt purpose of the charity.[35] As such, it is imperative that the contract be drafted in a manner that expressly establishes that the project will advance the charitable purposes of the organization, lest it endanger the charity's tax exemption.

Partnering with an established tax-exempt organization through a fiscal sponsorship arrangement may allow a social enterprise to undertake a wide range of projects that might not otherwise be cost-effective or attainable. This trend appears to be catching on, as many tax-exempt organizations are now formed for the specific purpose of acting as a fiscal sponsor for various projects. Social enterprises wishing to pursue a fiscal sponsorship arrangement with a tax-exempt organization can consult a number of resources to assist them, both on-line and in print. One useful place to start the search for a fiscal sponsor is with the Fiscal Sponsor Directory (FSD) (http://www .fiscalsponsordirectory.org/index.php). This online directory lists fiscal sponsors in 33 states and provides many other tools that may be helpful to entities searching for such assistance.

---

34. Jane C. Nober, *Fiscal Agent Versus Financial Sponsor,* FOUND. NEWS & COMMENTARY (Nov./Dec. 2004), *available at* http://www.foundationnews.org/CME/article.cfm?ID=3069.

35. Rev. Rul. 68-484, 1968-2 C.B. 105.

Governmental Assistance

Governmental support for social enterprise may come from federal, state, and/or local government agencies. Typically, governmental support is available both to subsidize the performance of activities and to assist in the generation of goods and services. Governmental support may be available in areas in which the government either cannot or chooses not to provide those services that are furnished by the social enterprise.

Social enterprises should determine how the government would benefit from the establishment and support of its mission when deciding which governmental agency or program it will target for support. It may also be helpful to look for examples of other organizations with similar purposes that have received governmental support in the past.

The sources of governmental support available to be tapped are vast and wide-ranging. At the federal level, social enterprises may wish to search for available government funding by researching the Catalog of Federal Domestic Assistance (the CFDA, available at http://www.cfda.gov). The CFDA provides a full listing of all federal programs available to state and local governments; domestic public, quasi-public, and private profit and nonprofit organizations and institutions; specialized groups; and individuals. The CFDA is exhaustive and contains financial and non-financial assistance programs administered by departments and establishments of the federal government. The variety of options available at the state and local level is outside the scope of this text.

Social enterprises should be aware that applying for governmental assistance generally requires significant lead time and involves the completion of a substantial amount of paperwork. Because of the wide variety of possible funding sources, it is impossible to generalize about the filing particulars and procedures.

Community Development Financing Fund

The Community Development Financial Institutions Fund (CDFI Fund) is a program of the U.S. Department of the Treasury.[36] Its purpose is to assist community development financial institutions (CDFIs)—that is, loan funds, banks, credit unions, and venture capital funds that serve low-in-

---

36. Community Development Financial Institutions Fund, *Who We Are* (Sept. 11, 2009), *available at* http://www.cdfifund.gov/who_we_are/about_us.asp.

come people and communities that would otherwise lack access to afford-able financial services.[37]

CDFIs typically engage in activities such as financing mortgages for first-time homebuyers, low-income homebuyers, and nonprofit institutions; pro-viding flexible underwriting and risk capital for community facilities; and making commercial loans and investments to start-up businesses in low-income areas.[38] For a CDFI to be eligible for financial assistance from the CDFI Fund, it must be certified by the Fund.[39]

Financial assistance awards by the CDFI Fund to applicant CDFIs are made in the form of equity investments, loans, grants, or deposits, but must be matched by funds of the same amount and type received by the applicant from non-federal sources.[40]

The Nonprofit Finance Fund (the NFF, found at http://www.nonprofitfinancefund.org), based in New York, Boston, Newark, Philadel-phia, Washington, D.C., Detroit, San Francisco, and Los Angeles, is one of several CDFIs focused on nonprofits.

NFF offers a continuum of financing, consulting, and advocacy services to nonprofits and funders nationwide. It provides loans and lines of credit to help nonprofits fund growth, obtain working capital, and finance facility-related projects and equipment purchases. Through its New Markets Tax Credits program, it attracts private capital for nonprofit community facility projects in underserved communities. And through its Building for the Future program, it helps nonprofits plan and save for facility maintenance and repair costs.

United Farm Credit System

Another example of a fertile government funding source for social enter-prises is the Farm Credit System. This funding source was created by Con-

---

37. Community Development Financial Institutions Fund, *Community Development Financial Institutions Program* (Aug. 20, 2010), *available at* http://www.cdfifund.gov/what_we_do/programs_id.asp?programID=7.

38. Community Development Financial Institutions Fund, *CDFI Certification* (Aug. 9, 2010), *available at* http://www.cdfifund.gov/what_we_do/programs_id.asp?programID=9.

39. *Id.*

40. Community Development Financial Institutions Fund, *Community Development Financial Institutions Program* (Aug. 20, 2010), *available at* http://www.cdfifund.gov/what_we_do/programs_id.asp?programID=7.

gress and provides financing to a wide spectrum of agricultural businesses. The goal of the Farm Credit System is to get money into the hands of participants in a federally chartered network of cooperatives and related service organizations that serves farmers, ranchers, aquatic producers, and rural homeowners, as well as farm-related businesses and rural utilities. Federal oversight by the Farm Credit Administration ensures the safety and soundness of the institutions in the Farm Credit System.

The Federal Farm Credit Banks Funding Corporation is the fiscal agent for Farm Credit System banks, and it raises money for loans and leases through the sale of Farm Credit system-wide debt securities in the U.S. and international money markets. Responsible for managing the Investor Relations Program, it meets with current and potential investors to educate them on the Farm Credit System's mission, financials, debt issuance patterns, and overall agricultural and credit market conditions.

The Farm Credit System provides financing and lending opportunities to agricultural and rural communities. Aside from debt-financing alternatives, Farm Credit also provides philanthropic contributions. Farm Credit touts on its website (http://www.farmcreditnetwork.com) that it will provide nearly $2 million in national contributions, and system banks and associations will provide millions of dollars toward local and regional activities.

Economic Development Companies

Economic development companies are defined by the services they provide to their surrounding communities and by their relationship to the U.S. Small Business Administration (SBA, at http://www.sba.gov).[41] If certified, such economic development companies have the ability to provide federally backed financing to small businesses through the implementation, distribution, and servicing of loans made under sections 503 and 504 of the Small Business Investment Act (Investment Act)[42] and section 7(a) of the Small Business Act (Business Act).[43]

Certified economic development companies' importance stems from their ability to provide low interest rate, long-term, and fixed financing to small businesses. Such loans may be used to acquire fixed assets, for expansion, or

---

41. *See* http://www.sba.gov/tools/resourcelibrary/lawsandregulations/tool_lawsreg_Smallbusinvst.html.
42. Small Business Investment Act §§ 503–504, 15 U.S.C. §§ 697–697a.
43. Small Business Act § 7(a), 15 U.S.C § 636(a).

for the modernization of the business.[44] Because of this ability, certified development companies can fund social enterprises that promote expansion of minority employment, rural development, urban development of impoverished areas, and other goals that attend to a social need.

Economic development companies must be certified to gain the backing of the SBA. The certification process is detailed in Chapter 8.

Community Advantage

In December 2010, the Small Business Administration announced a new program to help nonprofit community groups make federally guaranteed business loans.[45] Under this program, known as Community Advantage, the types of eligible lenders able to make government-guaranteed loans under section 7(a) of the Small Business Act[46] will now include mission-focused financial institutions, such as nonprofit microlending intermediaries, as well as community development financial institutions and certified development companies.[47] Previously, government-guaranteed loans under section 7(a) could only be made by banks.[48] In addition, the SBA intends to streamline the application process for 7(a) loans that do not exceed $250,000.[49]

The 7(a) loans available under the Community Advdntage program will be made available to small businesses for plant acquisition, construction, conversion, or expansion, including the acquisition of land, material, supplies, equipment, and working capital.[50] The government guarantees 85 percent of such loans if the balance is less than or equal to $150,000, and 75 percent of such loans if the balance exceeds $150,000.[51]

---

44. U.S. Small Bus. Admin., CDC/504 Loan Program, *available at* http://www.sba.gov/financialassistance/borrowers/guaranteed/CDC504lp/index.html; *see also* Small Business Investment Act § 502, 15 U.S.C. § 696.

45. Paul Merrion, *Non-profits Get SBA Nod to Offer Business Loans*, CRAIN'S CHI. BUS. (Jan. 3, 2011), at 12.

46. Small Business Act § 7(a), 15 U.S.C. § 636(a).

47. Press Release, U.S. Small Business Administration, SBA Announces New Initiatives Aimed at Increasing Lending in Underserved Communities (Dec. 15, 2010), *available at* http://fwww.sba.gov/content/sba-announces-new-initiatives-aimed-increasing-lending-underserved-communities.

48. Paul Merrion, *supra* note 45.

49. *Id.*

50. Small Business Act § 7(a), 15 U.S.C. § 636(a).

51. Small Business Act § 7(a)(2)(A), 15 U.S.C. § 636(a)(2)(A).

As this book went to press, the SBA had announced that the Community Advantage program was scheduled to take effect by March 15, 2011.[52]

Startup America

Another potential funding source that the federal government has established is the "Startup America" initiative.[53] This initiative is a coordinated public-private effort designed to increase the number and scale of new high-growth firms that promote economic growth, innovation, and jobs.[54]

As part of this initiative, the SBA is committing $2 billion, in the form of SBA-guaranteed bonds, over a five-year period as a match to private capital.[55] Of this amount, $1 billion, to be known as the Impact Investment Fund, is being committed to funds that invest growth capital in companies located in underserved communities.[56] The SBA will match private capital raised by such funds up to a 2 to 1 match.[56] The other $1 billion, known as the Early-Stage Innovation Fund, will match private capital raised by early-stage seed funds at a 1 to 1 match.[58]

Among the private companies that have committed to support the Startup America initiative are Intel, which has pledged to invest $200 million in American startup companies, and IBM, which has committed $150 million to promoting entrepreneurship and new business opportunities.[59]

Catalog of Federal Domestic Assistance

Governmental agencies may be willing and able to either provide loans or guarantee loans made to or from a social enterprise depending on the circumstances and purpose of such lending. The process in this situation is likened to grant making, in which the social enterprise will be required to

---

52. Press Release, U.S. Small Business Administration, SBA Announces New Initiatives Aimed at Increasing Lending in Underserved Communities (Dec. 15, 2010), *available at* http://www.sba.gov/content/sba-announces-new-initiatives-aimecl-increasing-lending-underserved-communities.

53. *Fact Sheet: White House Launches "Startup* America " Initiative (2011), available at http://www.whitehouse.gov/startup-america-fact-sheet.

54. *Id.*

55. *Id.*

56. *Id.*

57. *Id.*

58. *Id.*

59. *Id.*

research and determine the appropriate agency or program to support its purposes. As such, the Catalog of Federal Domestic Assistance on-line at http://www.cdfa.gov may be helpful as a referential starting point to determine supportive programs at the federal level.

Issuance of Securities

Federal Securities Law Compliance

The issuance of securities,[60] such as stocks or debt instruments (debentures, bonds, notes, and the like), requires strict compliance with both federal and state securities laws. At the federal level, an issuer of securities must ensure compliance with the Securities Act of 1933, the Securities Exchange Act of 1934, the Investment Company Act of 1940, and the Investment Advisors Act of 1940. A social enterprise that issues securities will be primarily concerned with the Securities Act and the Securities Exchange Act.

In most instances, a social enterprise will not need to concern itself with the reporting and registration requirements of the Securities Exchange Act, as they generally apply only to publicly traded companies. What may be of concern are the registration requirements of the Securities Act dealing with the issuance of securities. Still, the federal securities laws mentioned above contain important offering exemptions from the registration requirements of the Securities Act. In fact, securities issued by an entity organized and operated exclusively for religious, educational, benevolent, fraternal, charitable, or reformatory purposes and not for pecuniary profit are exempt from the registration requirements of the Securities Act.[61] This is among many exempted classes of securities as specified in section 3 of the Securities Act.

Without regard to the entity type or the type of security offered, section 4 of the Securities Act offers exemptions from registration based on the type of transaction.[62] The most widely used exemption is section 4(2), which provides for the exemption from registration for a private placement of secu-

---

60. SEC v. W.J. Howey, Co., 329 U.S. 819 (1946) (defining a security in the context of an investment contract); United Housing Found., Inc. v. Forman, 421 U.S. 837 (1975) (defining a security in the context of stock); Reves v. Ernst & Young, 494 U.S. 56 (1990) (defining a security in the context of a debt security).
61. 15 U.S.C. § 77c(a)(4).
62. 15 U.S.C. § 77d.

rities not involving a public offering.[63] An offering is generally considered a private placement when it is made to a limited number of investors and adequate disclosures are made to those investors.[64] The Securities and Exchange Commission has issued a series of rules known as Regulation D to provide a safe harbor for compliance with section 4(2).[65] The regulation is fairly complex and provides offering and disclosure requirements that look to, among other things, the number of purchasers, the nature of the purchasers, the amount of the offering, the timing of the offering, and the location of the offering.[66] Section 4(2) and all other applicable exemptions apply equally to all securities, regardless of the debt or equity nature of such securities.[67]

Documentation, Disclosures, and Reporting Suggested in a Private Placement

The following items need to be supplied to any investor in a private placement of securities:

- Prospectus, private placement memorandum (PPM), or other documents explaining the terms of the offer, risks, and other information investors will need to aid in their due diligence;
- Subscription agreement or other contract for the purchase of securities;
- Investor questionnaire, used to ascertain the potential investor's suitability;
- Federal and state securities regulation filings; and
- Other related documents, such as buy-sell agreements, investor rights agreements, etc.

Finally, it is important to keep in mind that the anti-fraud provisions of the securities laws will always apply to any sale of securities. Sections 11 and 12 of the Securities Act create liability for misstatements and omissions made during the offering or sale of a security.[68] Arguably, the most powerful anti-fraud provision is section 10(b) of the Securities Exchange Act, which cre-

---

63. 15 U.S.C. § 77d(2).
64. SEC v. Ralston Purina Co., 346 U.S. 119 (1953).
65. 17 C.F.R. § 230.501–508.
66. Id.
67. Id.
68. 15 U.S.C. §§ 77k, 77l.

ates liability for all intentional misstatements or omissions connected with any purchase or sale of a security, including secondary market purchases.[69]

State Securities Law Compliance and Preemption by Federal Securities Laws

In addition to federal securities laws, securities laws also vary from state to state. Social enterprises should familiarize themselves with and comply with all state laws from states in and from which the securities will be issued. Still, there are important federal preemption issues that the social enterprise should be aware of.

Section 18 of the Securities Act provides for preemption of certain registration requirements of state securities laws for covered securities.[70] If a security is a covered security, state securities laws will apply to that security.[71] While there are many types of covered securities, including securities that trade on national or automated exchanges, social enterprises will generally be issuing securities under section 4(2) of the Securities Act. Securities issued under this section and pursuant to the requirements of Regulation D are considered covered securities.[72] Nevertheless, states may still require notice filings of securities offerings issued under 4(2) and the accompanying regulation.[73]

Every state has exemptions from registration that track the exemptions found in federal securities laws. For example, California provides a statutory exemption for securities issued by certain social enterprises which effectively tracks the section 3(4) exemption of the Securities Act. California exempts from registration securities offered by an issuer organized exclusively for educational, benevolent, fraternal, religious, charitable, social, or reformatory purposes and not for pecuniary profit, if no part of the net earnings of the issuer inures to the benefit of any private shareholder or individual.[74] Many jurisdictions follow California's lead and pattern their securities laws after federal securities laws.[75]

---

69. 15 U.S.C. § 78j(b).
70. 15 U.S.C. § 77r.
71. 15 U.S.C. § 77r(a).
72. 15 U.S.C. § 77r(a)(4).
73. *Id.*
74. CAL. CORP. CODE § 25100(j).
75. ALA. CODE § 8-6-2; ALASKA STAT. § 45.55.101; ARIZ. REV. STAT § 44-1801; COLO. REV. STAT. § 11-51-101; FLA. STAT. § 517.021; 815 ILL. COMP. STAT. ANN. 5/1 (as examples of securities laws from other jurisdictions).

Funding Networks: Social Enterprises Helping Each Other

Today, the social enterprise movement is beginning to see new investment models whereby social enterprises are pooling funds with the sole purpose and intent of distributing them to other social enterprises. Many social enterprises, including RSF Financial, Slow Money, REDF, and others, are creating funds, sourced by both debt and equity contributions from outside, socially conscious investors, with the intent to distribute fund proceeds directly to social enterprises that have certain characteristics. For instance, Slow Money is concerned with investments in the farming and agriculture-producing industries. REDF is concerned with job creation for the homeless and the underprivileged. These "feeder" social enterprises may organize as a tax-exempt private foundation, an ordinary tax-exempt nonprofit corporation, or a for-profit business. The general tax and governance consequences of these organizational structures can be found in Chapters 4 and 5 of this book. The distribution requirements of the private foundation can be found in the section above.

This section focuses on how these "feeder" social enterprises can put money in the hands of other social enterprises.

Venture Philanthropy

The principles of venture capital have been applied in the social enterprise context through the emergence of venture philanthropy firms. These firms, social enterprises in their own right, gain funding through contributions and then invest the proceeds in other social enterprises. Venture philanthropy distinguishes itself by:

- its willingness to invest in start-up social enterprises with new approaches to solving social problems;
- its focus on measurable result (i.e., measuring the social impact of a target enterprise);
- its readiness to shift funds between organizations and goals based on the tracking of measurable results; and
- the high involvement of the venture philanthropy firm in the affairs of the target enterprise.

Although not all venture philanthropic enterprises share all these traits, most embrace at least some of them. Some of these enterprises have greater risk tolerances than others and are more willing to ride out a particular investment over a longer period of time (such as Slow Money and the Acumen Fund, discussed below). The core characteristic of venture philanthropy is its willingness to fund new and innovative social enterprises.

REDF and the Promotion of Venture Philanthropy

One prominent and very effective venture philanthropy firm is REDF (found at http://www.redf.org, formerly the Roberts Enterprise Development Fund).[76] REDF collects funds from donors and charitable investors, including private foundations.[77] These funds are pooled and managed by REDF, and dispersed to social, nonprofit enterprises that employ young people and adults who are lacking education or unable to find jobs. Specifically, the social enterprises invested in REDF employ individuals who are overcoming histories of homelessness, mental illness, addiction, incarceration, chronic poverty, and joblessness.[78] Of particular note, the funds are used not only to support and expand the enterprises in REDF's investment portfolio, but also to fund initiatives to measure the impact and success of their enterprises.[79]

The capital provided by REDF has been classified by the organization as start-up capital for the social enterprises in REDF's portfolio. As noted above, the funds used by REDF to provide this capital are gained through the contributions of individuals, corporations, and private foundations. Of note, REDF has recently received a $3 million grant from the Social Innovation Fund managed by the Corporation for National and Community Service, a federal agency that promotes social enterprise and volunteerism in the United States.[80] When combining private-sector funding—such as that provided by various depository banking institutions—with federal funding, venture philanthropy organizations, which are themselves social enterprises, can create a well of funds aimed at promoting the social good.

The Acumen Fund

Another example of venture philanthropy is the work being done by the Acumen Fund (http://www.acumenfund.org), which seeks to use "patient

---

76. See http://www.redf.org/about-redf.
77. See id.
78. See id.
79. See id.
80. See http://www.redf.org/about-redf/press-release.

capital" to build transformative businesses. Created on April 1, 2001, with seed capital from the Rockefeller Foundation, Cisco Systems Foundation, and three individual philanthropists, the Acumen Fund has now expanded its investor base and is committed to using entrepreneurial approaches to solve global poverty.

Patient capital is an innovative concept that brings market-based approaches in line with the social impact philanthropy and is the core of the Acumen Fund's philosophy. The Acumen Fund defines patient capital as having the following characteristics: (1) long-term horizons for investment; (2) risk tolerance; (3) a goal of maximizing social rather than financial returns; and (4) the flexibility to seek partnerships with governments and corporations through subsidy and co-investment when doing so may be beneficial to low-income customers. It seeks to provide assistance to entrepreneurial pioneers, which it believes will be the ultimate solution to global poverty.

An example of such a business model discussed on Acumen Fund's website is its investment of $600,000 in WaterHealth International, a company committed to bringing safe drinking water to rural people in India.[81] Since the initial investment, WaterHealth International has raised $11 million in private capital and has put more than 275 systems in place, providing help to more than 350,000 people.

Slow Money Investing

Slow Money (http://www.slowmoney.org), an IRC § 501(c)(3) tax-exempt organization, pioneered the "slow money investing" model that, like the patient capital model of the Acumen Fund, looks to long-term investment horizons. The aim of slow money investing is to get money from a particular community (a town, a city, a particular section of a city, etc.) into the hands of small food enterprises and local food-producing systems within that community that produce food and goods in a socially and environmentally conscious manner.[82] The slow money movement is, in some respects, an extension of the slow food movement, in which purchasers of food are concerned with

---

81. WILLIAM MEEHAN ET AL., ACUMEN FUND AND WATERHEALTH INTERNATIONAL: THE ROLE OF VENTURE PHILANTHROPY (Jan. 2007), *available at* http://www. acumenfund. org/knowledge-center.html?document=125; Press Release, WaterHealth Int'l, Inc., WaterHealth International Receives New Funding Totaling $1.8 Million (Nov. 22, 2004), *available at* http://www.waterhealth.com/press/22-Nov-04.php.

82. *See* http://www.slowmoney.org/about.html.

how the food they eat is produced, how it is prepared, and how that preparation affects the environment.[83] The mission of Slow Money is:

- to promote entrepreneurship that preserves and restores soil fertility, appropriate-scale organic farming, and local food communities;
- to catalyze increases in foundation grant-making and mission-related investing in support of sustainable agriculture and local economies; and
- to incubate next-generation socially responsible investment strategies, integrating principles of carry capacity, care of the commons, sense of place, and non-violence.[84]

The principles of the slow money movement center not only on investing in particular types of food producers but also on investing those funds in particular ways.[85]

Slow Money operates various funds, which it raises through contributions and other methods and then invests in certain food producers or groups of food producers.[86] All investments are integrated along industry and supplier lines.[87] These funds can be invested in the socially conscious food suppliers themselves or in nonprofit organizations that provide specific aid to specific types of suppliers.[88] The investment would not only be aimed at providing resources to help the actual production of food, but also at creating sustainable resources for the producers of certain foods.[89] For instance, instead of supplying funds just to build slaughterhouse facilities for meat producers in an area, money would also be invested to create new processing plants, start a meat producers' cooperative, establish marketing resources, establish sales resources, and promote educational programs for meat produc-

83. Katie McCaskey, *Like Slow Food? Try Slow Money* (Apr. 29, 2009), *available at* http://www.mainstreet.com/article/moneyinvesting/stocks-funds/slow-food-try-slow-money.

84. Tom Stearns, *Slow Money Seeks to Fund Vermont's 21st Century Healthy Food System, available at* http://www.slowmoneyvermont.com/img/nofavt_slowmoney.pdf.

85. *See* http://www.slowmoney.org/about.html.

86. Tom Stearns, *Slow Money Seeks to Fund Vermont's 21st Century Healthy Food System, available at* http://www.slowmoneyvermont.com/img/nofavt_slowmoney.pdf.

87. *Id.*

88. *Id.*

89. *Id.*

ers about safe and humane methods of meat production.[90] It is envisioned that all investors who contribute debt capital to any project will have their funds returned with a moderate (5 percent or less) return on investment. Because Slow Money itself is an IRC § 501(c)(3) charitable organization with limited ability to raise funds or have an unrelated profit-making business activity,[91] it may be difficult to generate such returns.

Slow Money has established the Soil Trust, which is meant to provide co-investment capital and guarantees for Slow Money investors. The Soil Trust was established and is operated by Slow Money, and will guarantee certain sums of debt capital invested into Slow Money as well as provide a matching amount of capital in certain circumstances. The goal of the Soil Trust is to encourage investment by third-party investors into Slow Money.[92] All returns garnered by the Soil Trust in its co-investment efforts will be returned to the trust for reinvestment into Slow Money and Slow Money initiatives.[93]

RSF Financial

RSF Financial (rsfsocialfinance.org) is a nonprofit enterprise that also engages in venture philanthropy by providing financial services and support to other nonprofits and social enterprises. In sum, this organization collects money and donations from third-party investors and then supplies funding and capital to enterprises that address a wide range of social, environmental, and educational concerns.[94] To date, RSF has made more than $200 million in loans and more than $90 million in grants to worthy charitable organizations.

Mission Markets

With more and more media attention devoted to social enterprise as the means to fight global poverty and generate social and environmental change, funding for such enterprises is becoming more available. Mission Markets (http://www.missionmarkets.com) operates a securities exchange for the

---

90. *Id.*

91. *See* I.R.C. § 511.

92. *See* https://org2.democracyinaction.org/o/6351/t/9125/shop/custom.jsp?donate_page_KEY=2234.

93. *See id.*

94. *See* http://rsfsocialfinance.org/about/.

social and environmental capital markets. This platform provides socially and environmentally responsible companies, organizations, and projects with cost-effective access to mission-aligned capital.

Its mission is to create a marketplace that improves the flow of capital for sustainable investments that generate measurable social and environmental impacts, thereby improving humanity and life on earth. It does so by providing investors with a wide array of social-impacting investment opportunities.

Mission Markets allows companies and organizations that meet its minimum listing requirements to promote their investment opportunities on its platform, where accredited and institutional investors can review and select offerings of interest. A small fee is charged by Mission Markets based on the percentage of funds raised or transacted, but as a rule there are no listing or membership fees assessed.

Mission Markets is required to meet all applicable legal standards as an automated exchange and broker dealer. Missionmarkets.com is both an automated exchange for privately placed and publicly offered securities and a broker-dealer engaged in secondary transactions on that exchange. As such, Mission Markets must comply with the strict rules of the Securities and Exchange Commission, as well as the rules set forth by the Financial Industry Regulatory Authority, commonly known as FINRA. Accordingly, the companies seeking to be listed on the Mission Markets marketplace will need to be aware of stringent federal regulations governing publically traded securities.

Pay-for-Success/Social Impact Bonds

In February 2011, President Obama's proposed federal budget for the year 2012 was released, including among its provisions pilot programs to be known as "pay-for-success bonds."[95] Pay-for-success bonds are also known as "social impact bonds," particularly in the United Kingdom, where they were introduced in 2010.

These instruments, under either name, are not "bonds" in the traditional definition of the term, for which investors are guaranteed a fixed

---

95. OFFICE OF MANAGEMENT AND BUDGET, FISCAL YEAR 2012 BUDGET OF THE U.S. GOVERNMENT 32, 70 (2011), *available at* http://www.whitehouse.gov/sites/default/files/omb/budget/fy2012/assets/budget.pdf.

return. Rather, they are created as contracts among a public-sector body (such as a government agency), a private financing intermediary (sometimes known as a "social impact bond-issuing organization"),[96] and private investors, in which the public-sector body agrees to pay for improved social outcomes. These improved social outcomes are to be achieved through the use of funds provided by the private investors.[97]

For example, the first social impact bond[98] was issued in 2010 to finance support for short-term prisoners with the goal of reducing the percentage of them who will become repeat offenders after release. In the U.K., 60% of prisoners serving short-term sentences go on to re-offend within one year after release. A social impact bond has raised funds from private investors to fund intensive support from experienced social-sector organizations to 3,000 short-term prisoners at Peterborough Prison, both before and after their release, to enable their resettlement into the community. If the re-offending rate drops by at least 7.5% compared to a control group of ex-prisoners, the Ministry of Justice will provide the investors with a share of the cost savings achieved accordingly. Additional reductions in the re-offending rate will result in higher payments, with a maximum potential return to the investors of 13%.[99] If the social-sector organizations are unsuccessful in reducing the re-offending rate sufficiently, the private investors will receive nothing.[100] Because the prisoners receiving these services are being released at various times, and their re-offending rate is determined based on the number of times they are convicted within

---

96. JEFFREY B. LIEBMAN, SOCIAL IMPACT BONDS, Center for American Progress (February 2011), at 11, *available at* http://www.americanprogress.org/issues/2011/02/pdf/social_impact_bonds.pdf.

97. *Social Impact Bonds: Rethinking Finance for Social Outcomes*, SOCIAL FINANCE 3 (August 2009), *available at* http://www.socialfinance.org.uk/downloads/SIB_report_web.pdf.

98. The social impact bond has been described as "the first programme of its kind in the world." Tom Whitehead, *World First in Rehabilitation Scheme*, THE TELEGRAPH (London), Sept. 10, 2010, *available at* http://www.telegraph.co.uk/news/uknews/law-and-order/7991948/World-first-in-rehabilitation-scheme.html.

99. *Re-Offending Social Impact Bond Launched by Social Finance*, SOCIAL FINANCE, *available at* http://www.socialfinance.org.uk/services/index.php?page_ID=15.

100. Alan Travis, *Will Social Impact Bonds Solve Society's Most Intractable Problems?*, THE GUARDIAN (Oct. 6, 2010), *available at* http://www.guardian.co.uk/society/2010/oct/06/social-impact-bonds-intractable-societal-problems.

a year after release from prison, it will take up to four years before investors start to see a return on their investment.[101]

Besides the initial use of these bonds to finance the goal of reducing the number of repeat offenders, such bonds could be used to finance new approaches to improving education (as in President Obama's budget),[102] health care, and other social goals.

A distinct feature of this kind of bond is that the government decides what social goals it will pay to be achieved but is not involved in deciding *how* those social goals are achieved; rather, that decision is made by the investors through the bond-issuing organization. For example, in the case of the Peterborough Prison social impact bond, the Ministry of Justice does not determine how much of the funds raised from investors are allocated to job training, how much to drug rehabilitation, or how much to other types of interventions.[103]

The Economist has stated that "[i]n many ways the social-impact bond epitomises the new approach to social ills. It provides long-term funds for promising ideas; it transfers risk to private capital markets; and it costs public money only if the scheme provides specific social benefits."[104]

Besides the proposal to include pay-for-success bonds in the federal budget, such bonds are also under consideration by the governments of Massachusetts and New York City.[105] The Rockefeller Foundation is involved in seeking to make such bonds a reality in the United States, having invested $500,000 in social impact bonds for the Peterborough Prison project.[106] Anthony Bugg-Levine, a managing director at Rockefeller, has

---

101. *Id.*

102. OFFICE OF MANAGEMENT AND BUDGET, FISCAL YEAR 2012 BUDGET OF THE U.S. GOVERNMENT 32, 70 (2011), *available at* http://www.whitehouse.gov/sites/default/files/omb/budget/fy2012/assets/budget.pdf.

103. JITINDER KOHLI, FINANCING WHAT WORKS: SOCIAL IMPACT BONDS HOLD PROMISE, Center for American Progress (Nov. 18, 2010), *available at* http://www.guardian.co.uk/society/2010/oct/06/social-impact-bonds-intractable-societal-problems.

104. *Social Innovation: Let's Hear Those Ideas*, THE ECONOMIST (Aug. 12, 2010), *available at* http://www.economist.com/node/16789766.

105. David Leonhardt, *For Federal Programs, a Taste of Market Discipline*, N.Y. TIMES (Feb. 9, 2011), at B1, *available at* http://www.nytimes.com/2011/02/09/business/economy/09leonhardt.html?_r=1&ref=business.

106. Shelly Banjo, *Rockefeller Foundation Sees Social-Change Dividend*, WALL ST. J. (Feb. 15, 2011), *available at* http://online.wsj.com/article/SB10001424052748703584804576144661629994864.html.

stated, "There simply isn't enough money in philanthropy and government alone to solve the problems that need to be solved. There's $80 trillion in for-profit capital markets, and we believe there's huge potential in unlocking some of that money and deploying it to solve social problems."[107] Rockefeller has granted $400,000 to the Nonprofit Finance Fund for projects that will help make these bonds viable in the United States.[108]

Jeffrey B. Liebman, a professor at Harvard's Kennedy School of Government and a former Office of Management and Budget official during the Obama Administration, notes that such bonds have the potential to achieve improved performance and lower costs, to accelerate the adoption of new solutions to social problems, and to make it possible to more quickly learn which approaches work and which do not.[109] However, he has also commented that the following criteria must be met for such bonds to be successful:

1. The interventions must have sufficiently high net benefits to enable investors to earn a satisfactory rate of return. This is particularly true given that it is likely that some projects will fail, resulting in a complete loss to the investors, and thus requiring the successful projects to earn a higher rate of return than might otherwise be required.[110]

2. The interventions must have measurable outcomes that can be evaluated by reliable performance measures. Such measures must be highly correlated with a comprehensive assessment of the program's net social benefits to prevent distorted measurements that could result from evaluating only a narrow component of the program's performance.[111]

3. The treatment population must be well-defined in a way that cannot be manipulated by the service provider. For example, in the U.K., the Peterborough Prison project is being evaluated based on the recidivism rate of all prisoners released from that prison during the program period, not just those receiving services. If a

---

107. *Id.*

108. *Id.*

109. JEFFREY B. LIEBMAN, SOCIAL IMPACT BONDS, Center for American Progress (February 2011), at 3, *available at* http://www.americanprogress.org/issues/2011/02/pdf/social_impact_bonds.pdf.

110. *Id.*

111. *Id.*

service provider were allowed to select the specific ex-convicts on whose performance it would be judged, it might direct its services only to those who were less likely to re-offend in the first place, thus artificially boosting its performance.[112]

4. The impact assessments must be credible and be able to assess what outcomes would have been achieved in the absence of the program.[113] For example, the recidivism rate of the ex-convicts from Peterborough Prison is being compared to a control group of similarly situated ex-convicts released from other prisons.

5. Unsuccessful performance must not result in excessive harm to the target population. Because bondholders might seek to shut down a program and cut their losses if the program is unlikely to meet performance targets, the bond contracts should include contingency plans in case of a performance or financial failure, to avoid leaving the beneficiaries of the program unserved.[114]

Additional Funding Sources

Beyond the funding sources already mentioned in this chapter, there are numerous other potential sources of funding for social enterprise. The following selected list has been compiled from information published by Ned.com[115] and SocialEarth.org (including information provided by commenters at the latter site).[116]

Angels and Venture Capital

Aavishkaar (http://www.aavishkaar.in)
ACCESS Community Capital Fund (http://www.accessccf.com)
The Adventure Project (theadventureproject.org)
Agora Partnerships (http://www.agorapartnerships.org)

---

112. *Id.* at 4.
113. *Id.*
114. *Id.*
115. *Social Entrepreneur, Social Enterprise and Social Innovation Sources of Funding*, Ned.com (Jan. 5, 2011), *available at* http://www.ned.com/group/seeb/ws/social_entrepreneur_funding/.
116. Tristan, *130 Ways to Fund Your Social Venture*, SocialEarth.org (Jan. 19, 2011), *available at* http://www.socialearth.org/130-ways-to-fund-your-social-venture?utm_source=feedburner&utm_medium=feed&utm_campaign=Feed:+Socialearth+%28SocialEarth%29.

Appropriate Infrastructure Development Group (http://www.aidg.org)

Bamboo Finance (http://www.bamboofinance.com)

Big Issue Invest (http://www.bigissueinvest.com)

Blue Ridge Foundation New York (http://www.brfny.org)

CEI Ventures (http://www.ceiventures.com)

City Light Capital (http://www.citylightcap.com)

The Community Development Venture Capital Alliance (http://www.cdvca.org)

Endeavor Global (http://www.endeavor.org)

Expansion Capital Partners (http://www.expansioncapital.com)

Good Capital (http://www.goodcap.net)

GoodCompany Ventures (http://www.goodcompanyventures.org)

Grand Challenges in Global Health (http://www.grandchallenges.org)

Gray Ghost Ventures (http://www.grayghostventures.com)

Humanity Fund (http://www.humanityfund.com)

IGNIA (http://www.ignia.com.mx)

Investors' Circle (http://www.investorscircle.net)

Jasmine Social Investments (http://www.jasmine.org.nz)

Joshua Venture Group (joshuaventuregroup.org)

Manhattan Institute Social Entrepreneurship Initiative (http://www.manhattan-institute.org)

The Mulago Foundation (mulagofoundation.org)

New Cycle Capital (http://www.newcyclecapital.com)

New Profit Inc. (http://www.newprofit.com)

New Ventures (http://www.new-ventures.org)

Next Street Financial LLC (http://www.nextstreet.com)

Nonprofit Finance Fund (nonprofitfinancefund.org)

NYC Seed (http://www.nycseed.com)

Omidyar Network (http://www.omidyar.com)

Pacific Community Ventures (http://www.pcvfund.com)

Pipeline Fund (pipelinefund.tumblr.com)

Presumed Abundance (http://www.presumedabundance.com)

Renewal2 Investment Fund (renewal2.ca)

Root Capital (http://www.rootcapital.org)

Satori Capital (http://www.satori-capital.com)

Schwab Foundation for Social Entrepreneurship (http://www.schwabfound.org)

Shared Interest Society (http://www.shared-interest.com)

SJF Ventures (http://www.sjfventures.com)
SME Finance Innovation Fund (http://www.changemakers.com)
Social Enterprise Fund (socialenterprisefund.ca)
Social Impact Exchange (http://www.socialimpactexchange.org)
Social Innovators Collective (http://www.socialinnovatorscollective.org)
SocialReturns (http://www.socialreturns.org)
TBL Capital (http://www.tblcapital.com)
TechnoServe (http://www.technoserve.org)
Thrust Fund (http://www.thrustfund.com)
Underdog Ventures (www2.underdogventures.com)
Union Square Ventures (http://www.usv.com)
UnLtd Advantage (unltdadvantage.org.uk)
Village Capital (http://www.vilcap.com)
Vox Capital (http://www.voxcapital.com.br)
ZeroDivide (http://www.zerodivide.org)

Banks and Loan Providers
Calvert Foundation (http://www.calvertfoundation.org)
New Resource Bank (http://www.newresourcebank.com)
Nonprofits Assistance Fund (http://www.nonprofitsassistancefund.org)
Partners for the Common Good (http://www.pcgloanfund.org)
Social Capital Partners (http://www.socialcapitalpartners.ca)
Triodos Bank (http://www.triodos.co.uk)
U.S. Small Business Administration (http://www.sba.gov)
Wainwright Bank (http://www.wainwrightbank.com)

Crowdfunding Sites
33 Needs (33needs.com)
CauseVox (http://www.causevox.com)
Changents (changents.com)
Chase Community Giving (http://www.facebook.com/
    ChaseCommunityGiving)
Crowdrise (http://www.crowdrise.com)
DonorsChoose.org (http://www.donorschoose.org)
FirstGiving (http://www.firstgiving.com)
GlobalGiving (http://www.globalgiving.org)
IndieGoGo (http://www.indiegogo.com)
Kickstarter (http://www.kickstarter.com)

Kiva (http://www.kiva.org)
MicroPlace (http://www.microplace.com)
Network for Good (www1.networkforgood.org)
Pepsi Refresh Project (http://www.refresheverything.com)
PledgeBank (http://www.pledgebank.com)
Profounder (http://www.profounder.com)
Razoo (http://www.razoo.com)
RocketHub (rockethub.com)
StartSomeGood (startsomegood.com)
TakeAction@GuideStar (www2.guidestar.org/)
United Prosperity (http://www.unitedprosperity.org)

Fellowships

Ashoka (ashoka.org)
Draper Richards Kaplan Foundation (http://www.draperrichards.org)
Echoing Green (http://www.echoinggreen.org)
PopTech (http://www.poptech.org)
PresenTense Group Social Entrepreneur Fellowship (presentense.org)
Rainer Arnhold Fellows (rainerfellows.org)
Skoll Foundation (http://www.skollfoundation.org)
The StartingBloc Fellowship (startingbloc.org)
TED Fellows (http://www.ted.com)
Unreasonable Institute (unreasonableinstitute.org)

Grants

The Awesome Foundation (awesomefoundation.org)
Chinook Fund (http://www.chinookfund.org)
Corporation for National and Community Service Social Innovation
    Fund (http://www.nationalservice.gov)
Do Something (http://www.dosomething.org)
Foundation Center (foundationcenter.org)
Fundsnet Services (http://www.fundsnetservices.com)
Google Grants (http://www.google.com/grants/)
Grantmakers for Effective Organizations (http://www.geofunders.org)
Grants.gov (http://www.grants.gov)
Kauffman Foundation (http://www.kauffman.org)
Philanthropy New York (http://www.philanthropynewyork.org)
USA.gov for Nonprofits (http://www.usa.gov/Business/Nonprofit.shtml)

Student Fellowships

C. V. Starr Social Entrepreneurship Fellowship
    (swearercenter.brown.edu)
Dartmouth College Class of 1982 Upper Valley Social Entrepreneurship
    Fellowship (http://www.dartmouth.edu/~tucker/)
Global Social Entrepreneurship Competition (http://
    www.foster.washington.edu)
Global Social Venture Competition (http://www.gsvc.org)
Harvard Business School Social Entrepreneurship Fellowship (http://
    www.hbs.edu)
Milken Family Foundation Social Entrepreneur Internship Program at
    Tulane University (tulane.edu/cps/)
New York University Reynolds Program in Social Entrepreneurship
    (http://www.nyu.edu/reynolds)
Sparkseed (http://www.sparkseed.org)
VentureWell (http://www.venturewell.org)
Wharton Social Enterprise Fellows (wlp.wharton.upenn.edu)

*   *   *   *

Ross Social Venture Fund

The Samuel Zell & Robert H. Lurie Institute for Entrepreneurial Studies at
the University of Michigan's Ross School of Business launched a Social Venture Fund to train students to invest in and manage for-profit enterprises
that respond to societal needs not otherwise met by market players. The
fund will make early-stage investments of up to $200,000 in "double-bot-
tom-line" organizations.

*   *   *   *

Securing initial and continuing funding sources can be tricky for any
business concern, and even more so for the social enterprise. Social purpose,
mission-driven, and tax-exempt considerations all affect what funding
sources are available to the social enterprise as well as methods of securing
such funding.

After issues of initial entity choice, governance, and funding have been
adequately addressed, the social enterprise may wish to pursue certification
of its products or services. Such certifications can be helpful in garnering
positive social recognition and give the social enterprise a competitive edge in
the market place.

Securing Certification

Certifying a business as an "accredited" social enterprise, as a particular type of social enterprise, or as an enterprise engaged in a certain type of business may afford the qualifying venture several privileges and advantages.

- First, it instantly affords the enterprise credibility when seeking investors and other funding opportunities. Such certifications are useful informational shortcuts for investors and contributors looking to fund social enterprises engaged in specific types of businesses.
- Second, it allows enterprises selling products or services to associate themselves with causes that are well known to their consumer bases. This, in turn, may encourage the purchase of products or services because of their association with a particular cause.
- Finally, in some instances, such as the certification of economic development companies, certification is legally required for the company to effectively do business.

Social Enterprise Accreditation

Social Enterprise Alliance (SEA), "North America's largest association of social enterprises working to solve some of the world's toughest challenges," has developed its own certification standards for social enterprises and, through its affiliate, The Center for Social Enterprise Accreditation (which the author chairs), certifies those enterprises that meet its strict criteria.

Accredited Social Enterprise
Certification Standards

What is a Social Enterprise?

A "Social Enterprise" is a nonprofit or private-sector entity, or any business unit thereof which maintains separate books and records, that:

- uses *earned* revenue strategies, either exclusively as a business or as a significant part of a nonprofit's revenue stream, and

- *directly* addresses social needs either through its goods and/or services or by employing people who are disabled or disadvantaged.

What is the purpose of certifying Social Enterprises as Accredited Social Enterprises?

The intent of the Accredited Social Enterprise certification is to support and promulgate commercial enterprises whose primary purpose is to promote the common good.

What standards must be met in order to become an Accredited Social Enterprise?

Any United States entity, irrespective of form, or any business unit thereof which maintains separate books and records, that meets the following standards is eligible for certification as an Accredited Social Enterprise:

-   If it is tax-exempt under section 501(c)(3) of the Internal Revenue Code (**required: favorable IRS determination letter**),

AND

-   is currently operating (required: certificate of good standing from its state of incorporation or organization),

AND

-   More than fifty (50) percent of its revenue (as reported on its most recently and timely filed Form 990, or its financial statements for the most recent fiscal year, certified by an authorized officer of the entity that it is accurate, complete and prepared in accordance with generally accepted accounting principles, consistently applied) is earned revenue (from the sale of goods and/or services) as opposed to gifts, grants, subsidies, unrelated taxable business income (UBTI), etc. (**required:**

1. **most recent, timely filed Form 990; or its financial statements for the most recent fiscal year, certified by an authorized officer of the entity that it is accurate, complete and prepared in accordance with generally accepted accounting principles consistently applied; or**

2. in the case of a business unit seeking certification, that unit's income statement for the most recent fiscal year, certified by an authorized officer of the entity that it is accurate, complete and prepared in accordance with generally accepted accounting principles, consistently applied),

AND

-   is directly addressing social needs by providing goods and/or services that directly address social needs or by using people who are disabled or disadvantaged for more than fifty (50) percent of its direct labor **(required: a certified statement by an authorized officer that the entity during the most recent fiscal year has provided goods and/or services that directly address social needs or that more than fifty (50) percent of its direct labor at the end of the most recent fiscal year was made up of people who are disabled or disadvantaged.)**

OR

-   If it is not tax-exempt under Section 501(c)(3), but its primary purpose is positive social impact rather than financial rewards (required:
1. governing instruments, such as articles of incorporation or organization, bylaws or mission statement, as amended to date, that reasonably evidence such purpose;
2. the entity's most recent, timely filed federal income tax return; or
3. in the case of a business unit seeking certification, that unit's income statement for its most recent fiscal year, certified by an authorized officer of the entity that it is accurate, complete, and prepared in accordance with generally accepted accounting principles, consistently applied),

AND

-   is currently operating (required: certificate of good standing from its state of incorporation or organization),

AND

-   is directly addressing social needs by providing goods and/or services that directly address social needs or by using people who are disabled or disadvantaged for more than fifty (50) percent of its direct labor (required: a certified statement by an authorized officer that the entity during the most recent fiscal year has provided goods and/or services that directly address social needs or that more than fifty (50) percent of its direct labor at the end of the most recent fiscal year was made up of people who are disabled or disadvantaged.)

SEA hopes that government and corporate procurement as well as tax benefits may eventually be awarded to these accredited social enterprises.

Fair Trade Movement Certifications

The Fair Trade Movement is an organized social movement and market-based approach that aims to help farmers and producers of goods in developing countries obtain better trading conditions and promote sustainability. The movement is seeking to change the purchasing habits of individuals and to heighten awareness of and solve the plight of third-world farmers and producers of marketable goods (collectively "producers").[1]

The Fair Trade Labeling Organizations International (FLO) is made up of 24 organizations working to secure better trading for producers. From its headquarters in Bonn, Germany, FLO sets international fair trade standards.[2] FLO's mission is to connect disadvantaged producers with consumers through promoting fairer trading conditions that also account for environmentally safe production of products and goods.

To accomplish this goal, the FLO has established fair trade certification standards to ensure that products are marketed and sold according to principles of fair trade.[3] Once certification standards are met, the product sold by the enterprise will be allowed to portray the fair trade label.

There are several fair trade certification standards, depending on the type of product involved. Each standard has a certification agency, which is a part of the FLO, that verifies all the stages of the production and trading processes to ensure that the production and trading process complies with the fair trade certification standards.[4] Importantly, fair trade certification applies not only to the actions of those companies involved in the selling of the products but also to the actions of the producers of those products.

If a social enterprise seeks to have its products certified as complying with the fair trade standards, specific certification standards for the particular type of product must be met, along with generic certification standards based on the size and type of enterprise involved in selling the product.[5] The specific product types include food products, such as produce, and

---

1. *See* http://www.fairtrade.net/standards.html.
2. *See id.*
3. *See id.*
4. *See id.*
5. *See id.*

non-food products, such as cotton and textile materials. These two general categories are then broken down into subcategories, such as bananas, coffee, dried fruit, etc., each with its own certification standards. The certification standards for each category and subcategory of product can be located on the FLO's webpage at http://www.fairtrade.net/716.html.

In the United States, fair trade certification is available through Fair Trade USA (formerly TransFair USA), a nonprofit organization exempt from federal taxation under IRC § 501(c)(3). Fair Trade USA audits transactions between U.S. companies offering Fair Trade Certified products and the international suppliers from which they source. For more information, the organization's website is www.transfairusa.com.

Goods produced under fair trade standards are all around us in our everyday lives, but may often go unnoticed to the untrained eye not actively searching the products out for consumption. One example of fair trade certification at work is the CraftNetwork, a commercial social enterprise organization that empowers disadvantaged artisans in developing countries located in Southeast Asia. The CraftNetwork distributes jewelry, paintings, sculptures, home décor, and other accessories to a number of high-end retail outlets. Purchasers of such goods can be assured that the member producers are provided a fair living wage for the work they perform.

Another example of a social enterprise that is currently taking advantage of the fair trade certification process is Guayaki, a for-profit social enterprise that uses a market-driven business model to champion the restoration of the rainforest and the creation of living-wage jobs.[6]

Guayaki refines and sells yerba mate–based energy drinks and supplements through partnerships with South American farmers, who grow and cultivate the yerba mate plants. The farmers, utilizing fair trade standards of production, grow the plants through the aid and stewardship of Guayaki and its managers. Guayaki then buys the plants utilizing the fair trade standards of commerce, ensuring fair prices and sufficient working conditions. This acts as a form of job creation. In exchange for the creation of farming jobs, Guayaki requires farmers to plant trees to aid in the reforestation of the rainforest. The yerba mate–based energy supplements and drinks are then sold to consumers. In purchasing the products, consumers are actually aiding in the reforestation of the rainforest and the creation of sustainable living-wage jobs.

6. *See* http://guayaki.com/about/131/Market-Driven-Restoration.html.

"Green" Companies

The Federal Trade Commission warns manufacturers and marketers against using labels that make broad, "eco-friendly" claims. Of great concern to the Commission is the use of environmental seals and certifications. According to the Ecolabel Index, there are 349 seals and certifications for marketing green products worldwide, 88 of them in use in North America.

In October 2010, the FTC proposed revisions to its *Green Guides*, last updated in 1998. The new Guides are expected to clearly handle certification issues, requiring companies to tell customers if the seals they use are certified by a third party and if the companies are members of a trade organization that certifies their products.

The proposed rules will also require seals and certifications that suggest general environmental claims to be more specific, using a label like "Green Smart, Recyclable Certified," rather than merely "Green Smart." Most important, companies that use third-party certifications will be required to substantiate their claims.

FTC Chairman Jon Leibowitz believes that "the proposed updates to the Green Guides will help businesses better align their product claims with consumer expectations."[7]

---

7. Press Release, Federal Trade Commission, Federal Trade Commission Proposes Revised "Green Guides" (Oct. 6, 2010), *available at* http://www.ftc.gov/opa/2010/10/greenguide.shtm.

Summary of the FTC's Proposed Revisions to Its *Green Guides*[8]

General Environmental Benefit (e.g., "green," "eco-friendly")
- Marketers should not make unqualified general environmental benefit claims. They are difficult, if not impossible, to substantiate. *(The current Guides state that marketers can make unqualified claims if they can substantiate all express and implied claims. Otherwise, they should qualify the claim.)*
- Qualifications should be clear and prominent, and should limit the claim to a specific benefit. Marketers should ensure that the advertisement's context does not imply deceptive environmental claims. *(In the current Guides, this guidance appears only in examples.)*

Certifications and Seals of Approval
- This new section emphasizes that certifications/seals are endorsements covered by the Commission's Endorsement Guides and provides new examples illustrating how those Guides apply to environmental claims (e.g., marketers should disclose material connections to the certifier). *(The current Guides address certifications/seals in only one example in the general environmental benefit section. 16CFR 260.7, Example 5.)*
- Because an unqualified certification/seal (one that does not state the basis for certification) likely conveys a general environmental benefit claim, marketers should use clear and prominent language limiting the claim to particular attribute(s) for which they have substantiation. *(This provision highlights guidance already provided in current Guides' Example 5.)*
- Third-party certification does not eliminate a marketer's obligation to have substantiation for all conveyed claims.

Recyclable
- The proposal highlights the three-tiered analysis for disclosing the limited availability of recycling programs. *(This guidance currently appears in examples only.)*
  1. "Substantial majority" of consumers/communities have access to recycling facilities—Marketer can make an unqualified recyclable claim.
  2. "Significant percentage" of consumers/communities have access to recycling facilities—Marketer should qualify recyclable claim (e.g., package may not be recyclable in your area.)

---

8. Federal Trade Commission, *Green Guides: Summary of Proposal,* available at http://www.ftc.gov/os/2010/10/101006greenguidesproposal.pdf.

3. Less than a "significant percentage" of consumer/communities have access to recycling facilities—Marketer should qualify recyclable claim (e.g., product is recyclable only in the few communities that have recycling programs).

Made with Renewable Materials
- Marketers should qualify claims with specific information about the renewable material (what it is; how it is sourced; why it is renewable).
- Additionally, marketers should qualify renewable materials claims if the item is not made entirely with renewable materials (excluding minor, incidental components).

Made with Renewable Energy
- Marketers should not make unqualified renewable energy claims if the power used to manufacture any part of the product was derived from fossil fuels.
- Marketers should qualify claims by specifying the source of renewable energy (e.g., wind or solar). Additionally, marketers should qualify claims if less than all, or virtually all, of the significant manufacturing processes involved in making the product/package were powered with renewable energy or conventional energy offset by renewable energy certificates (RECs).
- Marketers that generate renewable energy (e.g., by using solar panels) but sell RECs for all of the renewable energy they generate should not represent that they use renewable energy.

Degradable
- For solid waste products other than those destined for landfills, incinerators, or recycling facilities, the proposal clarifies that the "reasonably short period of time" for complete decomposition is no more than one year after customary disposal. *(The current Guides state that a marketer should qualify a degradable claim unless it can substantiate that the "entire product or package will completely break down and return to nature within a reasonably short period of time after customary disposal.")*
- Marketers should not make unqualified degradable claims for items destined for landfills, incinerators, or recycling facilities because decomposition will not occur within one year.

Compostable

- The proposal clarifies that the time period referenced in the current Guides for an unqualified compostable claim ("All materials in product/package will break down into, or otherwise become a part of, usable compost . . . in a safe and *timely manner . . .*") means that a product or package will break down in approximately the same time as the materials with which it is composted.

Ozone-Safe/Ozone-Friendly

- The proposal contains minor updates to examples to reflect changes in regulations concerning ozone-depleting chemicals.

Free-of/Non-toxic

- **Free-of:** This new section expands the current guidance, advising that even if true, claims that an item is free of a substance may be deceptive if:
  (1) the item has substances that pose the same or similar environmental risk as the substance not present (*currently covered in an example*); and
  (2) the substance has never been associated with the product category (*new guidance*). Also, under certain circumstances, free-of claims may be appropriate even where an item contains a de minimis amount of a substance (*new guidance*). Free-of claims may convey additional environmental claims, including general benefit or comparative superiority claims (*new guidance*).
- **Non-toxic:** Such claims likely convey that an item is non-toxic both for humans and for the environment generally. *(This guidance was in an example in the general environmental benefit section.)*

Carbon Offsets

- Marketers should have competent and reliable scientific evidence to support their carbon offset claims, including using appropriate accounting methods to ensure that they are properly quantifying emission reductions and are not selling those reductions more than once.
- Marketers should disclose if the offset purchase funds emission reductions that will not occur for two years or longer.
- Marketers should not advertise a carbon offset if the activity that forms the basis of the offset is already required by law.

Certified Economic Development Companies

Economic development companies can receive government assistance in order to advance their mission of providing financial support to small community businesses. Such government assistance comes in the form of federal guarantees for all debentures issued and used to fund loans to small business, a financing method specified in the Small Business Investment Act (Investment Act).[9] To be eligible for this assistance, provided directly by the Small Business Association (SBA), economic development companies must be certified by the SBA.

Certification Requirements under the Small Business Investment Act

The requirements that an entity must meet in order to be a certified economic development company under the Investment Act are governed exclusively by federal law under both the Investment Act itself and rules issued by the SBA. Under federal law, a company must first fit the definition of an "economic development company" and thereafter meet the qualifications for certification.

Determining Status as a Development Company

Under the Investment Act, the term "economic development company" is defined as a company that has been organized with the authority to promote and to assist the growth of and development of small-business concerns in the area covered by their operations.[10] A "small business" is defined under the Small Business Act as a business concern, including but not limited to enterprises that are engaged in the business of producing food and fiber, ranching and raising of livestock, aquaculture, and all other farming and agricultural-related industries, that is independently owned and operated and is not dominant in its field of operation.[11] Regardless of any other characteristic or any other requirement of law, an agricultural concern will be considered a small business if its annual receipts (including its affiliates) do not exceed $750,000.[12]

---

9. Small Business Investment Act §§ 503–504, 15 U.S.C. §§ 697–697a.
10. Small Business Investment Act § 103(7), 15 U.S.C. § 662(6).
11. Small Business Act § 3(a)(1), 15 U.S.C. § 632(a)(1).
12. *Id.*

Meeting the Qualifications for Certification

To meet the requirements set forth in sections 503 and 504 of the Investment Act, an economic development company must be a certified economic development company (referred to as a CDC).[13]

Along with certain specific requirements of the SBA listed below, a CDC is an economic development company that has:

(A) a full-time professional staff;

(B) professional management ability (including adequate accounting, legal, and business-servicing abilities); and

(C) a board of directors, or membership, which meets on a regular basis to make management decisions for such company, including decisions relating to the making and servicing of loans by such company.[14]

If an economic development company is in a rural area, it will be deemed to have a full-time professional staff and professional management ability if it contracts with a CDC to provide such services that is also located within the same geographical area.[15]

Certification Requirements under SBA Rules and Guidelines

The SBA has promulgated additional guidelines necessary to be met for the conferral of CDC status. Although not specified in the statute, a CDC must be organized as a nonprofit organization.[16] The SBA's other requirements are listed below and can also be found directly on the SBA website.[17]

Nonprofit Status—13 CFR § 120.820

A CDC must be a nonprofit corporation and must:

* Be in good standing in the state in which the CDC is incorporated;

---

13. Small Business Investment Act §§ 503–504, 15 U.S.C. §§ 697–697a.
14. Small Business Investment Act § 503(e), 15 U.S.C. §§ 697(e).
15. Small Business Investment Act § 503(e), 15 U.S.C. §§ 697(e)(2).
16. 13 C.F.R. § 120.820.
17. *Available at* http://www.sba.gov/financialassistance/borrowers/guaranteed/.

- Be in compliance with all laws, including taxation requirements, in the state in which the CDC is incorporated and any other state in which the CDC conducts business; and
- Provide a copy of its IRS tax exemption.

Area of Operations—13 CFR § 120.821

A CDC must operate only within its designated area of operations, as approved by the SBA. The area of operations is the state of the CDC's incorporation.

CDC Membership—13 CFR § 120.822

A CDC must have at least 25 members who actively support economic development in their area of operations. Members are responsible for electing the board of directors of the CDC. The members must be represented by the following four membership groups:

- Government organizations;
- Financial institutions (lenders);
- Community organizations such as chambers of commerce, foundations, trade associations, colleges, universities, and small-business development centers; and
- Businesses in the area of operations.

CDC Membership Requirements—13 CFR § 120.822

- CDC members must meet annually;
- No person or entity can own or control more than 10 percent of the CDC's voting membership; and
- No employee or staff of the CDC can qualify as a member of the CDC for the purpose of meeting the membership requirements.

CDC Board of Directors—13 CFR § 120.823

The CDC must have a board of directors chosen by the members. In addition:

- At least three of the four membership groups must be represented on the board;
- No single membership group shall control the board;

- No person who is a member of a CDC's staff may be a voting member of the board except for a CDC manager;
- At least one member other than a CDC manager must possess commercial lending experience;
- The board must meet at least quarterly and shall be responsible for CDC staff decisions and actions; and
- A quorum shall require at least five directors authorized to vote. The board meetings require a quorum to transact business. A quorum must be present for the duration of the meeting.

When the board votes on SBA loan approval or servicing actions, at least one board member with commercial loan experience acceptable to the SBA other than a CDC manager must be present and vote. There must be no actual or apparent conflict of interest with respect to any actions of the board.

Loan Committees—13 CFR § 120.823(a)
The board may establish a loan committee of non-board members that reports to the board. The following requirements apply to such a loan committee:

- Loan committee members must include at least one member with commercial lending experience acceptable to the SBA;
- All members of the loan committee must live or work in the area of operations of the state where the 504 project they are voting on is located;
- No CDC staff may serve on a loan committee;
- A quorum must include at least five committee members authorized to vote;
- The CDC's board must ratify the actions of any loan committee; and
- There must be no actual or apparent conflict of interest with respect to any actions of the loan committee.

CDC Staff—13 CFR § 120.824
A CDC must have:

- A full-time professional management staff, including an executive director (or an equivalent) managing daily operations;

- A full-time professional staff qualified by training and experience to market the 504 program, package and process loan applications, close loans, and service the loans; and
- At least one salaried professional employee who is employed directly by the CDC (not an independent contractor or an associate of an independent contractor) full-time to manage the CDC. Note: CDCs may obtain additional professional services under written contract.

A CDC may petition the SBA to waive the requirement that its manager be employed directly if:

(1) Another nonprofit entity that has the economic development of the CDC's area of operations as one of its principal activities will contribute the management of the CDC; and

(2) The CDC petitioning the SBA for such waiver has insufficient loan volume to justify having management employed directly by the CDC.
   - The SBA must pre-approve professional service contracts with the exception of accounting and legal services.
   - Contracts must clearly identify terms and conditions satisfactory to the SBA.
   - The CDC must provide copies of these contracts to the SBA for review annually.
   - If a CDC's board believes that it is in the best interest of the CDC to contract for professional services, the CDC's board must explain its reasoning to the SBA.
   - No contractor or associate of a contractor may be a voting or non-voting member of the CDC's board.

Financial Ability to Operate—13 CFR § 120.825

A CDC must be able to sustain its operations continuously, with reliable sources of funds (such as income from services rendered and contributions from government or other sponsors). Any funds generated from 504 loan activity by a CDC remaining after payment of staff and overhead expenses must be retained by the CDC as a reserve for future operations or for investment in other local economic development activity in its area of operations.

SBA Form 1246 Application

A CDC must submit SBA Form 1246 in order to obtain certification. This form can be obtained from the SBA's website at www.sba.gov or from any SBA office.

Documents to Be Included with Application

- Listing of those persons/entities organized by membership groups;
- Listing of the board of directors organized by membership groups and accompanied by SBA Form 1081 (Statement of Personal History);
- Plan of operation, which is a narrative describing the applicant's ability to package, process, and service the loans. The plan should state the applicant's financial and legal capacity, explain how it plans to market the 504 program, and identify the geographic area it plans to serve;
- An organizational chart;
- Listing of all officers and paid staff of the CDC (including all contracted staff and contractors performing loan packaging, processing, and servicing for the CDC) accompanied by SBA Form 1081 (Statement of Personal History) and fingerprint cards;
- Certificate or Articles of Incorporation;
- Bylaws;
- Board resolution(s) authoring the certification of the economic development company as a CDC; and
- Financial statements and projections demonstrating the CDC's ability to financially operate.

B Corp. Certification

For-profit entities that blend mission with profit objectives may seek B (for Beneficial) Corp. certification through B Lab, a nonprofit, tax-exempt organization that certifies and then audits entities that respect stakeholder and mission-driven concerns. Despite the name, B Corp. certification is not solely limited to corporations. The certification is available to all types of qualifying for-profit entities, such as LLCs (including the low-profit limited liability company, or L³C), LLPs, business corporations, and benefit corporations.[18]

B Corp. status is conferred upon companies that meet a strict set of criteria established and governed by B Lab, but B Corp. branding carries no legal weight.[19]

B Lab Certification Process

B Lab has established criteria that must be satisfied for an entity to attain B Corp. status. Essentially, in order to be considered a B Corp., an entity must have an eye toward corporate social responsibility. This generally includes considering stakeholder interests rather than just shareholder or member interests.

To qualify as a B Corp., an entity must attain a score of 80 out of 200 points on the B Lab's certification test. The factors considered during the certification process are:

- a core commitment to a social purpose, which is embedded in the organizational structure;
- freedom to engage in any legitimate activity in the pursuit of the social purpose;
- equitable distribution of ownership rights and distribution rights among stakeholders;
- equitable compensation of employees, investors, and other stakeholders in proportion to their contributions and risk, subject to

---

18. Although a B Corp. is not itself a form of legal entity and is thus taxed as it was before it earned certification, the city of Philadelphia, creating a financial incentive for sustainable businesses, has passed an ordinance to give 25 B Corps. that are classified as certified sustainable businesses a $4,000 tax credit against the gross receipts portion of the city's business privilege tax for tax years 2012 through 2017. Other cities are expected to offer similar incentives to B Corps. *Philadelphia First City to Offer Green B12 Tax Incentives*, SUSTAINABLE BUSINESS.COM NEWS, December 2009, www.sustainablebusiness.com/index.cm/go/news.display/id/19350.

19. Alissa Mickels, *Beyond Corporate Social Responsibility: Reconciling the Ideals of a For-Benefit Corporation with Director Fiduciary Duties in the U.S. and Europe*, 32 HASTINGS INT'L COMP. L. REV. 271 (2009).

reasonable limitations that protect the ability of the organization to achieve its mission;
- commitment to having a net positive social and environmental impact;
- commitment to full and accurate assessment and reporting of social, environmental, and financial performance;
- limited liability structure so that directors of the organization will not be held personally responsible for the actions of the organization as long as the directors conduct business activity that is consistent with its social purpose and stakeholder obligation;
- ability to accept debt and equity investments as well as tax-deductible donations;
- exemption from certain business taxes; and
- locks on assets that prevent them from being privatized upon terminal events.[20]

These principles—and the general duty to look beyond shareholder or member profits—must be embodied in the governance documents of the entity for it to be certified as a B Corp.[21] (See box on following page.)

One example of a social enterprise that has taken advantage of B Corp. certification is Impact Makers, Inc. This consulting firm is a certified B Corp. that provides professional consulting services that range from information technology services to project management for various companies and health-care institutions. Impact Makers is organized as a non-stock Virginia corporation, does not have equity holders, and is overseen by the secretary of state of Virginia. Importantly, it is not tax-exempt and generates profits from the consulting services provided to its private-sector clients. In fact, Impact Makers seeks to maximize profits from its operations.[22] What qualifies Impact Makers as a B Corp. is that 100 percent of profits, after expenses, taxes, and salaries are paid, are given to

---

20. *Id.* at 281.
21. *Id.*
22. *See* Impact Makers, *Frequently Asked Questions, available at* http://www.impactmakers.org/faq.htm.

> **Using the corporate form as an example, a variation of the following language should be incorporated into the entity's governing documents:**
>
> - "In discharging his or her duties, and in determining what is in the best interests of the Company and its shareholders, a Director or Officer shall consider such factors as the Director or Officer deems relevant, including but not limited to the long-term prospects and interests of the Company and its shareholders, and the social, economic, legal, or other effects of any action on the current and retired employees, the suppliers and customers of the Company or its subsidiaries, and the communities and the society in which the Company or its subsidiaries operate (collectively the 'Stakeholders'), together with the short-term, as well as long-term, interests of its shareholders and the effect of the Company's operations (and its subsidiaries' operations) on the environment and the economy of the state, the region and the nation."
> - "Nothing in this Article/Bylaw, express or implied, is intended to create or shall create or grant any right in or for any person or any cause of action by or for any person."
> - "Notwithstanding the foregoing, any Director or Officer is entitled to rely upon the definition of 'best interests' as set forth above in enforcing his or her rights hereunder and under state law, and such reliance shall not, absent another breach, be construed as a breach of a Director's or Officer's fiduciary duty of care, even in the context of a Change of Control Transaction where, as a result of weighing other Stakeholders' interests, a Director determines to accept an offer, between two competing offers, with a lower price per share."

community partners, who themselves are nonprofit corporations.[23] These partners serve the greater Virginia community and are involved in allowing free medicine and health-care supplies to be delivered to free clinics throughout Virginia. This directive is included in the corporate charter. There are several things to take note of with this example when considering Impact Makers' existence as a certified B Corp.:

- Impact Makers has memorialized its social purpose in its charter.

---

23. *See id.*

This is a critical requirement for B Corp. certification.

- Because profit maximization is the ultimate goal for Impact Makers and because there are no equity holders, there is less chance that management will face liability for not pursuing profits.
- Impact Makers' social purpose is specifically targeted at its surrounding community. This makes it more likely that a court will determine that the actions of the managers, as they relate to its social purposes, are protected by Virginia's constituency statute.

Another example of B Corp. certification is found in CleanFish. CleanFish is organized as a corporate concern that is involved in the buying and selling of seafood. CleanFish serves as a middleman, linking fishermen with other market participants, such as wholesale distributors and restaurants.[24] CleanFish, while creating a fee structure based on what the end-term consumer pays for the fish, ensures that the fishermen in question use sustainable methods to catch and harvest fish. This enterprise, while operating for profit through membership fees collected from fishermen, also keeps the standards of production at an environmentally friendly level. Accordingly, it has been granted B Corp. certification.

*   *   *   *

Thus, securing a certification is one effective way to gain credibility for a social enterprise. Doing so allows the business to connect with consumers more directly by promoting its mission, which will ultimately increase its potential for business success and social impact.

---

24. *See* CleanFish, *Join the CleanFish Alliance!*, available at http://www.cleanfish.com/join.htm.

CHAPTER NINE

To What End?
Measuring the Impact of the Social Enterprise

The performance of profit-driven businesses is measured by cash flows, asset valuation, and statements of income, but the performance—or impact—of social enterprises can be much harder to quantify. Unlike profit-driven ventures, social enterprises are in the business of producing an intangible bottom line: social good. Still, the demand for metrics to evaluate social impact has never been stronger.[1]

Among the constituencies that require appropriate measures of social impacts are these:

- Private foundations, which not only need to guard against jeopardizing investments but also want to ensure that their investments and grants are directed at the most effective social programs.
- Donors, especially those who have a stake in the outcomes the enterprise drives.
- Policy makers and lawmakers who want to ensure that their efforts are spent on the most worthwhile and impactful segments of social enterprise.
- Government budget officials who need to allocate funds among the most worthwhile enterprises.

---

1. Geoff Mulgan, *Measuring Social Values*, STANFORD SOCIAL INNOVATION REV. (Summer 2010), at 38, *available at* http://www.ssireview.org/images/articles/2010SU-Feature_Mulgan.pdf.

- Social investors who yearn for accurate metrics of social impact, analogous to the measure of profit in profit-driven enterprises.[2]
- Most critically, social entrepreneurs themselves, along with their boards and their leaders, who need to make informed decisions about their enterprises based on hard empirical data.

Revisiting the Social Impact Theory: Knowing Where You Are Going

In fact, the savvy social entrepreneur will have gauged the venture's potential for social impact before its launch.[3] The entrepreneur will have concluded that his or her idea for positive social change had the requisite potential to justify the time and money he or she will have committed to organizing and running the social enterprise. This analysis will have relied upon a social impact theory, against which the social entrepreneur can accurately assess the potential impact of the social enterprise.[4]

The social impact theory of a particular enterprise is created by clearly defining the enterprise's intended outcomes and articulating how the enterprise's inputs will produce a sequence of outcomes, both in the short and long term.[5] This essentially calls for the social entrepreneur to conceptualize an outcome, or a series of outcomes, that his or her social enterprise would like to achieve.

Once the desired outcome is matched with the inputs necessary to be considered, the social entrepreneur will begin to have an idea of the enterprise's actual impact. Based on that calculus, the social entrepreneur must consider whether the enterprise should or should not be pursued, based on the allocation of resources necessary to pursue it.[6]

---

2. *Id.*
3. *See supra* Chapter 2.
4. *See id.*
5. Ayse Guclu et al., *The Process of Social Entrepreneurship: Creating Opportunities Worthy of Serious Pursuit,* CENTER FOR THE ADVANCEMENT OF SOCIAL ENTREPRENEURSHIP, at 7 (2002); *see supra* Chapter 2.
6. *See supra* Chapter 2.

Performance Measurement

Root Cause (www.rootcause.org), a nonprofit research and consulting firm, has published a guide to performance measurement that social enterprises may find helpful in evaluating their success.[7] Root Cause's model of a performance measurement system is a cycle that starts with an organization's mission, vision of success, activities, and operations.[8] From there, the organization should do the following:

1. **Measure:** track its performance using selected indicators,
2. **Report:** communicate its performance both within the organization and to outsiders.
3. **Learn:** use the report to make decisions and identify ways in which the organization can improve.
4. **Improve:** implement decisions to improve activities and operations.[9]

More specifically, Root Cause describes a five-step process that an organization can follow to build a performance measurement system:

1. **Planning to measure.** The organization should form a performance measurement working group, which should include anyone who will be critical to getting the performance measurement system running, as well as the organization's leader and key program staff.[10] The organization should also conduct a performance measurement audit to determine what indicators the organization is already tracking, how and when such indicators are being tracked, how the data is stored, how and to whom the data is reported, and how the data is being reviewed and used.[11]
2. **Choosing what to measure.** The organization should choose the indicators that it will use to track its progress in carrying out its rnission.[12] Root Cause describes three types of indicators: (1) *orga-*

7. Andrew Wolk et al., Building a Performance Measurement System: Using Data to Accelerate Social Impact (Root Cause 2009).
8. *Id.* at 5.
9. *Id.* at 5-6.
10. *Id.* at 11.
11. *Id.* at 11-12.
12. *Id.* at 15.

nizational health indicators—such us statistics describing the organization's cash flow and budgeting, the number of staff members, and the percentage of milestones the organization has met or goals it has achieved; (2) *program performance indicators*—such as measurements of the activities the organization is conducting, the short-term results of those activities, the cost of those activities, and the quality of those activities; and (3) *social and economic impact indicators*—such as measurements of the long-term progress of the organization in meeting its goals and achieving desired social impacts.[13] Once the organization determines what indicators it will track, it should compile a master indicator list to check off which indicators are being tracked and whether those indicators should be reported based on particular activities or with respect to the entire organization.[14]

3. **Determining how to measure.** The organization should determine how it will measure each of the indicators it seeks to take into consideration.[15] In many cases, particularly with regard to social and economic impact indicators, this may require the organization to conduct a survey.[16] In some cases, the data that an organization wishes to measure may be difficult to acquire. For example, an organization may want to determine the number of low-income people participating in its activities, yet may not want to require its participants to disclose their household income. In such a case, the organization may instead choose to ask participants for their zip codes instead, and then use census data to determine how many of the participants are residents of low-income zip code areas.[17] The organization must also determine how to store the data collected, such as in a spreadsheet or a standardized or customized database.[18]

4. **Preparing to use the data.** The organization should create "dashboards" for reviewing data and drawing conclusions.[19] These dash-

---

13. *Id.* at 15-19.
14. *Id.* at 27.
15. *Id.* at 31.
16. *Id.* at 32.
17. *Id.* at 34.
18. *Id.* at 35.
19. *Id.* at 37.

boards should display a focused selection of indicators drawn from the master indicator list.[20] For each indicator, the current result should be displayed along with a baseline (the initial measurement for that indicator) and a target (the organizations goal for that indicator).[21]

5. **Putting the performance measurement system into action.** It is possible that the organization may be unable at first to measure all of the indicators it wants to measure. However, it should start analyzing the data available to it and add other indicators as they become available.[22] The organization should update its baselines and targets as appropriate.[23] The organization may refine its performance measurement system to add new indicators if necessary or remove indicators that are no longer believed to be useful, but such changes should be kept to a minimum so that the organization will be able to collect consistent data over an extended period of time.[24] Once the organization has completed a few measurement cycles, it should begin to report relevant data to outside stakeholders by means of a report card.[25]

Creating a Universal Method of Measuring Social Impact and Ultimate Value

While one can measure the financial performance of a social enterprise in ways that can be summarized in dollar amounts—such as revenues, expenses, assets, and liabilities—measuring its social performance is less intuitive and more challenging.

The IRIS Model

Several social enterprises and socially conscious investors have joined forces in recent years to develop the Impact Reporting and Investment Standards (IRIS) (http://iris.thegiin.org/). This is a joint effort by the Acumen Fund

---

20. *Id.* at 37-38.
21. *Id.* at 38.
22. *Id.* at 55.
23. *Id.* at 55-56.
24. *Id.* at 56.
25. *Id.* at 57.

(www.acumenfund.org), B Lab (www.bcorporation.net), the Rockefeller Foundation (www.rockefellerfoundation.org), and Deloitte (www.deloitte. com), and consists of an evolving method to measure the impact of a social enterprise that can be used across various sectors.

The goal of the IRIS is to afford stakeholders, investors, government agencies, and those invested in social enterprise an accurate method of knowing which social enterprises have the greatest impact and, thus, the highest value. At its core, IRIS is an information-gathering and -reporting system that collects and collates data from various social enterprises in various social sectors. Each enterprise that chooses to report to the IRIS data-gathering repository, held by the Global Impact Investing Network, is asked to transmit information that is common to all participating social enterprises, specific to the particular social enterprise, and specific to its social sector. For example, social enterprises involved in education will transmit a certain set of information, while social enterprises involved in microfinance will transmit a different set of information. All of this information is used to create an impact report.

The IRIS framework for measuring social impact consists of three categories of impact measurement indicators, all of which request certain information. Those indicators are the following:[26]

1) Financial Impact Indicators—request information that focuses on past, present, and future financial gains and outputs;

2) Operational Impact Indicators—request information that looks at the organization's policies as they are related to employees and governance of the enterprise; and

3) Product Impact Indicators—request information that looks at the performance and reach of the organization's products and services.

Additionally, there are two categories of descriptor indicators that are used to gather general information about the enterprise and its mission. Those indicators are the following:[27]

1) Organizational Descriptor Indicators—request information describing the organization's mission, operational model/structure, and area of operation; and

---

26. *Available at* http://iris.thegiin.org/.
27. *Id.*

2) Product Descriptor Indicators—request information describing the organization's products, services, and target markets.

The system, which is still growing, should be used as a comparative tool by socially conscious investors and other individuals and organizations looking to find the right social enterprise in which to invest. For our purposes, social enterprises may want to rely on the IRIS data-gathering and - reporting system to see where they stand among their peers in achieving social impact.

It is important to understand that IRIS is not a self-contained valuation system; rather, it provides the impact measurement tools to create these systems. B Lab, discussed in Chapter 8 and responsible for B Corp. certification, is in the process of using the IRIS system to create a rating system for social enterprises in which B Lab would rate the impact of the social enterprise.[28] This rating system could, in turn, create informational shortcuts for consumers and investors and be used as a component of the valuation process. Additionally, IRIS could be used to create socially responsible investing models[29] used by investment managers and other financial professionals.

Feeding the Social Enterprise's Information into the IRIS Data Repository

A social enterprise that chooses to place data in the IRIS data repository will be able to do so based on the indicators on which it chooses to report. Based on the data imputed, an impact report will be generated. Impact reports can then be accessed by other social enterprises, and by investors or their intermediaries, for comparative purposes. Social impact can then be translated into value. Ultimate value is subjective, so how each social investor may read or interpret particular indicators will not necessarily be the same. The IRIS standard, while creating a system through which ultimate value may be measured, does not assign a specific value to any participating social enterprise.

---

28. *Available at* http://iris.thegiin.org/.
29. *See generally* Marc J. Lane, Profitable Socially Responsible Investing? An Institutional Investor's Guide (Institutional Investor Books 2005)

How IRIS Indicators Measure Impact

Each indicator category will request information that is general to all reporting enterprises, as well as information that is specific to a particular reporting enterprise. All of the information gathered from the indicators is then used to generate an impact report. The following example, taken from the IRIS website,[30] demonstrates how the IRIS system is applied to a fictitious social enterprise to generate an impact report. Note that the example has consolidated some of the information requested from each indicator.

---

30. *Available at* http://iris.thegiin.org/report/banco-si.

Banco Si

Banco Si is a microfinance[31] institution operating out of Peru that offers small loans, mostly to women (clients), for its clients to create sustainable businesses. It also offers savings accounts and other financial products, such as insurance. Operating in both urban and rural areas, it also provides job traning and education opporunties for the communities and clients that its serves.

The left side of each chart represents the information requested from the enterprise and the right side represents the information submitted by the enterprise.

Organizational Descriptor Indicators

Name of Organization:	Banco Si
Year Found:	2001
Type of Financial Institution:	NBFI/NBFC
Mission Statement:	To provide financial services to urban and rural poor, allowing them to create self-sustaining businesses and accrue savings

Product Descriptor Indicators:
Microcredit Products

Product/Service Type:	Financial services
Product/Service Description:	Small micro loans intended to spur the creation of small sustaining businesses
Target Beneficiary:	Women (although not exclusively)
Socioeconomic State of Beneficiary:	Poor (below poverty line)
Area of Operation:	Peru, South America
Microfinance Method:	Group lending
Interest Rate:	40% with a declining balance method
Small Business Services Offered:	Workshops and skill development on starting and running small businesses

---

31. *See supra* Chapter 1.

Non-microfinance services offered:	Women empowerment seminars, youth education, health services, other services

Financial Impact Measurement Indicators: *Income Statement*	
Earned Revenue:	+$21,500,000
Financial Revenue:	+$19,800,000
Contributed Revenue:	+$450,000
Interest Expense:	-$4,950,000
Impartment Loss:	-$920,00
Financial Expense:	-$5,910,00
Operating Expense:	-$10,400,000

Operational Impact Measurement Indicators *Governance and Policies*	
Number of Full-Time Employees:	531
Social Performance Training and Management Programs for Employees:	Yes
Social Performance Incentives for Employees:	Yes
Facilitating Communication with Clients:	- Mechanisms are in place to handle client complaints;
	- Acceptable and unacceptable collection practices are clearly spelled out in various company policies;
	- All staff have been instructed on how to communicate in a nontechnical manner so clients understand their rights and obligations;

| | - Price, terms, and conditions of all financial products are disclosed to clients prior to sale; |
| | - Loan approval does not rely solely on the existence of sureties and other guarantors, but also on the ability of the clients to repay the loans. |

Product Impact Measurement Indicators *Microcredit Products*	
Loan Portfolio—Outstanding	
Value of Investments	$43,000,000
Total Clients	90,219
Clients: Female	62,156
Clients: Poor	19,470
Clients: Very Poor	20,000
Communities served	173
Effective Interest Rate	40.5%

As should be evident from the microfinance example above, indicators will request information that is specific to the social enterprise. All information compiled will be used to generate an impact report.

A breakdown of each indicator category, including all information requested in each category, is available on the IRIS website at http://iris.thegiin.org/.

Center for What Works Model

The Center for What Works (www.whatworks.org) is a nonprofit organization that has aimed its efforts at creating impact measurement tools for social enterprises and other nonprofits, and for those interested in funding them. The Center has created a benchmarking framework to measure and evaluate the impact of social enterprises based on isolating desired outcomes and indicators of success for social enterprises. A list of desired outcomes has been developed along with a list of outcome indicators to assess whether or not a particular outcome of the social enterprise has a sufficient impact.[32] In the Center for What Works model, each sector of social enterprise (14 are tracked) has its own specific desired outcomes and indicators of outcome success, which, taken together, can be used to assess the impact of the enterprise.[33] The social entrepreneur looking to adequately measure the impact of the social enterprise should consult the material located at http://whatworks.org/displaycommon.cfm?an=4. Below is a generalized list of desired outcomes and indicators of success, based on different aspects of operation, which the social entrepreneur may consider when he or she begins assessing impact.[34] (Not all of these desired outcomes will be applicable to all social enterprises.)

32. *Available at* http://whatworks.org/displaycommon.cfm?an=4.

33. *Id.*

34. The following table is based on the *Nonprofit Taxonomy of Outcomes* found in THE CENTER FOR WHAT WORKS, THE NONPROFIT TAXONOMY OF OUTCOMES: CREATING A COMMON LANGUAGE FOR THE SECTOR (December 2006), at 3–6, *available at* http://www.urban.org/center/met/projects/upload/taxonomy_of_outcomes.pdf.

Program-Centered Outcomes and Indicators

Desired Outcomes	Indicators of Success/Impact
Striving to reach a large number of target constituents of services or programs	Percentage of target constituency aware of services or programs
	Percentage of constituency enrolled in the programs
	Percentage of constituency that actually participate in the programs (including overall rates of attendance, attendance rates at specific events, subscription rates, number of subscriptions to services offered)
	Percentage of services offered for below cost or at no charge
Striving for continued constituent engagement	Percentage of constituency that continue with the program after initial experience
	Percentage of constituency that use multiple services and offerings
	Percentage of constituency that return to receive further services
Striving to have a reputation of success in the particular social sector	Number of favorable reviews
	Number/size of other social enterprises that partner with the social enterprise
	If constituency is polled, the number that are satisfied with the program and its results, noting that their needs were met
Striving for high graduation and completion rates for those enrolled in social programs	Percentage who successfully complete the program
	Average length of time it takes for a participant to complete the program.

Participant/Constituency-Centered Outcomes and Indicators

Desired Outcomes	Indicators of Success/Impact
Striving to increase the skill set of individuals who participate in education and social programs	Increase in test scores for participants
	Percentage of participants who move to the next levels of the program
	Improvement in aptitude of participants as reported by parents, co-workers, etc.
	Percentage of participants who are qualified for employment after graduating from the program
Striving to reduce incidents of crime and drug abuse	Reduced incidence rates by participants of the program
	Reduced rates of relapse
	Passage of time since new incidents or relapse
	Percentage of participants who do not reenter the program
Striving to better the economic condition of participants	Percentage who find employment after participating in social programs
	Percentage who retain employment after participating in social programs
	Percentage who move into long-term housing after the program
	Percentage who choose to move on to higher education
Striving to improve the health of the participant	Percentage of participants with reduced incidences of health problems
	Percentage with immediate positive responses
	Percentage with positive responses 120 days out

Community/Environmentally-Centered Outcomes and Indicators

Desired Outcomes	Indicators of Success/Impact
Striving to increase awareness about environmental or community issues	Percentage of target constituents that are aware of issues
	Actual number of individuals reached through communications Number of legislative and law-making contacts (percentage of lawmakers who are aware of the issues)
Striving to increase public health and safety	Percentage of public aware of the issues
	Percentage of public willing to take precautions to cure the issues
	Percentage of public actually taking steps to cure the issues
	Actual measurable results of environmental conservation
	Decrease in crime and increase in crime prevention in certain areas

The Gates Foundation and Actionable Measurement

The Bill and Melinda Gates Foundation (www.gatesfoundation.org), a private foundation set up to improve the health and stability of populations in developing countries as well as the education system in the United States, has developed its own method of valuation through its actionable measurement model of valuation, which looks to several variables, including impact. As a private foundation, the Gates Foundation is subject to minimum distribution requirements as prescribed by the Internal Revenue Code.[35] Accordingly, the foundation is involved in the process of making grants, contributions, and investments in other charitable organizations and in social enterprises. The actionable measurement model has

---

35. I.R.C. § 4942.

been developed to determine the success of the foundation itself by analyzing its overall strategies and investment decisions. The Gates Foundation defines this model as a "measurement [model] with the potential to be
acted upon, or is designed with action in mind."[36] The success of the foundation is measured at the strategy stage, the initiative stage, and the grant-
making stage.[37] The model is ultimately based on a hierarchy of results,
ranging from inputs to impacts, with inputs eventually leading to impacts:[38]

Inputs	→ Activities	→ Outputs	→ Outcomes	→ Impact
The resources used by the foundation and grantees to implement activities	The process taken to achieve outputs	The direct result of an activity	Intermediate, measurable results and changes that result from activities	Ultimate sustainable change

Success at the strategy stage can be quantified by the long-term results
that come from the actions of the Gates Foundation as well as actions of its
grantees and investees. At this level, sheer outcome rather than actual impact is the measurement of success—for example, tracking the level of vaccinations (outcomes) throughout the world rather than the effect of the
vaccinations on mortality rates (actual impact).[39] Nevertheless, where impact can be identified, it should be accounted for. The purpose of measuring success at this level is to help revise the overall goals and general aims of
the foundation.

Success at the initiative stage can be quantified by the progress actually
made toward the foundation's intended target levels of impact.[40] At this
level, the success of the Gates Foundation is measured through the close
tracking of grants and program-related investments made by the foundation.[41] Common indicators of target impact for a particular initiative are

---

36. The Bill and Melinda Gates Foundation, A Guide to Actionable Measurement (2010), *available at* http://www.gatesfoundation.org/learning/Documents/
guide-to-actionable-measurement.pdf.
37. *Id.*
38. *See id.*
39. *Id.*
40. *Id.*
41. *Id.*

developed with grantees that look to specific inputs, activities, outputs, and outcomes of grants. Grantees are asked to report on these indicators. All the information collected from grant-making for a particular initiative will be analyzed by the foundation to evaluate target impact.

Success at the grant stage can be quantified by the efficiency found in the grant-making process as measured by the tracking of inputs, activities, outputs, and outcomes from grants (collectively, "results").[42] The foundation identifies a clear set of results to be accrued from each grant and then ensures that these results are aligned with the specific initiatives that the grant is meant to fund. After the grant is made, the efficiency of the grant-making (or investment) process can be evaluated by asking the grantee for a report on the results of the grant-making during specific critical moments during the lifetime of a grant. These progress reports should be submitted by grantees from time to time. The foundation will not ask the grantees for a measurement of impact through this reporting process. The purpose of measuring success at this stage is to allow the foundation to make decisions about renewal requests and inform decisions about future grant-making to similar grantees.[43]

Finally, all stages of measuring the success of the foundation will be interwoven so that the Gates Foundation can accurately gauge the success of its overall strategy, its initiatives, and its grant-making activities. Although this method was created specifically for the Gates Foundation, it may be useful for the social entrepreneur when trying to craft his or her own valuation technique.

Supply and Demand Model: Looking to Value without Direct Reference to Social Impact

Over the course of the past 100 years or so, modern economics has developed a unifying concept in judging value. How something is valued is not based on an ultimate truth or principle, but on how much value people assign to it based on the concept of supply and demand. Several commentators have tried to apply this simple concept to the complex field of social

---

42. *Id.*
43. *Id.*

enterprise valuation.[44] Using supply and demand as a predictive tool is not as informative as one might hope, because the demand side of the equation varies based on social need. Still, a supply-and-demand method can be an effective tool for gauging the current value of a social enterprise.

One simple, unifying way of determining the value of a social enterprise is through comparing effective demand with effective supply.[45] Effective demand is what someone is willing to pay for a particular service or outcome produced by the social enterprise. Effective supply means that the service or outcome can be implemented, is affordable, and works (in that order).[46] The key to assessing value is to see if the social enterprise provides services that people are willing to fund, as investors and donors, or use, as a consumers of the services, and then to see if the services can be adequately provided.

Take a program aimed at curing substance abuse in lower-income communities. If investors and funders are lining up to pay for the outcome of the program—and indigents are willing and able to the use the program—then there is adequate effective demand for the program. If the social enterprise running the program is able to provide initiatives that adequately address the problem to the point that the demand is met, there is adequate effective supply. Adequately meeting supply may require fragmenting the different tasks among various programs (such as drug counseling, education programs, and health care).[47] Measuring adequate demand requires that the social entrepreneur recognize that the social enterprise's programs may be attractive to multiple and diverse groups who want to see the same outcomes.

The closer the social enterprise is to matching effective demand with effective supply, the more valuable the social enterprise is. Although the underlying analysis can be complex, how to measure the sum of the supply-and-demand equation is fairly simple. If there is excess demand, the social enterprise is not running efficiently or simply does not have the tools

---

44. Geoff Mulgan, *Measuring Social Values*, STANFORD SOCIAL INNOVATION REV. (Summer 2010), at 38, 42, *available at* http://www.ssireview.org/images/articles/2010SU-Feature_Mulgan.pdf (developing the concept of effective supply and effective demand in the social enterprise setting); *see also* C.J. Barrow, *Social Impact Assessment: An Introduction*, Cabinet Office, London (2009).

45. Geoff Mulgan, *supra* note 44.

46. *Id.* at 42.

47. *Id.* at 42.

to meet the demand adequately. If there is excess supply, there is inadequate demand. In both cases, the social enterprise may not be achieving its true value or may be incapable of achieving a value necessary for its continuing operation. The social enterprise must be attractive enough to investors and contributors—and useful enough to its consumers—that there is a reason for its continuing existence.

The Importance of Measuring Social Impact

It is important that social entrepreneurs discover an effective method for measuring the impact that their enterprises are having—and will have—on society. Where hard numbers may not be adequate predictors or measures of success, the task of measurement can be difficult. Still, measuring social impact should be a goal of the social entrepreneur: if social impact isn't reliably measured, it surely won't be valued by the stakeholders on which the venture depends and to whom it is accountable.

Bibliography

Primary Sources

Table of Cases

Baron v. Strawbridge & Clothier, 646 F. Supp. 690 (E.D. Pa. 1986)

Brehm v. Eisner, 746 A.2d 244, 263 (Del. 2000)

Britt v. United States, 431 F.2d 227 (5th Cir. 1970)

Business Bureau of Washington, D.C. v. United States, 326 U.S. 279 (1945)

In re Caremark Derivative Litigation, 698 A.2d 959 (Del. Ch. 1996)

Cede & Co. v. Technicolor, 663 A.2d 1156 (Del. 1995)

Commissioner v. Bollinger, 485 U.S. 340 (1988)

Driver v. Producers Cooperative Inc., 345 S.W.2d 16 (Ark. 1961)

Edwin's Inc. v. United States, 501 F.2d 675 (7th Cir. 1974)

Eldridge v. Tymshare, Inc., 230 Cal. Rptr. 815 (Ct. App. 1986)

Eurich v. Korean Foundation, Inc., 176 N.E.2d 692 (Ill. App. Ct. 1961)

Ferris Elevator Co, Inc. v. Neffco, Inc. 674 N.E.2d 448 (Ill. App. Ct. 1996)

Gaillard v. Natomas Co., 256 Cal. Rptr. 702 (Ct. App. 1989)

Gantler v. Stephens, 965 A.2d 695 (Del. 2009)

Guth v. Loft Inc., 5 A.2d 503 (Del. 1930)

Iowa Cooperative v. Schewe, 149 F. Supp. 2d 709 (N.D. Iowa 2001)

Johnston v. Greene, 121 A.2d 919 (Del. Ch. 1956)

Jones Bros. Bakery, Inc. v. United States, 411 F.2d 1282 (Ct. Cl. 1969)

Kamin v. American Express Co., 383 N.Y.S.2d 807 (Sup. Ct. 1976)

Krivo Industrial Supply Co. v. Nat'l Distillers & Chemical Corp., 483 F.2d 1098 (5th Cir. 1970)

Levandusky v. One Fifth Avenue Apartment Corp., 553 N.E. 2d 1321 (N.Y. 1990)

Levien v. Sinclair Oil, 261 A.2d 911 (Del. Ch. 1966)

Lewis v. Vogelstein, 699 A.2d 327 (Del. Ch. 1997)

Mile-o-Mo Fishing Club, Inc. v. Noble, 210 N.E.2d 12 (Ill. App. Ct. 1965)

Miller v. American Tel. & Tel. Co, 507 F.2d 759 (3d Cir. 1974)

Miller & Son Drywall, Inc v. Commissioner, 89 T.C. 1279 (2005)

National Foundation, Inc. v. United States, 13 Cl. Ct. 486 (1987)

Nursing Home Building Corp. v. DeHart, 535 P.2d 137 (Wash. Ct. App. 1975)

Puget Sound Plywood, Inc. v. Commissioner, 44 T.C. 305 (1965)

Revlon v. MacAndrews & Forbes Holdings Inc., 506 A.2d 173 (Del. 1986)

SEC v. Edwards, 540 U.S. 389 (2003)

SEC v. Ralston Purina Co., 346 U.S. 119 (1953)

SEC v. W.J. Howey Co., 328 U.S. 293 (1946)

S.H. & Helen R. Scheuer Family Found. v. 61 Assocs., 582 N.Y.S.2d 662 (App. Div. 1992)

Smith v. Van Gorkom, 488 A.2d 858 (Del. 1985)

Stern v. Lucy Webb Hayes National Training School, 381 F. Supp. 1003 (D.C. Cir. 1974)

Summers v. Cherokee Children & Family Servs., 112 S.W.3d 486 (Tenn. Ct. App. 2002)

Unocal Corp. v. Mesa Petroleum Co., 493 A.2d 946 (Del. 1985)

Walling v. Portland Terminal Co., 330 U.S. 148 (1947)

Weinberger v. UOP, Inc., 457 A.2d 701 (Del. 1983)

Administrative and Legislative Materials

H. Rep. 104-506, 104th Cong., 2d Sess. 56 (1996)

IRS, Election Year Activities and the Prohibition on Politial Campaign Intervention for Scetion501(c)(3) Organizations, F.S.-2006-17, February 2006

IRS Gen. Couns. Mem. 38459 (July 31, 1980)

IRS Gen. Couns. Mem. 39326 (Jan. 17, 1985)

IRS Gen. Couns. Mem. 39598 (Feb. 4, 1987)

IRS Gen. Couns. Mem. 39862 (Dec. 2, 1991)

IRS Priv. Ltr. Rul. 9130002 (Mar. 19, 1991)

IRS Priv. Ltr. Rul. 199938041 (Sept. 27, 1999)

IRS Priv. Ltr. Rul. 200132040 (Aug. 13, 2001)

IRS Priv. Ltr. Rul. 200326035 (June 27, 2003)

IRS Priv. Ltr. Rul. 200603031 (Jan. 20, 2006)

IRS Priv. Ltr. Rul. 200610020 (Mar. 10, 2006)

IRS Rev. Rul. 68-484, 1968-2 C.B. 105

IRS Rev. Rul. 69-316, 1969-1 C.B. 263

IRS Rev. Rul. 74-390, 1974-2 C.B. 331

IRS Rev. Rul. 80-106, 1980-1 C.B. 113

IRS Rev. Rul. 81-178, 1981-2 C.B. 135

IRS Rev. Rul. 98-15, 1998-1 C.B. 718

Secondary Sources

Jerr Boschee, *Eight Basic Principles for Nonprofit Entrepreneurs*, NONPROFIT WORLD, July/Aug. 2001, at 15, *at* http://www.community-wealth.org/_pdfs/articles-publications/social/article-boschee.pdf.

W. Derrick Britt et al., *Frequently Asked Questions: Proposed Amendments to the California Corporations Code for a New Corporate Form: The Flexible Purpose Corporation,* California Working Group for New Corporate Forms (Jan. 5, 2010), *at* http://www.primakers.net.

The Center for What Works, *The Nonprofit Taxonomy of Outcomes: Creating a Common Language for the Sector* (last updated Dec. 2006), *at* http://www.urban.org/center/met/projects/upload/taxonomy_of_outcomes.pdf.

Dorsey & Whitney, *Wisconsin Adopts Second Cooperative Statute: The Wisconsin Cooperative Associations Act* (last updated Mar. 2007) *at* http://www.dorsey.com/agribusiness_news_mar_2007/.

Douglas Fee & Allan C. Hoberg, *Potential Liability of Directors of Agricultural Cooperatives*, 37 ARK. L. REV. 60 (1983).

Daniel Fischel & Frank Easterbrook, *Corporate Control Transactions*, 91 YALE L.J. 698 (1982).

James J. Fishman, *Improving Charitable Accountability*, 62 MD. L. REV. 218 (2003).

Bill & Melinda Gates Foundation, *Program-Related Investments: Leveraging Our Resources to Catalyze Broader Support for Our Mission* (last visited Oct. 4, 2010), *at* http://www.gatesfoundation.org/about/Pages/program-related-investments-faq.aspx.

General Principles and Problems of Cooperatives: An Introduction, 1954 WIS. L. REV. 533.

Suzanne K. Golden, *Board of Directors' Fiduciary Duties: Are They Compromised in Agricultural Cooperatives?*, 10 SAN JOAQUIN AGRIC. L. REV. 201 (2000).

Harvey J. Goldschmid, *The Fiduciary Duties of Nonprofit Directors and Officers: Paradoxes, Problems, and Proposed Reforms*, 23 J. CORP. L. 631 (1998).

Ayse Guclu et al., *The Process of Social Entrepreneurship: Creating Opportunities Worthy of Serious Pursuit*, Center for the Advancement of Social Entrepreneurship (November 2002).

Terry Lynn Helge, *Policing the Good Guys: Regulation of the Charitable Sector Through a Federal Charity Board*, 19 CORNELL J.L. & PUB. POL'Y 1 (2009).

Bruce R. Hopkins, *Planning Guide for the Law of Tax-Exempt Organizations* (John Wiley & Sons, Inc. 2007).

R. William Ide, *Post-Enron Corporate Governance Opportunities: Creating a Culture of Greater Board Collaboration and Oversight*, 54 MERCER L. REV. 829 (2003).

Marc J. Lane, *Advising Entrepreneurs: Dynamic Strategies for Financial Growth* (John Wiley & Sons, Inc. 2001).

Marc J. Lane, *Legal Handbook for Nonprofit Organizations* (Amacom 1981).

Marc J. Lane, *Legal Handbook for Small Business* (Amacom, rev. ed. 1989).

Marc J. Lane, *Profitable Socially Responsible Investing? An Institutional Investor's Guide* (Institutional Investor Books 2005).

Marc J. Lane, *Representing Corporate Officers, Directors, Managers, and Trustees* (Aspen Publishers, 2d ed. 2010).

David T. Leibell, *Gates Embraces Philanthro-capitalism*, TRUSTSANDESTATES.COM, Dec. 30, 2009, *at* http://trustsandestates.com/wealth_watch/gates-foundation-venture-philanthropy1230/.

Letter from Stuart M. Lewis, Chair, Section of Taxation, American Bar Association, to Commissioner of the Internal Revenue Service, Re: Comments on Proposed Additional Examples of Program-Related Investments (Mar. 3, 2010), *at* http://www.abanet.org/tax/pubpolicy/2010/Comments_Concerning_ Proposed_Additional_ Examples_ on_Program_Related_Investments.pdf.

Elisabeth Mattsson, *Social Economy and New Cooperatives Create Jobs?*, COPAC Open Forum, *at* http://www.copacgva.org/about/2000/cecop-text.pdf.

Alissa Mickels, *Beyond Corporate Social Responsibility: Reconciling the Ideals of a For-Benefit Corporation with Director Fiduciary Duties in the U.S. and Europe*, 32 HASTINGS INT'L COMP. L. REV. 271 (2009).

Elizabeth Carrott Minnigh, *Low-Profit Limited Liability Companies: An Unlikely Marriage of For-Profit Entities and Private Foundation*, TAX MANAGEMENT, ESTATE, GIFTS, AND TRUST JOURNAL, September 2010, at 1, *at* http://www.americansforcommunitydevelopment.org/downloads/MinnighL3CCompaniesArticle.pdf.

Lawrence E. Mitchell, *A Theoretical and Practical Framework for Enforcing Corporate Constituency Statutes*, 70 TEX. L. REV. 579 (1992).

Mosher & Wagenmaker, LLC, *Not-for-Profit Directors' and Officers' Responsibilities* (last visited Oct. 4, 2010), *at* http://www.mosherlaw.com/featuredarticles.htm.

Geoff Mulgan, *Measuring Social Values*, STANFORD SOCIAL INNOVATION REV., Summer 2010, at 38, *at* http://www.ssireview.org/images/articles/2010SU-Feature_Mulgan.pdf.

Jennifer Mullen, *Performance-Based Corporate Philanthropy: How "Giving Smart" Can Further Corporate Goals*, PUBLIC RELATIONS QUARTERLY, June 1997 at 42.

Jane Nober, *Fiscal Agent versus Financial Sponsor*, FOUNDATION NEWS AND COMMENTARY, Nov./Dec. 2004, *at* http://www.foundationnews.org/CME/article.cfm?ID=3069.

Eric Otis, *Beyond Shareholders: Interpreting Corporate Constituency Statutes*, 61 GEO. WASH. L. REV. 14 (1996).

Ronald L. Perl, *Legal Standards by Which Community Association Boards Are Judged*, NEW JERSEY LAWYER, Oct. 2006, at 41.

Katherine J. Sedo, *The Application of Securities Laws to Cooperatives: A Call for Equal Treatment for Nonagricultural Cooperatives*, 46 DRAKE L. REV. 259, 261 (1997).

Social Enterprise Alliance, *Social Enterprise: A Powerful Engine for Economic and Social Development* (last visited Oct. 4, 2010), *at* http://www.sageglobal.org/files/pdf/social-enterprise-white-paper.pdf.

Tom Stearns, *Slow Money Seeks to Fund Vermont's 21st Century Healthy Food System* (last visited Oct. 4, 2010), *at* http://www.slowmoneyvermont.com/img/nofavt_slowmoney.pdf.

Fay Twersky et al., *The Bill and Melinda Gates Foundation, A Guide to Actionable Measurement* (2010), *at* http://www.gatesfoundation.org/learning/Documents/guide-to-actionable-measurement.pdf.

Robert A. Wexler, *Effective Social Enterprise—A Menu of Legal Structures*, 63 EXEMPT ORG. TAX REV. 565 (2009).

John Winward, *The Organized Consumer and Consumer Information Co-operatives, in* THE AUTHORITY OF THE CONSUMER 76–77 (Russell Keat et al. eds., 1994).

Muhammad Yunus, *Building Social Business: The New Kind of Capitalism That Serves Humanity's Most Pressing Needs*, PUBLIC AFFAIRS (2010).

Social Enterprises and Related Organizations

The following is a list of all social enterprises and related organizations mentioned in this book, along with their web addresses.

33 Needs (33needs.com)
A Safe Haven (www.asafehaven.com)
Aavishkaar (www.aavishkaar.in)
ACCESS Community Capital Fund (www.accessccf.com)
The Acumen Fund (www.acumenfund.org)
The Adventure Project (theadventureproject.org)
Agora Partnerships (www.agorapartnerships.org)
Appropriate Infrastructure Development Group (www.aidg.org)
Ashoka (ashoka.org)
The Awesome Foundation (awesomefoundation.org)
B Lab (www.bcorporation.net)

Bamboo Finance (www.bamboofinance.com)
Benetech (www.benetech.org)
Better World Books (www.betterworldbooks.com)
BigBelly Solar (www.bigbellysolar.com)
Big Tree Organic Farms (www.bigtreeorganic.com)
Big Issue Invest (www.bigissueinvest.com)
The Bill and Melinda Gates Foundation (www.gatesfoundation.org).
Blue Ridge Foundation New York (www.brfny.org)
The Calvert Foundation (www.calvertfoundation.org)
CauseVox (www.causevox.com)
CEI Ventures (www.ceiventures.com)
The Center for What Works (www.whatworks.org)
Changents (changents.com)
Chase Community Giving (www.facebook.com/ChaseCommunityGiving)
Chinook Fund (www.chinookfund.org)
City Light Capital (www.citylightcap.com)
CleanFish (www.cleanfish.com)
The Clinton Foundation (www.clintonfoundation.org)
The Community Development Venture Capital Alliance (www.cdvca.org)
The Co-operative Group (www.co-operative.coop)
Corporation for National and Community Service Social Innovation Fund
     (www.nationalservice.gov)
CraftNetwork (www.craftnetwork.com)
Crowdrise (www.crowdrise.com)
C. V. Starr Social Entrepreneurship Fellowship (swearercenter.brown.edu)
CyberAngels (www.cyberangels.org)
Dartmouth College Class of 1982 Upper Valley Social Entrepreneurship
     Fellowship (www.dartmouth.edu/~tucker/)
Do Something (www.dosomething.org)
DonorsChoose.org (www.donorschoose.org)
Draper Richards Kaplan Foundation (www.draperrichards.org)
Echoing Green (www.echoinggreen.org)
Endeavor Global (www.endeavor.org)
Expansion Capital Partners (www.expansioncapital.com)
Fair Trade Labeling Organizations International (FLO) (www.fairtrade.net)
Fair Trade USA (www.transfairusa.org)
FirstGiving (www.firstgiving.com)0

The Ford Foundation (www.fordfoundation.org)
Foundation Center (foundationcenter.org)
Fundsnet Services (www.fundsnetservices.com)
Future For Kids (www.f4k.org)
The Global Fund (www.theglobalfund.org/en)
GlobalGiving (www.globalgiving.org)
Global Social Entrepreneurship Competition (www.foster.washington.edu)
Global Social Venture Competition (www.gsvc.org)
Good Capital (www.goodcap.net)
GoodCompany Ventures (www.goodcompanyventures.org)
Google Grants (www.google.com/grants/)
Grameen Bank (www.grameenfoundation.org)
Grand Challenges in Global Health (www.grandchallenges.org)
Grantmakers for Effective Organizations (www.geofunders.org)
Grants.gov (www.grants.gov)
Gray Ghost Ventures (www.grayghostventures.com)
The Greyston Foundation (www.greyston.org)
Guardian Angels (www.theglobalfund.org/en)
Guayaki (www.guayaki.com)
Harborquest, Inc. (www.harborquest.com)
Harvard Business School Social Entrepreneurship Fellowship
    (www.hbs.edu)
Humanity Fund (www.humanityfund.com)
IGNIA (www.ignia.com.mx)
Impact Makers (www.impactmakers.org)
IndieGoGo (www.indiegogo.com)
International Co-operative Alliance (www.ica.coop)
Investors' Circle (www.investorscircle.net)
Jasmine Social Investments (www.jasmine.org.nz)
Jobs for Youth (www.jfychicago.org)
The John D. and Catherine T. MacArthur Foundation (www.macfound.org)
Joshua Venture Group (joshuaventuregroup.org)
Juma Ventures (www.jumaventures.org)
Kauffman Foundation (www.kauffman.org)
Kickstarter (www.kickstarter.com)
Kiva (www.kiva.org)
Land O'Lakes, Inc. (www.landolakes.com)

Manhattan Institute Social Entrepreneurship Initiative (www.manhattan-institute.org)

Materials Matter (www.materialsmatter.org)

MicroPlace (www.microplace.com)

Milken Family Foundation Social Entrepreneur Internship Program at Tulane University (tulane.edu/cps/)

Mission Markets (www.missionmarkets.com)

The Mulago Foundation (mulagofoundation.org)

Network for Good (www1.networkforgood.org)

New Cycle Capital (www.newcyclecapital.com)

New Profit Inc. (www.newprofit.com)

New Resource Bank (www.newresourcebank.com)

New Ventures (www.new-ventures.org)

New York University Reynolds Program in Social Entrepreneurship (www.nyu.edu/reynolds)

Next Street Financial LLC (www.nextstreet.com)

Nonprofit Finance Fund (nonprofitfinancefund.org)

Nonprofits Assistance Fund (www.nonprofitsassistancefund.org)

NYC Seed (www.nycseed.com)

Omidyar Network (www.omidyar.com)

Open Books (www.open-books.org)

Pacific Community Ventures (www.pcvfund.com)

The Paradigm Project (www.theparadigmproject.org)

Partners for the Common Good (www.pcgloanfund.org)

Pepsi Refresh Project (www.refresheverything.com)

Philanthropy New York (www.philanthropynewyork.org)

Pipeline Fund (pipelinefund.tumblr.com)

PledgeBank (www.pledgebank.com)

PopTech (www.poptech.org)

PresenTense Group Social Entrepreneur Fellowship (presentense.org)

Presumed Abundance (www.presumedabundance.com)

Profounder (www.profounder.com)

Rainer Arnhold Fellows (rainerfellows.org)

Razoo (www.razoo.com)

REDF (www.redf.org)

Renewal2 Investment Fund (renewal2.ca)

The Rockefeller Foundation (www.rockefellerfoundation.org)

RocketHub (rockethub.com)
Root Capital (www.rootcapital.org)
RSF Financial (www.rsfsocialfinance.org)
Satori Capital (www.satori-capital.com)
Schwab Foundation for Social Entrepreneurship (www.schwabfound.org)
Shared Interest Society (www.shared-interest.com)
SJF Ventures (www.sjfventures.com)
Skoll Foundation (www.skollfoundation.org)
Slow Money (www.slowmoney.org)
SME Finance Innovation Fund (www.changemakers.com)
Social Capital Partners (www.socialcapitalpartners.ca)
Social Enterprise Fund (socialenterprisefund.ca)
Social Impact Exchange (www.socialimpactexchange.org)
Social Innovators Collective (www.socialinnovatorscollective.org)
SocialReturns (www.socialreturns.org)
Sparkseed (www.sparkseed.org)
The StartingBloc Fellowship (startingbloc.org)
StartSomeGood (startsomegood.com)
Stonyfield Farms (www.stonyfield.com)
TakeAction@GuideStar (www2.guidestar.org/)
TBL Capital (www.tblcapital.com)
TechnoServe (www.technoserve.org)
TED Fellows (www.ted.com)
Thrust Fund (www.thrustfund.com)
TOMS Shoes (www.toms.com)
Triodos Bank (www.triodos.co.uk)
Underdog Ventures (www2.underdogventures.com)
Union Square Ventures (www.usv.com)
United Prosperity (www.unitedprosperity.org)
UnLtd Advantage (unltdadvantage.org.uk)
Unreasonable Institute (unreasonableinstitute.org)
U.S. Small Business Administration (www.sba.gov)
USA.gov for Nonprofits (www.usa.gov/Business/Nonprofit.shtml)
VentureWell (www.venturewell.org)
Village Capital (www.vilcap.com)
Vox Capital (www.voxcapital.com.br)
Wainwright Bank (www.wainwrightbank.com)

Wharton Social Enterprise Fellows (wlp.wharton.upenn.edu)
Wisconsin Women's Business Initiative Corporation (www.wwbic.com)
The Women's Bean Project (www.womensbeanproject.com)
The Young Foundation (www.youngfoundation.org)
ZeroDivide (www.zerodivide.org)

Glossary

Actionable measurement model
A method of measuring the grant-making or investment success of a private foundation by looking at overall donation and investment strategies in three stages: the initial strategy stage, the initiative stage, and the grant-making stage. The system is based on a hierarchy of results that range from inputs to impacts.

B Corporation
A certification issued by B Lab, an independent IRC § 501(c)(3) organization, which is bestowed upon businesses that are formed to solve social and/or environmental problems. Certified B Corporations must operate and be governed in a manner that allows the company to achieve comprehensive and transparent social and environmental performance standards. See http://www.bcorporation.net/.

Benefit corporation
A legal entity recognized in two states, Maryland and Vermont, which requires the directors and officers to take into account certain social purposes through the governance of the corporation.

C corporation
A legal business form in the United States that, for federal income tax purposes, is taxed under Subchapter C of the Internal Revenue Code. A C corporation is a separate legal entity apart from its owners (shareholders). The net income of a C corporation is subject to double taxation at both the

corporate level and the shareholder level upon the issuance of dividend distributions.

Cause-related marketing
A marketing strategy whereby a for-profit business organization markets and promotes a nonprofit organization's cause in an effort to produce mutual benefits for both organizations.

CDC (Certified Economic Development Company)
An economic development company that has undergone the certification process dictated by the Small Business Administration (SBA), thereby making it an eligible participant in the SBA loan program and enabling the CDC to provide federally backed financing to small and developing businesses within a particular geographic area.

CDFI Fund (Community Development Financial Institutions Fund)
A program of the U.S. Department of the Treasury to assist community development financial institutions (i.e., loan funds, banks, credit unions, and venture capital funds) that serve low-income people and communities that would otherwise lack access to affordable financial services.

CFDA (Catalog of Federal Domestic Assistance)
The Catalog of Federal Domestic Assistance is a compilation of all federal programs, projects, services, and activities administered by the federal government that provide assistance or benefits to the American public.

Chinese wall
A method of separating a manager from a transaction between two business entities when that manager owes conflicting fiduciary duties to both.

Consumer-side cooperative
A legal entity that provides services to members, thereby giving them greater purchasing power when purchasing products and services.

Corporate social responsibility
A method of running a for-profit business organization in which certain social and environmental issues are considered and factored into the day-to-day management and operations of the business.

Cost-benefit/cost-effective analysis
An analysis that considers the cost-effectiveness of various alternatives to determine whether the benefits of a certain action or inaction outweigh the costs.

CRA (Community Reinvestment Act)
Title VIII of the Housing and Community Development Act of 1977. This federal law was enacted with the intent of ensuring that banks satisfy the lending needs of the areas in which they operate, including low- to moderate-income communities.

Disqualified person
Any person who was in a position to exercise substantial control or influence over the affairs of a tax-exempt organization at any time within a five-year period prior to an alleged excess benefit transaction.

Disregarded entity
A business entity that is disregarded for federal tax purposes and not treated as a separate entity apart from its owners.

Earned revenue strategies
Any business strategy by which a tax-exempt organization engages in business activities and generates income. Income earned through an earned revenue strategy is distinguishable from income generated through charitable solicitations and resulting charitable contributions.

Economic development company
A company that has been organized with the authority to promote and assist the growth of small businesses in a particular geographic area.

Endorsement
The utilization of one organization's intellectual property (name, logos, etc.) by another organization in connection with that organization's distribution, sale, advertising, and/or promotion of merchandise or services. The endorsement is effectuated through a contractual licensing arrangement. Payments made to a nonprofit, tax-exempt entity for the use of its intellectual property, if characterized as royalties under IRC § 512(b), are not classified as unrelated business taxable income.

Excess benefit transaction
An excess benefit transaction occurs when an economic benefit is provided by a tax-exempt organization directly or indirectly to or for the use of any disqualified person if the value of the economic benefit provided by the tax-exempt organization exceeds the consideration (including the performance of services) received for providing the benefit.

Expenditure responsibility
The requirement under IRC § 4945(h) by which a private foundation is responsible to exert all reasonable efforts and establish adequate procedures to ensure that the funds expended by the private foundation are being used for their legitimate purpose. The responsibility is met by obtaining reports detailing how the funds were utilized and making such reports available to the IRS for inspection.

FINRA (Financial Industry Regulatory Authority)
A quasi-governmental body, overseen and empowered by the Securities and Exchange Commission (SEC), that regulates financial marketplaces (securities exchanges) and financial professionals interacting with those marketplaces.

Flexible purpose corporation
A hybrid entity form currently being considered by the California legislature that requires corporate fiduciaries to consider certain social concerns when operating the corporation.

FLO (Fair Trade Labeling Organizations International)
A collection of 24 organizations headquartered in Bonn, Germany, that sets standards for the certification of fair trade organizations.

Fund manager
A director, officer, or trustee (or an individual with powers similar to a director, officer, or trustee) of a sponsoring organization that has been delegated control over donor-advised fund assets.

Hybrid business entity
A business formed under state statute that operates and is governed in a manner that permits the pursuit of profit while addressing social problems. The most common examples of hybrid business entities are the low-profit limited liability company (L^{3}C) and the benefit corporation.

Hybrid structuring
Structuring affiliated for-profit and tax-exempt organizations in a manner that permits the most effective utilization of each entity's capabilities in an effort to advance a social purpose.

Insider
In respect to the general prohibition against private inurement in the governance of tax-exempt enterprises, "insider" refers to any individual who has a relationship with a tax-exempt organization that allows him or her to exercise control over the organization or its assets.

Intermediate sanctions
Penalties imposed upon nonprofit organizations and individuals who engage in transactions that cause assets to improperly inure to the benefit of a person or affiliated entity. Intermediate sanctions may range from monetary penalties to possible revocation of tax-exempt status.

L³C (low-profit limited liability company)
A legal form of doing business that requires operation with a significant purpose of advancing a charitable or educational purpose while earning a profit or permitting capital appreciation as a secondary motive. L³Cs are prohibited from engaging in political or legislative activities.

IRIS (Impact Reporting and Investment Standards)
A data-gathering system that provides a method of measuring an organization's social impact by analyzing metrics and other indicators to provide a basis for performance reporting.

Jeopardizing investment
A questionable investment made by a private foundation that might jeopardize its tax-exempt purpose due to the lack of care and prudence of foundation managers in making the investment. Jeopardizing Investments are not considered qualifying distributions.

Microcredit
Providing credit in relatively small dollar amounts to poor and underserved populations throughout the world to induce the creation of sustainable businesses to alleviate poverty. The concept of providing microcredit was originally conceived by Muhammad Yunus.

Microfinance
In conjunction with microcredit transactions, this refers to providing broader financial services and products to poor and underserved populations, such as savings accounts and insurance coverage.

MRI (mission-related investment)
The investment of a foundation's assets in opportunities that pursue the foundation's organizational mission, the primary purpose of which may be financial return on the investment.

Multi-stakeholder cooperative
A cooperative that is owned and democratically controlled by multiple stakeholders (e.g., groups of workers, producers, consumers, or members of a particular community) bound together for a common purpose.

NASCO (National Association of State Charity Officials)
An association of state offices charged with oversight of charitable organizations and charitable solicitations in the United States.

Pay-for-success bond
Also known as *social impact bond*, a financing arrangement in which a government agency contracts with a private-sector bond issuing organization to achieve a specific social outcome. The bond issuing organization raises funds from private investors and uses those funds to contract with service providers to provide social services intended to achieve the social outcome. Only if the social outcome is achieved does the government agency pay the bond issuing organization and thus enable the private investors to recoup their investments and earn a profit.

PRI (program-related investment)
Direct debt and/or equity investments made by a private foundation that are presumptively considered qualifying distributions in satisfaction of the foundation's annual distribution requirement under IRC § 4942. PRIs are an exception to jeopardizing investments.

Private benefit rule
The tax doctrine that charitable organizations, which must operate primarily for exempt purposes, may not be operated for private ends. When considering transactions with a charity's "insiders," the less-forgiving "private inurement" rule applies.

Private placement memorandum
A disclosure document that contains select offering and company information that may be provided to investors during a private placement of securities under § 4(2) of the Securities Act of 1933.

Producer-side cooperative
A cooperative that serves its members by providing marketing services, supply chain services, and other services as needed. Membership is made up of producers and manufacturers of goods.

Qualifying distribution
The annual distribution of assets made by a private foundation that are distributed for the purposes described in IRC § 4942.

Qualifying sponsorship payments
Payments to a tax-exempt organization by a person engaged in a trade or business when there is no arrangement or expectation that the payer will receive a "substantial return benefit" in exchange for the payment other than the use or acknowledgment of the name or logo (or product lines) of the payer's trade or business in connection with the tax-exempt organization's activities.

SBA
Small Business Association.

SEC
Securities and Exchange Commission.

Small business
For the purposes of establishing the existence of an economic development company, under the Small Business Act, this term refers to a business that is independently owned and operated and is not dominant in its field of operation.

Social impact theory
A method of measuring the potential social impact of a social enterprise by analyzing the desired outcome of the enterprise and considering all inputs necessary for achieving it.

Sponsorship income
Income earned by a tax-exempt organization in exchange for the acknowledgment of another company/sponsor's name, logo, and/or product lines in connection with the activities or events of the tax-exempt organization.

Sponsoring organization
The nonprofit, tax-exempt organization that holds, maintains, operates, and at all times has legal control over the assets and operations of a donor-advised fund.

Socially responsible investment
An investment made under a broad-based investment strategy that takes into account not only financial returns generated, but also non-financial and societal benefits that may be achieved as part of the overall return on investment.

Triple-benefit corporation
A hybrid legal form of entity currently under consideration by the Michigan legislature. This corporate form would require fiduciaries to consider both profit-driven and mission-driven purposes. If legislation is enacted, a triple-benefit corporation would be run primarily for the promotion of charitable or educational purposes, with the production of income as a secondary purpose.

UBIT (unrelated business income tax)
A federal tax levied against tax-exempt organizations on their unrelated business taxable income.

UBTI (unrelated business taxable income)
Income generated by a tax-exempt entity as a result of engaging in a trade or business that is regularly carried on and is not substantially related to the purposes for which tax exemption was granted to the organization.

Venture philanthropy
An investment practice that utilizes proven venture capital models to make investments in organizations that have the purpose of achieving philanthropic goals.

Index

A

accreditation of social enterprises
203–06
 Center for Social Enterprise Accreditation, standards of 203–06
 Social Enterprise Alliance, standards
of 203
actionable measurement model of
valuation 237–39
 grant stage success 239
 investment decisions, analysis of
238
 initiative stage success 238
 results, hierarchy of 238
 strategies, analysis of 238
 strategy stage success 238
Acumen Fund 13, 189–90
 Impact Reporting and Investment
Standards (IRIS) model, development of 227
 patient capital 189–90
  defined 190
  use of 189
 transformative businesses, creation
of 189
 WaterHealth International
investment in 190
Allen, William 126
American Bar Association, Section of
Taxation
 program-related investments,
examples of 168
American Recovery and Reinvention
Act of 2009
 compensation, for-profit entities,
application to 143

Anderson, Beth Battle 21
associations, unincorporated nonprofit
83–87
 IRS provisions for 83
 managers, duties of 87
 members, duties of 87
 Revised Uniform Unincorporated
Nonprofit Association Act 85
 tax exemption requirements 86
 Uniform Unincorporated Nonprofit
Association Act
  application to 84

B

B Corp. certification 12–13. *Also see*
B Lab certification process
 for-profit entities, eligibility of 12
 requirements for 12
B Lab. *Also see* B Lab certification
process
 B Lab, defined 217
 Impact Reporting and Investment
Standards (IRIS) model 228–29
  development of 228
  use in creating social enterprise
rating system 229
B Lab certification process 217–20
 certification test 218
  key factors 218–19
 corporate social responsibility,
importance of 218
 governance document requirements
220
 granting of certification 221
 profits, looking beyond 219

bad faith
    business corporations 124
    nonprofit directors and officers 72
Ben & Jerry's Homemade, Inc. 48
benefit corporations, certification of.
    See B Lab certification process
benefit corporations 2, 9, 26, 43–48
    annual benefit report 46–47
    authorization for 43–44
    benefit director 46–47
        appointment of 46
        independence requirement for
        46
        responsibilities of 46
        statement by, requirement for
        47
    capital sources for 43
    creation of 9
    directors of 45–48
        immunity issues 48
        standards of conduct for 45–46
    distributions from 43
    general public benefit 44
    governance of 43
    liquidation of 43
    management of 43
    motives of 11
    permitted profit motives of 26
    philanthropic donors, appeal to 26
    public benefits, impact on business
    11
    specific public benefits 44
    state approval of 11, 43–44
    tax considerations 43
    third-party standard for 45
    Vermont requirements for 47
benefit corporations, governance of
    127–29
    duty of care 129
    duty of loyalty 129
    fiduciary duty issues 128–29
    management of 128
    ownership of 128
    social enterprise, advantages to 128

    socially beneficial factors, consider-
    ation of 127
    tax status of 128
        C Corporation 128
        S Corporation 128
Benetech 1
Better Business Bureau recommenda-
    tions regarding cause-related
    marketing 174
Better World Books 1
BigBelly Solar 22–23
branding appeal
    low-profit limited liability company,
    advantages for 42
Bugg-Levine, Anthony 195
Building for the Future program
    purpose of 181
Bureau of Labor Statistics
    volunteerism survey 27
business corporations, governance of
    119–27. *Also see* business
    judgment rule; loyalty, duty of,
    business corporations
    fiduciary duty issues 120–21
        returns, maximization of 120
        shareholder responsibilities
        121
    management of 120
    ownership of 120
    shareholder concerns, consideration
    of 119–20
    social entrepreneurs, concerns for
    119
    tax status of 120
        C corporations 120
        S corporations 120
business judgment protection 73
    nonprofit directors and officers 73
business judgment rule 68–69
    application to nonprofit entities 68
    business judgment presumption
        business corporations, applica-
        tion to 121

compensation, for-profit entities, application to 141
cooperatives, application to 61
corporations, presumption of validity, application of 119
nonprofit directors and officers, application to 69
purpose of 69
business plans 20
focus of 20
legal form options 20
market research for 20
mission statement, development of 20

C

C corporations, benefit corporations as 128
Calvert Foundation 14
capital, accessing 163–64
expected financial returns, consideration of 163
sources of 163
care, duty of, benefit corporations 129
care, duty of, business corporations 125–26
business decisions, focus on 125
intrinsic fairness test 127
Model Business Corporation Act, application to 125
ordinary negligence issues 125
procedural due care issues 125–26
reasonable person standard, application of 125
waste issues 126–27
care, duty of, nonprofit directors and officers 75–77
decision-making process, application to 75–77
jurisdiction standards of care, application to 75
reliance on counsel, allowance for 75

reporting requirements, awareness of 76
requirements of 75
wasting of corporate assets 77–78
Catalog of Federal Domestic Assistance 180, 185
cause-related marketing 173–75
benefits of 175
Better Business Bureau recommendations regarding 174
charity benefits, disclosure of 174
defined 173
forms of 174
opportunity provided by 173
research regarding, advisability of 175
sponsorship, differentiation from 175
Center for Social Enterprise Accreditation, certification standards of 203
Center for What Works 233–34
desired outcomes, selection of 234
outcome indicators, list of 234
certification of social enterprises 203–06. *Also see* certifications, Fair Trade Movement; economic development companies, certification of; green companies, certification of
accreditation, standards for 203–06
advantages of 203
privileges of 203
Social Enterprise Alliance certification standards 192-93 203–04
certifications, Fair Trade Movement 206–08. *Also see* Fair Trade Labeling Organizations International
CraftNetwork, purpose 207
developing countries, focus of 206
fair trade standards, raising awareness of 207
Fair Trade USA 207

Guayaki, purpose of 207
purpose of 206
sustainability, promotion of 206
trading conditions, improvement of
    206
charitable donations
government restrictions on 25
grants and contributions 165
    donor substantiation require-
        ments 165
tax-exempt entities, receipt of 66
charitable organizations. *Also see*
    Illinois Charitable Trust Act;
    Illinois Solicitation for Charity
    Act; Maryland Solicitation Act;
    New York's charitable solicitation
    laws
compliance failures, consequences
    of 101
private inurement, prohibitions
    against 88
registration of 25
state laws regarding 101–10
    state-specific registration
        requirements 105–10
Civic Staffing L³C 2
Clayton Act 55
CleanFish 221
Co-operative Group 57
Cohen, Ben 48
commercial reasonableness 90
compensation for nonprofit officers
    and directors 90
outside expert use in determining
    90
standard of 90
Commodity Futures Trading Commis-
    sion regulations for compensa-
    tion, for-profit entities 143
Community Advantage program 183
application process for 183
loans made, uses for 183
purpose of 183–84

Small Business Administration,
    management of 183
Community Development Financial
    Institutions Fund 180–81
activities of 181
Building for the Future program,
    purpose of 181
financial assistance awards, form of
    181
New Markets Tax Credits program
    181
purpose of 180
compensation, for-profit entities 141–
    44
applicable legislation 143
    American Recovery and
        Reinvention Act of 2009 143
    Dodd-Frank Wall Street Reform
        and Consumer Protection Act
        143
    Emergency Economic Stabili-
        zation Act of 2008 143
    Investment Company Act of
        1940 143
    Sarbanes-Oxley Act of 2002
        143
    Securities Exchange Act of
        1934 143
business judgment protection,
    application of 141
conflicts of interest, avoidance of
    142–43
due care considerations 141–42
key issues to consider 142
procedures for setting, correctness of
    142
compensation, nonprofit officers and
    directors 91–95
compensation, defined 91
key questions regarding 95
reasonableness of, determining 91–
    92
conflicted transactions
private inurement, potential for 73

conflicts of interests
  addressing 80–81
  disclosure duties regarding 80
  existence of, determining 80
  financial interest, defined 79
  interested person, defined 79
  IRS sample policy for 79–83
  loyalty, duty of, nonprofit directors
    and officers 69
  loyalty, duty of, business corpora-
    tions 123–24
  policies, violations of 81
constituency statutes, for-profit
    entities 13, 137–40
  advantages provided to social
    enterprises 139
  change-of-control transactions 137
  duties, specification of 138
  interpretation of 137
  legal issues raised by 138–39
  liability issues 140
  nonshareholder stakeholder con-
    cerns, consideration 13
  purpose of 13
  scope of 137
  stakeholder, definition, importance
    of 137
  takeovers, application to 137
Control Data Corporation 8
cooperatives 53–57. *Also see* coopera-
    tives, governance of
  consumer 57
  defined 53
  fair business practices, assurance of
    56
  fair labor practices, assurance of 56
  federal taxation issues 59–60
    characteristics, required 59
    IRS classification of 59
  formation issues 58–59
  laws applicable to 58–59
  multistakeholder 57
  principles of 54
  producer 55–57

Rochford Principles, guidance for
    53
  social needs, response to 53
  values of 54
cooperatives, governance of 60–63
  board of directors 61
    membership restrictions 61
  business judgment rule, application
    to 61
  conflicted transactions 62
    self-dealing, avoidance of 62
  duty of care 62
  duty of loyalty 62
  duty of obedience 63
  fundamental duties 60
  membership fees 61
  non-stock enterprises 61
  stock enterprises 61
corporate opportunity, usurping
  loyalty, duty of, business corpora-
    tion, breach of 122
  loyalty, duty of, nonprofit directors
    and officers 70–72
corporate social responsibility, defined
    3
Corporation for National and Commu-
    nity Service 189
  purpose of 189
  Social Innovation Fund, creation of
    189
corporations, tax-exempt subsidiaries
    as 148–52
  benefits of 148
    liability, shareholder shield
      from 148
  boards of directors, interlocking
    150
  bona fide business purpose, need for
    151
  control issues 151–52
  directives, conflicts between 151
  double taxation, potential for 149
  revenue as dividend, benefits of
    149

separate entity requirements 149–50

tax exemption, protection of 149

unrelated business taxable income, avoidance of 148

CraftNetwork, purpose of 207

Cramer, Geoff 21

CyberAngels 21

D

Dees, Gregory 21

Deloitte

Impact Reporting and Investment Standards (IRIS) model, development of 228

Department of Labor requirements regarding volunteerism 28

Department of the Treasury

Community Development Financial Institutions Fund 180

disadvantaged people

defined 5

social enterprise mission focus on 5

Dodd-Frank Wall Street Reform and Consumer Protection Act

compensation, for-profit entities, application to 143

E

Early-Stage Innovation Fund, purpose of 184

earned revenue 5–8

defined 5

entity choices, social enterprise 6

nonprofit, tax-exempt entities growing reliance on 8

strategies for social enterprise 5–6

eco-friendly claims, FTC warnings about 208

economic development companies 182–83, 212–17

certification of 212–17

qualifications for 213

Small Business Association

assistance from, eligibility for 212

Small Business Investment Act, economic development company, defined 212

importance of 182

loans made, uses for 182–83

purpose of 182

Emergency Economic Stabilization Act of 2008 143

compensation, for-profit entities, application to 143

endorsements 177–78

intellectual property, use of 177

licensing agreements 177

private inurement rules, application of 178

royalties, payment classification as 177

unrelated business taxable income, avoidance of 178

entity structure, choice of 24–28. *Also see* hybrid entities; resource conservation; tax-exempt entities

for-profit businesses, advantages of 24

excess benefit rules 94

charities, application to 94

social welfare organizations, application to 94

excess benefit transactions 92–94

compensation, application to 94

determining 92

founding members/management, impact on 92

intermediate sanctions, IRS invocation of 94

management's personal liability for 92–94

private inurement restrictions on 92

rebuttable presumptions, application to 93

repeated offenses 93
excess business holdings rules 171
private foundation investments,
application to 171
excise tax, application to excess
benefit transactions 94
expenditure test, application to
lobbying activities, nonprofit
entities 100

F

Fair Labor Standards Act requirements
for volunteerism 28
Fair Trade Labeling Organizations
International 206–07
fair trade certification standards
establishment of 206
products covered 206–07
verification provisions 206
international fair trade standards,
setting of 206
mission of 206
Fair Trade Movement. _See_ certifications, Fair Trade Movement
Fair Trade USA 207–08
Farm Credit System 181–82
Farm Credit Administration,
oversight by 182
Farm Credit system-wide debt
securities, sale of 182
Federal Farm Credit Banks Funding
Corporation, fiscal agent of 182
goal of 182
philanthropic contributions of 182
Federal Deposit Insurance Company
compensation, for-profit entities,
regulations for 143
Federal Farm Credit Banks Funding
Corporation 182
Investor Relations Program, manage-
ment of 182
federal securities law, compliance with
185–87

anti-fraud provisions, impact of 186
disclosure requirements 186
documentation requirements 186
Investment Advisors Act 185
Investment Company Act 185
preemption of state laws 187
reporting requirements 186
Securities Exchange Act 185–86
applicability to social enterprises 185
registration requirements,
exemption from 185
Federal Trade Commission warnings
about eco-friendly claims 208
Green Guides, revisions to 208
feeder social enterprises fund distribution activities 188
Financial Industry Regulatory Authority 193
security exchange compliance with
10
socially conscious companies,
listing of 14
Fiscal Sponsor Directory 179
fiscal sponsorship 178–79
administrative support services,
providing 178
benefits of 179
contractual agreements covering
179
direct capacity-building assistance,
providing 178
financial management services,
providing 178
Fiscal Sponsor Directory, content of
179
growing popularity of 179
IRS requirements for 178
project incubation assistance,
providing 178
services, categories of 178
technical assistance, providing 178
flexible purpose corporations 12, 49–
52

annual report requirements 50
classification as, requirements for
  49
performance evaluation requirements 50–51
profit motives, consideration of 12
proposal for creation of 49
purposes of 12, 50
social interests, pursuit of 12
special purpose MD&A, requirements for 50–51
flow-through entities, tax-exempt
  subsidiaries as 152–55
activities, IRS consideration of 152
co-investor options 152
control, consideration of 154–55
internal operation, IRS concerns
  regarding 153–54
IRS rulings regarding 154
liability protection provisions 152
options for 152
private inurement issues 153
sole owner option 152
unrelated business taxable income
  issues 153
for-profit entities
B Corp. certification, eligibility for
  12
challenges facing 9
collaboration with nonprofit entities
  26
constituency statutes, impact on 13
hybrid entities as 31
profit motive, importance of 9
socially responsible corporate
  practices, implementation of 9
structured with nonprofit organizations 89
for-profit entities, governance of. *See*
  benefit corporations, governance
  of; business corporations,
  governance of; compensation,
  for-profit entities; constituency
  statutes, for-profit entities;

limited liability companies,
  governance of; low-profit limited
  liability companies, governance
  of
for-profit subsidiaries of nonprofit
  entities. *See* multi-organizational
  structures
Ford Foundation 170
Foundation Center 28
fraud
business corporation, potential for
  123
nonprofit directors and officers,
  consequences of 72
funding networks 187
feeder social enterprises, funding of
  188
fund distribution considerations
  188
pooling funds, intent of 188
purpose of 188
Roberts Enterprise Development
  Fund 188
RSF Financial 188
Slow Money 188
funding sources for social enterprises
  197–200
banks and loan providers 199
crowdfunding sites 199
fellowships 200
grants 200
student fellowships 201
venture capital 197
funds, pooling of, social enterprises
  188
Fuqua School of Business 21
Futures for Kids 21

G

Gates Foundation, Bill and Melinda
  31–32, 170. *Also see* actionable
  measurement model of valuation

Global Impact Investing Network
  Impact Reporting and Investment
  Standards (IRIS) model
    data gathering for 228
good faith
  nonprofit directors and officers,
    requirements for 72
governmental support for social
  enterprises. *Also see* Community
    Advantage; Community Develop-
    ment Financial Institutions Fund;
    economic development compa-
    nies; Startup America; United
    Farm Credit System
  applying for, requirements 180
  benefits for agency, determining
    180
  cutbacks, impact of 22
  positive social values, promotion of
    22
  sources of 180, 185
    *Catalog of Federal Domestic
      Assistance* 180, 185
Grameen Bank 1, 4
grants and contributions 164–67
  attractiveness of 164
    unrequired repayment 164
    unrequired financial return 164
  categories of 165
  contingency pledges 164
  expected returns for 164–65
  forms of 164
  program-related investments 164–
    67
  restrictions on 165
  sources for 164
  substantiation for donor require-
    ments for 165–66
grants
  government, tax-exempt entities,
    eligibility for 66
  private foundation, tax-exempt
    entities, eligibility for 66

green companies, certification of 208
  eco-friendly claims, warnings about
    208
  Federal Trade Commission revision
    of *Green Guide* 208
  third-party certifications, substantia-
    tion of 208
Greenfield, Jerry 48
Greyston Foundation 118
Guardian Angels 21
Guclu, Ayse 21

H

Habitat for Humanity 9
Harborquest, Inc. 2
HIV/AIDS in Africa, efforts to eliminate 174
hybrid entities. *Also see* benefit
  corporations; flexible purpose
  corporations; low-profit limited
  liability companies; Minnesota
  community enhancement
  corporations; program-related
  investments; public benefit
  corporations; triple benefit
  corporations
  for-profit entities, classification as
    31
  motives, options regarding 26
  nonprofit/for-profit collaborations
    26
hybrid structuring models. *Also see*
  benefit corporations; flexible
  purpose corporations; low-profit
  limited liability company; triple
  benefit corporation
  advantages of 9–10
  social enterprises, application to 10

I

Idealist.org 28
Illinois Charitable Trust Act 102–05
  conflicts of interest, regulations
    regarding 104–05

property, obligations regarding 102
registration requirements under 103
reporting requirements under 103
self-dealing, regulations regarding
    104–05
trustee duties under 103
wasting of corporate assets, prohibi-
    tion against 77
Illinois Cooperative Act 58
Illinois Solicitation for Charity Act
    105–06
registration requirements under 105
reporting requirements under 105
solicitation requirements of 105
Impact Investment Fund
purpose of 184
Impact Makers, Inc. 219–21
impact of social enterprises, measur-
    ing. *See* social impact, measure-
    ment of
Impact Reporting and Investment
    Standards (IRIS) model 227–29
comparative tool, use as 229
data, input of 229
descriptor indicators 228
development of 227–28
Global Impact Investing Network
    data repository 228
goal of 228
impact measurement indicators
    228–33
impact reports, generation of 229
rating system for social enterprises,
    use for 229
insiders 89
defined 89
private inurement implications for
    89
intellectual property, payments for. *See*
    endorsements
intermediate sanctions, excess benefit
    transactions, application to 94
Internal Revenue Service

charitable donations, substantiation
    requirements for 165–66
conflicted transactions, procedures
    regarding 69–71
cooperatives, designation for 59
corporations, tax-exempt subsidiar-
    ies as 149–50
endorsements, requirements for 177
excess benefit transactions, regula-
    tions regarding 92–94
expenditure test, application to
    lobbying activities of nonprofit
    entities 100
flow-through entities, rulings
    regarding tax-exempt subsidiaries
    152–54
legislation, definition of 98
low-profit limited liability compa-
    nies, tax requirements for 39
mission-related investments,
    requirements for 172
personnel sharing with for-profit
    subsidiaries, requirements for
    155
Philanthropic Facilitation Act,
    proposed amendments to 38
political activities, nonprofit
    entities, rulings on 96–98
private foundations
    defined 166
    investments, requirements for
    167
private inurement, regulations
    regarding 88
program-related investment rulings
    36–39, 167, 170
substantial part test, application to
    lobbying activities of nonprofit
    entities 100
tax-exempt entities, identification of
    7
tax-exempt status, requirements for
    67

International Co-operative Alliance 53–54
  Statement on the Co-operative Identity 54
intrinsic fairness test
  care, duty of, business corporations, application to 127
  nonprofit, tax-exempt corporations, application to 78
Investment Advisors Act 185
Investment Company Act of 1940 143, 185
  compensation, for-profit entities, application to 143

J

jeopardizing investment rule, application to program-related investments 167
job and career training services as social enterprise mission 5
Johnson & Johnson 9
Juma Ventures 1

L

L³C. *See* low-profit limited liability companies
Land O'Lakes, Inc. 56
Leibowitz, Jon 208
licensing agreements. *See* endorsements
Liebman, Jeffrey B. 196
limited liability companies, governance of 129–34
  duty of care 132
  duty of loyalty 132
  fiduciary duty issues 131–34
    obligations, contracting around 133–34
  good faith issues 132–33
  litigation issues 129
  management of 130
  ownership of 130

pass-through taxation option 129
tax status of 130
Uniform Limited Liability Company Act, application to 131
lobbying activities, nonprofit entities 98–100
  expenditure test for 100
  legislation, IRS definition of 98
  substantial part test for 100
low-profit limited liability companies (L³C) 2, 9, 32–43; 134–37. *Also see* program-related investments
  acceptance for, broadening of 42
  advantages of 33
  authorization of 34
  branding appeal, significance of 42
  capital sources for 32
  charitable contributions, ineligibility for 40
  charitable purposes of 35, 134
  controversy surrounding 41–43
  creation of 9
  distributions of 33
  due diligence issues 42
  duty of care 136
  duty of good faith 136
  duty of loyalty 136
  educational purposes of 35, 134
  fiduciary responsibilities within 40–41, 135–37
    obligations, contracting around 136–37
  for-profit and nonprofit functions, combining 33
  governance of 32
  legislative purposes, lack of 35
  liquidation of 33
  management of 11, 32, 40, 135
  membership, lack of limitation on 40
  ownership of 135
  Paradigm Project, description of 33
  permitted profit motives of 26
  philanthropic donors, appeal to 26

political purposes, lack of 35
positive social change, driving 34
primary focus of 33
private foundation investments,
  access to 170
production of income, no significant
  purpose for 35
resource conservation issues 27
social purpose, requirement for 135
state approval of 35
tax considerations 32, 39–40, 135
loyalty, duty of, benefit corporations
  129
loyalty, duty of, business corporations
  121–24
  bad faith, acts of 124
  breach of 122
  business judgment rule, inapplica-
    bility of 122–23
  conflicts of interest issues 123–24
  corporate opportunity, usurping
    122
  fraud, acts of 123
  illegal acts, commission of 123
  ultra vires liability, potential for
    123
loyalty, duty of, limited liability
  companies 131–32
loyalty, duty of, nonprofit directors
  and officers 69–75. *Also see*
  obedience, duty of, nonprofit
  directors and officers
  bad faith, consequences of 72
  breaches of, tax penalties for 69
  business judgment protection,
    loss of, potential for 73
  conflicts of interest 69–70
  corporate opportunity, usurping
    70–72
  fraud, consequences of 72
  good faith requirements for 72
  illegal actions, consequences of 72
  misappropriation of corporate
    information of 70–72

M

MacArthur Foundation, John D. and
  Catherine T. 170
Maryland Solicitation Act 106
  charitable organization, defined
    106
  registration requirements under 106
  reporting requirements under 107
Materials Matter 2
microfinance agencies
  business funding method 10
  defined 10
Minnesota Community Enhancement
  Corporation Act, purpose of 12
Minnesota community enhancement
  corporations 52
  directors, requirements for 52
  purpose of 52
misappropriation of corporate information, consequences of 70
mission, execution of, social enterprise
  4–5
  disadvantaged people
    defined 5
    focus of 5
  job and career training services 5
  social need, addressing 5
Mission Markets, Inc. 14, 192
  Financial Industry Regulatory
    Authority rules for 193
  mission of 192–93
  Securities and Exchange Commis-
    sion rules, application to 193
  securities exchange, operation of
    192–93
mission-driven entities. *Also see*
  hybrid entities; tax-exempt
  entities
  products and services of, demand for
    29
  social enterprises, conflict with 25
  social-purpose branding, impact of
    29

mission-related investments 3, 171–73
  capital, return on 172
  excise taxes imposition, potential
    for 173
  IRS requirements for 172
  philanthropic foundation contribu-
    tions 172
  purpose of 172
  Revised Model Nonprofit Corpora-
    tion Act, application to 172
  social purposes, promotion of 172
Model Business Corporation Act
  requirements for duty of care,
  business corporations
multi-organizational structures. *Also*
  see corporations, tax-exempt
  subsidiaries as; flow-through
  entities, tax-exempt subsidiaries;
  office sharing with for-profit
  subsidiaries; personnel sharing
  with for-profit subsidiaries;
  private inurement; unrelated
  business taxable income issues
  asset protection advantages of 146
  benefits for social enterprises 145–
    46
  private inurement restrictions 89
  revenue-generating options of 145–
    46
  subsidiaries, legal form of 147–48
    corporate vs. flow-through
      considerations 148
    determination, importance of
      148
    options regarding 148
multiplier effect, program-related
  investments, treatment of 169
multistakeholder cooperatives 57

N

National Association of State Charity
  Officials
  L³C, position regarding 41

Unified Registration Statement,
  development of 109
National Conference of Commissioners on Uniform State Laws
  Uniform Unincorporated Nonprofit
    Association Act, drafting of 84
Native American nations
  low-profit limited liability compa-
    nies, establishment of 34
New Markets tax credits program,
  purpose of 181
New York's charitable solicitation laws
  107–08
  charitable organization, defined
    107
  registration requirement under 108
  reporting requirement under 108
Nike 9
Nonprofit Finance Fund 181
nonprofit officers and directors. *Also*
  see commercial reasonableness;
  compensation, nonprofit officers
  and directors
nonprofit, tax-exempt corporations
  66–78. *Also see* associations,
  unincorporated nonprofit;
  business judgment rule; care,
  duty of, nonprofit directors and
  officer; commercial reasonableness; loyalty, duty of, nonprofit
  directors and officers; political
  activities, nonprofit entities;
  private inurement
  board of directors, duties of 67–68
    fiduciary obligations 67
    obedience 68
    social mission, fulfillment of
      67–68
  derivative suits, potential for 68
  for-profit organizations, structured
    with 89
  intrinsic fairness, application to 78
  membership interests 67
  public interests, service to 67

tax-exempt status, obtaining 67
volunteer labor, issues regarding
    101
nonprofit, tax-exempt entities 7–8
    dwindling support for 8
    earned revenue, growing reliance on
        8
    operating costs, escalation of 8
    prevalence among social enterprise
        entities 11
    section 501(c)(3) organizations,
        purpose of 8
    section 501 requirements for 8
    services, increased demand for 8
    support for 8
Norris, William C. 8

O

Obama administration introduction of
    pay-for-success bonds 193
obedience, duty of, nonprofit directors
    and officers 68, 73–74
    corporate purpose, respect for 73
    loans to officers or directors, issues
        regarding 74
    private inurement 73–74
    tax-exempt status, ensuring 73–74
    ultra vires liability 74–75
Office of the Comptroller of the
    Currency regulations for compen-
    sation for-profit entities 143
office sharing with for-profit subsidiar-
    ies 160
Open Books 2
Organized Crime Control Act 66
    charitable organization exemption
        from 66

P

Paradigm Project 33
pass-through taxation options for
    limited liability companies 129
patient capital 190

Acumen Fund, use of 190
    defined 190
pay-for-success bonds 193–97
    criteria for success of 196–97
    features of 195
    improved social outcomes, goal of
        194
    introduction of 193
    Obama administration support for
        193
    Peterborough Prison project 194–
        95
    Rockefeller Foundation sponsorship
        of 195
    United Kingdom use of 194–96
performance measurement of social
    enterprises. *See* social impact,
    measurement of
personnel sharing with for-profit
    subsidiaries 155–60
    employee benefit plan consider-
        ations 160
    employer, determining, IRS ruling
        on 158–59
    federal employment tax issues
        156, 159
    IRS requirements for 155–56
    key questions regarding 156
    officer issues 157
    wages payment, control of 157
Peterborough Prison project
    pay-for-success bonds, use in 194
Philanthropic Facilitation Act 37–39
    Department of the Treasury regula-
        tions for 39
    drafting of 37
    IRC code amendments within 38
philanthropic foundation fiduciary
    standards for trustees 172
political activities, nonprofit entities
    95–97. *Also see* lobbying
    activities, nonprofit entities
    business activities with political
        intent, prohibition against 98

candidate support, acceptable
actions 96–97
IRS regulations regarding 96–98
political campaign intervention
issues 95–96
promotion of, options for 95
private foundation investments 166.
Also see cause-related marketing;
endorsements; fiscal sponsorship;
mission-related investments;
program-related investments;
socially responsible investments;
sponsorships
debt and/or equity investments from
166
excess business holdings rules,
impact of 171
expenditure responsibility 170
grants, issuance of 167
jeopardizing investment rule,
requirements of 167
low-profit limited liability companies, access to 170–71
private foundations, IRS definition
of 166
program-related investments as
alternatives to grants 169
qualifying distributions requirements for 167
private inurement. *Also see* excess
benefit transactions
charities, regulations regarding 88
compensation, commercial reasonableness of 90
compensation, restrictions on 91
defined 88
endorsements, application to 178
flow-through entities, tax-exempt
subsidiaries as 153
insiders
defined 89
implications for 89
IRS regulations regarding 88
multi-organizational structures,

application to 89–90
nonprofit directors and officers
compensation issues 73–74
producer cooperatives 55–57
program-related investments 31, 36–
41, 166–71
ABA Section of Taxation
examples of, identifying 168
accounting treatment of 169
advantages over grants 169–70
capital investments by private
foundations 36
complexity of 170
creative financing, options for 36
defined 31
examples of 168
favored recipient status, impact of
41
growing appeal of 170–71
Internal Revenue Code provisions
regarding 36
investment strategies employing
36–39
IRS private letter rulings, need for
39
IRS requirements for 37, 167–68
jeopardizing investment rules 167
legislation efforts, prohibitions
against 168
limited risks of 36
market-rate returns of 37
multiplier effect, potential for 169
of private foundations, leverage of
36
Philanthropic Facilitation Act
potential impact of 37
private letter rulings, securing 170
purpose of 31–32, 168
qualification as 36
requirements for 35, 167
Tax Reform Act of 1969, application
to 41
public benefit corporations 52
purpose of 52

public benefits 11
  defined 11
  role in benefit corporations 11

R

"RED" campaign to eliminate
    HIV/AIDS in Africa 174–75
REDF. *See* Roberts Enterprise Devel-
    opment Fund
resource conservation 26–27
  benefit corporation, issues regarding
    27
  low-profit limited liability compa-
    nies, issues regarding 27
  tax-exempt entities, advantages of
    26
  volunteerism
        Department of Labor require-
          ments regarding 28
        Fair Labor Standards Act,
          application to 28
        role in 27–28
        trends toward 27
Revised Model Nonprofit Corporation
    Act 68, 172
  business judgment rule, application
    to nonprofit entities 68
  religious entities, application to 77
  ultra vires liability provisions 75
Revised Uniform Unincorporated
    Nonprofit Association
  associations, unincorporated
    nonprofit, application to 85–86
  provisions of 85–86
Roberts Enterprise Development Fund
    188
  employees of 189
  funding intents 189
  program impact, measurement of
    189
  start-up capital, provision of 189
Rochdale Society of Equitable
    Pioneers 53

Rochford Principles 53
  cooperatives, guidance for 53
Rockefeller Foundation
  Acumen Fund, support of 190
  Impact Reporting and Investment
    Standards (IRIS) model, develop-
    ment of 228
  pay-for-success bonds, sponsorship
    of 195
Root Cause 225
  performance measurement of social
    enterprises, guide for 225
Ross Social Venture Fund, purpose of
    201
RSF Financial 188, 192
Revised Uniform Unincorporated
    Nonprofit Association Act 85–87
  fiduciary requirements of 87

S

S corporation
  benefit corporations as 128
Safe Haven, A 2
Samuel Zell & Robert H. Lurie
    Institute for Entrepreneurial
    Studies 201
Sarbanes-Oxley Act of 2002
  compensation, for-profit entities,
    application to 143
section 501(c)(3) organizations 8
  purpose of 8
  requirements for 8
Securities Act of 1933 185–87
  preemption of state laws, provisions
    for 187
  requirements inapplicable to social
    enterprises 185
Securities and Exchange Commission
  compensation, for-profit entities,
    regulations for 143
  rules of 193
Securities Exchange Act of 1934
  compensation, for-profit entities,
    application to 143

social enterprises requirements 185
securities exchanges 10–15
  federal and state regulation of 10
  social enterprises, securities trading
    of 10
  socially conscious companies,
    listing of 14–15
      Financial Industry Regulatory
        Authority regulation 14
      requirements for listing 14
      SEC requirements for 14
securities, issuance of 185–87. *Also
  see* federal securities law, compliance with
  state securities laws, compliance
    with 187
      federal preemption of 187
      registration requirements,
        exemption from 187
self-sustaining requirement
  social enterprises, funding of 5
Sliwa, Curtis 21
Slow Money 188
  funds, operation of 191
  investments, focus of 191
  mission of 190
  slow money investing, defined
  Soil Trust 192
Small Business Act 182–83
  Community Advantage program,
    creation of 183
  economic development companies,
    authorization of 182
  small business, defined 212
Small Business Administration
  Community Advantage program,
    establishment of 183
  economic development companies,
    relationship to 182
Small Business Association
  assistance from, eligibility for 212
  economic development companies,
    certification of 217

Small Business Investment Act
  economic development companies
    authorization of 182
    certification of 212
Social Enterprise Alliance 4–6
  certification standards of 192-193,
    203–04
  earned revenue strategies for social
    enterprises 5–6
  social enterprise, defined 4
social enterprises
  appeal, growth in 9
  bettering lives of others as basic
    goal 7
  business model, vetting of 18
  challenges for 17
  curing social maladies, goal of 4
  defined 4, 7
  distinguished from social entrepre-
    neurship 6
  earned revenue strategies as
    funding means 5
  hybrid structuring models 10
  impact of, measuring 14
  mission-driven motive of 7
  nonprofit, tax-exempt structures,
    prevalence of 11
  origins of 7
  purpose of 4
  self-sustaining, requirement for 5
  social good trap, danger of 6
  sound business principles, applica-
    tion of 7
  trading of securities 10
  venture philanthropy organiza-
    tions, classification 13
social entrepreneurship as distinguished from social enterprise 6
social good trap as danger to social
  enterprise 6
social impact bonds. *See* pay-for-
  success bonds
social impact, forecasting 23–24
  available inputs, analysis of 23–24

desired outcomes 23–24
    defined 23
    failure to achieve 24
    new research and analysis,
        application to 23
    social reality, testing against
        23
    purpose, testing of 23
social impact, measurement of 224–
    26. *Also see* actionable measure-
    ment model of valuation; Center
    for What Works; Impact Report-
    ing and Investment Standards
    (IRIS) model; performance;
    supply and demand model
    measurement of social enterprises
    guide to 225
    intended outcomes, defined 224
    necessary resources, consideration
        of 224
    process for 225
        choosing what to measure 225
        data, preparation of 226
        determining how to measure
            226
        performance measurement
            system, implementing 227
        planning to measure 225
social impact theory. *See* social
    impact, forecasting
Social Innovation Fund 189
social opportunity, determining
    viability of 19–20. *Also see*
    social impact, forecasting
    key factors 21
    key questions regarding 20
    values, agreeable, identifying 22
social-purpose branding, advantages
    of 29
socially responsible investments 3,
    173
    financial goals of 3
    investment evaluations, key issues
        173

screening procedures for 173
societal benefits, achievement of
    173
Soil Trust 192
    Slow Money establishment of 192
sponsorships 175–77
    objective, promotion of 175
    ordinary taxable income, payments
        as 175
    qualified sponsorship payments
        defined 176
    substantial return benefits 176
    unrelated business taxable income
        issues 175
Startup America 184
    Early-Stage Innovation Fund,
        purpose of 184
    Impact Investment Fund, purpose of
        184
Stonyfield Farms 118
substantial part test for lobbying
    activities of nonprofit entities
    100
supply and demand model 239–41
    effective demand, determining 240
    effective supply, determining 240
    excess demand, impact of 240
    excess supply, impact of 241
    predictive qualities, limitations of
        240
sustainable social needs, identification
    of 22

T

Tax Reform Act of 1969 41
    program-related investments,
        requirements for 41
tax-exempt entities 25–26, 65–66
    advantages of 65–66
        charitable donations to 66
        funding 66
        grants, eligibility for 66
    charitable contributions, restrictions
        on 25

compensation issues for 95
funding opportunities for 25
Organized Crime Control Act
    exemption from 66
qualifying for exemption 73
resource conservation advantages
    26
third-party investment, limitations
    on 25
venture philanthropic organiza-
    tions, funding from 26
taxation issues
    C Corporations
        benefit corporations as 128
        tax status of 120
    cooperatives 59
    limited liability companies
        tax exemption, option for 130
    pass-through taxation options for
        limited liability companies 129
    S corporations
        benefit corporation as 128
        tax status of 120
third-party standard requirement for
    benefit corporations 45
TOMS Shoes 29
triple benefit corporation
    charitable and educational activi-
        ties of 12
    purpose of 52
Trust for Conservation Innovation
    178

U

ultra vires liability
    loyalty, duty of, business corpora-
        tions 123
    obedience, duty of, nonprofit
        directors and office 74–75
Unified Registration Statement 109
    jurisdictions accepting 109
    supplemental forms, requirements
        for 109

Uniform Limited Liability Company
    Act application to limited
    liability companies 131
Uniform Unincorporated Nonprofit
    Association Act application to
    associations, unincorporated
    nonprofit 84–85
    revision of 85
Unilever 48
United Nations Volunteers 28
University of Michigan Ross School of
    Business 201
unrelated business taxable income
    (UBTI) issues
    corporate avoidance of 148
    dividend payments, treatment of 148
    endorsements, avoidance of 178
    flow-through entities, tax-exempt
        subsidiaries as 153
    sponsorships, application to 175
    tax consequences, favorableness of
        147
    tax-exempt corporations, volunteer
        labor, impact on 101
    unfair competition, elimination of
        146–47
    unrelated activities, determining 147

V

Valspar 9
venture philanthropy 188–201. *Also
    see* Acumen Fund; Mission
    Markets; Roberts Enterprise
    Development Fund; RSF Finan-
    cial; Slow Money
    funding, private-sector and federal
        combined 189
    funding, sources of 188, 192
    key features of 188
    principles of 188
    Ross Social Venture Fund, purpose of
        201
    tax-exempt entities, funding of 26

venture philanthropy organizations
    10–14
  defined 10
  funding of 13
  management of funds 13
  purpose of 13
  social enterprises, classification as
    13
  target social enterprise, impact on
    14
Vermont benefit corporations
  requirements for 47–48
Volunteer Match 28
volunteerism
  Department of Labor, requirements
    regarding 28
  Fair Labor Standards Act, applica-
    tion to 28
  promotion of 27–28
  resource conservation, role in 27–
    28
  trends toward 27

W

wasting corporate assets
  duty of care issues 77, 126
  mismanaging funds 78
  waste, defined 77
WaterHealth International
  purpose of 190
Wisconsin Cooperative Association
    Act 58
Wisconsin Women's Business Initia-
    tive Corporation 2
Women's Bean Project 1

Y

Yunus, Muhammed 1, 4

About the Author

Marc J. Lane, a business and tax attorney and financial advisor, practices law at The Law Offices of Marc J. Lane, P.C. (www.MarcJLane.com). Marc is an expert on entrepreneurship and entrepreneurial finance, and an influential advocate of best corporate governance practices. Twice a recipient of the Illinois State Bar Association's Lincoln Award, Marc, a "Leading Illinois Attorney" and "Illinois Super Lawyer," has consistently earned an "AV® Preeminent™" rating in the Martindale-Hubbell Legal Directory, the highest ranking awarded. Martindale-Hubbell also includes him in its *Bar Registry of Preeminent Attorneys*.

An innovator in helping social enterprises, investors, lenders and philanthropists leverage capital to maximize financial results while driving positive social change, Marc teaches social enterprise at Northwestern University School of Law. He is the pioneer behind the Advocacy Investing® approach to socially responsible and mission-related investing (www.AdvocacyInvesting.com).

A director of Social Enterprise Alliance, Marc spearheaded the launch of its Chicago chapter, which he serves as president and a director. He also chairs SEA's affiliate, The Center for Social Enterprise Accreditation.

This is Marc Lane's 34th book.